TREASURY OF WITCHCRAFT

treasury of
witchcraft

HARRY E. WEDECK

Lecturer in Classics, Brooklyn College, N. Y.

Fellow of the International Institute of Arts

and Letters.

Philosophical Library - New York

This edition published by Bonanza Books,
a division of Crown Publishers, Inc.,
by arrangement with Philosophical Library

k l m n o p

Library of Congress Catalog Card Number: 60-15949

Printed in the United States of America

TABLE OF CONTENTS

Chapter III

OPERATIONS OF MAGIC, SYMPATHETIC MAGIC, HERB LORE, MAGIC INSTRUMENTS, POTIONS, WANDS, MAGIC CIRCLES, PENTACLES

Chapter IV

RAISING THE DEVIL—AND THE DEAD, SATAN THE ARCH FIEND, SATANIC HIERARCHY, SATANIC REALMS, SATANIC PACT, RITES, EXORCISMS, NECROMANTIC RITES

Chapter V

BLACK MASS, SABBAT   117

Chapter VI

WITCHES AND WARLOCKS, APPEARANCE, CHARACTERISTICS, HABITS

Chapter VII

LYCANTHROPY, VAMPIRES, VOODOO 169

Chapter VIII

MANUALS OF MAGIC 181

Abaris
Adamantius
Agamede
Agonaces
Agrippa
Agrusadapariksay
Albert Magnus
Alexander the Paphlagonian
Allen, Jonet
Amalaric, Madeleine
Anania
Ansuperomin
Anthony, Francis
Apollonius of Tyana
Apuleius
Apusorus of Media
Arabantiphocus
Arnold of Villanova
Arnuphis
Artemidorus
Artephius
Ascletarion
Ashmole, Elias
Astrampsychos
Avenar
Bacis
Bacon, Roger
Balcoin, Marie
Barchusen, Johann Conrad
Basilides
Bavan, Madeleine
Becher, J. Joachim
Beckford, William
Belephantes
Benedict IX
Berosus
Beuther, David
Biscar, Jeannette
Bocal
Bodin, Jean
Bogomils
Boguet, Henri
Bolingbroke, Roger
Bonatti, Guido
Bragadini, Mark Antony
Bulwer Lytton
Cagliostro
Calmet, Augustin
Cardan, Jerome
Casanova, Giacomo
Catalin

Cellini, Benvenuto
Cham-Zoroaster
Chymierastes, J. C.
Cobham, Eleanor
Craca
Crollius, Osvaldus
Crowley, Aleister
Dashwood, Sir Francis
Dee, Dr. John
Delrio, Martin
Diodorus of Catania
Dipsias
Earl of Bothwell
Elich, Philip Ludwig
Epimenides
Erichtho
Faustus, Dr. Johannes
Fian, John
Flamel, Nicholas
Flaque, Louis Eugène
Fludd, Robert
Forman, Dr.
Gafferel, Jacques
Gaufridi, Louis
Gerbert, Pope Sylvester II
Gilles de Rais
Glanvil, Joseph
Gnostics
Gobryas
Gowdie, Isobel
Graterakes, Valentine
Gregory VI
Grierson, Isobel
Grillando, Paolo
Gross, Allison
Grossetête, Robert
Guazzo, Francesco Maria
Guibourg
Guido de Monteroquer
Guillaume de Paris
Hacks, Charles
Hakim
Harries, Dr. John
Hecate
Hermes Trismegistus
Hermotimus
Hildebrand, Pope Gregory VIII
Hu-Jum-Sin
Iamblicus
Iannes et Iambres
Idris

Imhetep
Isaac of Holland
Jechiel, Rabbi
John XX
Johnson, Margaret
Julianus
Khamuas
Khunrath, Heinrich
Knights Templar
Koh Hung
Kramer, Heinrich
Kyteler, Lady Alice
Lamont, Marie
L'Ancre, Pierre de
La Voisin, Catherine
Libanius
Libo Drusus
Lilith
Lotapes
Lully, Raymund
Marmarus of Babylonia
Martines de Pasqually
Mary the Jewess
Master John
Maternus, Julius Firmicus
Medea
Megain, Perrenon
Melampus
Merlin
Meroë
Mme. de Montespan
Mora, Pietro
Nectanebus
Nider, Johannes
Nostradamus
Oenothea
Osthanes
Pamphile
Pamphilos
Paracelsus
Pazalas
Pendragon, Uther

Perkins, William
Peter of Abano
Porta, Giovanni Battista della
Postel, Guillaume de
Priests of Sekhnet
Pythia
Richelieu, Duc de
Ripley, George
Rocail
Sabellicus, Georgius
Sadur and Ghadur
Sagana
Saint-Germain
Salvius Julianus
Sammonicus, Quintus Serenus
Sampson, Agnes
Schröpfer, Johann Georg
Scot, Michael
Setnau Kha-em-Uast
Sibly, Ebenezer
Simon Magus
Sinclair, George
Sinistrari, Ludovico Maria
    d'Ameno
Smith, Isobel
Solomon
Sons of Cham-Zoroaster
Sprenger, Jacob
Stevenote de Audebert
Style, Elizabeth
Tarmoendas
Tchatcha-em-ankh
Theodoris de Lemnos
Tiresias
Trithemius, Johannes
Tuchet, Eleanor
Vellada
Weishaupt, Adam
Wierus, John
Zaratus of Media
Zlito

Chapter X

GOETIC DIVERSIONS – DIVINATION – ASTROLOGY
LEVITATION – ALCHEMY   217

Chapter XI

WITCHCRAFT VERSUS THE STATE

Chapter I

General Introduction
Black and white magic, Effects on individuals and communities

Chapter 1

BLACK AND WHITE MAGIC

EFFECTS ON INDIVIDUALS AND COMMUNITIES

"Goe, and catche a falling starre,
Get with child a mandrake root,
Tell me, where all past yeares are,
Or who cleft the Divels foot."

John Donne

Introduction

The term magic has, through the ages, acquired such varied connotations, by means of accretions and undertones of implications and extensions of reference and adaptations that a summary definition is elusive. In a rigid sense, magic signifies the operation of phenomena in an inexplicable manner. Such operations encourage a belief that the magic act is attributable to obscure forces without human control, or to these same obscure forces subjected, by esoteric devices, to human discretion.

Some demographers assert distinctions between magic and witchcraft. They make formal classifications into ritual witchcraft and operative witchcraft, as Dr. Margaret Murray does. Again, they break down the Black Arts into wizardry and necromancy, divination and soothsaying, as if these were completely isolated and disparate branches. Such categories have their use, of course, in organizing the vast material of magic. But they all belong to witchcraft, or magic, or goety, or thaumaturgy—which are merely semantically distinctive but not generically different facets of one basically identical operation. For they are, in essence, variant phases, different approaches, techniques, or manifestations of one fundamental concept common to all the variants, that the normally accepted laws of nature can be subdued or transcended.

Fundamentally, magic is the imposition of the human will on the phenomena of nature: and that imposition extends, in the actual practice of Black Magic, into a conflict between two forces, one beneficent, the other malefic: constantly at war, over the entire cosmos. That was the primary concept of the ancient cult of the Manicheans, of the equally mystic cult of Zoroaster.

The mediaeval demonographer, Martin Delrio, in his Disquisitionum Magicarum Libri Sex, gives a succinct and essentially similar definition of magic:

> An art or skill that, by means of a not supernatural force, produces certain strange and unusual phenomena whose rationale eludes common sense. . . .

Magic is protean. It has multiple names, numberless forms. It is thaumaturgy and goety. It is witchcraft and it is religion. It is superstition and legend, tested by its potency, its primary effects on the individual, sometimes on the community, and not rarely on large ethnic groups. It enters into private domestic life and pervades the tribal community. On occasion, it dominates, in its malignant impact, an entire nation, upheaving governments, creating devastation and civic chaos. It pierces the very basic roots of existence, and sometimes forms itself into a religious cult, capable of overthrowing an established religious system. Impalpable sometimes, at all times secretive and cryptically esoteric, its powers rest in the grip of small dedicated hieratic groups: or in the control of an arch adept: or even, as in ancient Italy, as in the antique Chinese dynasties, in the supreme ruler himself, who is both first citizen and thaumaturgic priest.

Two aspects of witchcraft manifest themselves: White Magic, and the Black Art. Certain demonographers, and magicians as well, have assigned to White Magic an ethical motive: to benefit both the living and the dead. Black Magic, on the other hand, is completely malefic in its operations and its intent. It performs maleficently against its victims, against enemies, and contrary to the normal, commonly accepted view of the orderly sequence of cosmic rhythms in harmony with beneficent mankind.

Witchcraft, in its necromantic, thaumaturgic, and apotropaic diversity, has invariably been a significant phenomenon of all cultures, at whatever level of development.

It has never been a mere academic diversion. On the contrary, it has been an integral element, coloring and molding religious, political, and social situations and attitudes. And its impact, in these three directions, has been impressively pronounced, in a very realistic sense.

In early ages there was no demarcation between religion and magic. Religion was largely magic, for all religion was directed toward communication with the divine agencies and toward a degree of cooperation of these deities for the advantage of man. The pagan rites, the mystic ceremonials of the priestly castes—Egyptian and Assyrian, Hittite and Babylonian—the Eleusinian Mysteries, the Dionysiac performances, the cult of Mithra, the festal glorifications involving dedications and sacrifices, paeans and supplications and invocations —were associated with thaumaturgic arcana. The flow of folk thoughts and tendencies was all directed toward a projection of the self beyond the material, normally observable limitations of the human frame and the human spirit. Ancient witchcraft and wizardry in all their multiple permutations and impacts, like their modern counterparts, constituted virtually an ultimate faith. Magic was a stubborn credo that would not be refused. It was belief without reservation. Whether belief in beneficent principles or in actively malefic potencies, is another matter. But it was credence that equated man with these agencies, unseen yet real, that governed the cosmos. It was, in short, man's attempt toward divinity.

And through the long and perplexed centuries, although magic assumed crudities and accretions of bestiality and demoniac contacts, it was basically the spiritual means, though perverted, made manifest toward this consummation. Magic was the epiphany of man's ultimate faculty.

This treasury offers a representative conspectus of the magic arts, their motifs and techniques, personalities and impacts, from proto-history to modern times, from Babylonia to Scotland.

This division of the book is by chapters. A general introduction covers the subject of magic, while each chapter has a special introduction treating a significant phase of magic. The contents of each chapter are arranged chronologically and are furnished with explanatory comment wherever necessary, in addition to bibliographical or biographical material.

H. E. W.

[5]

What is Magic?

We may rest quite assured that magic is a thing detestable in itself. Frivolous and false, it still contains some element of truth in it.

Pliny the Elder (23-79 A.D.), Roman encyclopedist. Author of voluminous *Natural History*.

Nero as a Magician

There are many sorts of Magic, as Osthanes has set down in writing; for it works by the means of Water (hydromantia), Globes or Balls (sphaeromantia), Air (aeromantia), Stars (astrologia), Firelights (pyromantia), Basins (buanomantia), and Axes (axinomantia); means by which they promise the foreknowledge of things to come, also the raising up and conjuring of departed ghosts and conference with Familiars and infernal spirits.

All of these things were found out by the Emperor Nero in our days to be no better than vanities and vain illusions, and yet he was inclined to study the Magical art as assiduously as to play upon the cythera and to hear and sing tragic songs. Nor is it to be wondered at that he was given to such strange courses, having wealth and world at will and his fortune besides accompanied with many deep corruptions of the mind. But amid those many vices to which he had sold himself he had a chief desire to command the gods (forsooth) and familiar spirits, thinking that if he could attain to that, then he had climbed to the highest point and

pitch of magnanimity. There was never a man who studied harder and followed an art more earnestly than he did Magic. He had enough riches and power under his hands, his wit was quick and pregnant to apprehend and learn anything, and yet he gave it over in the end; an undoubted and peremptory argument to convince the vanity of this Art, when such an one as Nero rejected it.

As to this Art-magic which Nero would so fain have learned, what might be the reason which he could not reach unto it? These Magicians are not without their shifts and means of evasion to save the credit of their Art; as, for instance, that ghosts and spirits will not appear nor yield any service to people who are freckled and full of pimples, and haply Nero was such an one. As for his limbs otherwise he had them all sound, and then besides he could choose at his good will and pleasure the set days and times fit for this practice. It was an easy matter, too, for him to meet with sheep coal black, and such as had not a speck of white or any other colour; and as to sacrificing men nothing gave him greater delight. Furthermore, he had about him Tyridates the King of Armenia, a great Magician, to give him instruction. This prince travelled to Rome all the way by land because he had a scruple and thought it unlawful (as all magicians do) either to spit into the sea or otherwise to discharge into it from men's bodies what might pollute and defile that Element. He instructed Nero in the principles of Magic, yea and admitted him to sacred feasts and solemn suppers to initiate him into the profession; but all to no purpose, for Nero could never receive at his hands the skill of this Science. Therefore we may be fully assured that it is a detestable and abominable Art, grounded on no certain rules, full of lies and vanities, for, to tell the truth, the certitude which it has in effecting anything proceeds rather from the devilish cast of poisoning practised therewith than from the Art itself of Magic. But why need any man listen to the lies which the Magicians in old time have sent abroad, when I myself in my youth have seen and heard Apion (that great and famous Grammarian) tell strange tales of the herb Cynocephalia, that it has a divine and heavenly virtue as a preservative against all poisons, charms and enchantments, but that whoever plucked it out of the ground could not escape instant death. The same Apion reported in my hearing that he had conjured up spirits to enquire of Homer what country he was born in, and from what parents he was descended; but he dared not say what answer was given.

Pliny the Elder (23-79 A.D.). Roman encyclopedist who wrote a voluminous *Natural History*. Translated by Philemon Holland, 1601.

Egyptian Memphis as Seat of Magic

Let secret Memphis reveal all the arcane knowledge of the ancient magicians.

Lucan (39-65 A.D.), Roman poet. Author of *Pharsalia*.

MEMPHIS: ancient city of Lower Egypt, noted for witchcraft.

Magic has Divine Associations

Have you heard that magic is an art acceptable to the immortal gods: a noble art since the age of Zoroaster and Oromazus, the inventors, and handmaiden to the heavenly beings?

Apuleius (2nd century A.D.), Roman novelist and philosopher. Author of *De Magia*.

ZOROASTER: ancient Persian philosopher and magician. Founder of religious cult.
OROMAZUS: a variant form of Ormuzd, divine spirit associated with White Magic.

Deities Associated with Magic

Mercury inventor of incantations was wont to be invoked in the rites of magicians and Venus who entices the mind and the Moon aware of night's mystery and Hecate, mistress of the spirits of the dead.

Apuleius (2nd century A.D.), Roman novelist. Author of *De Magia*, a refutation against charges of witchcraft.

Origin of Witchcraft

The evil angels had sown the seeds of that strange art among men and had introduced every kind of sorcery and magic among them.

Eusebius (d. 309 A.D.), *Praeparatio Evangelica*.

Power of Symbolism

Theurgic union is achieved only by observing ineffable ceremonies, ritually

[8]

performed operations, worthy of the gods and surpassing all understanding, and by the inexplicable power of the symbols known only to the gods.

Iamblichus (4th century A.D.), *The Mysteries of the Egyptians, Chaldeans and Assyrians.*

General View of Magic

Custom and common talk accept the magi as wizards.

St. Jerome (c. 340-420 A.D.), *Commentary on Daniel.*

Miracles and Witchcraft

Miracles occurred by simple faith and pious devotion, not by incantations and spells composed by the evil occult art that is called magic, or, by a more detestable name, goetia, or, by a more dishonorable term, theurgia.

St. Augustine (354-430 A.D.), *De Civitate Dei.*

Magic for Knowledge

Men seek the magic arts, not for themselves but for earthly happiness or from an overpowering curiosity.

St. Augustine (354-430 A.D.), Roman Church Father. *De Civitate Dei.*

Mediaeval Definition of Magician

Magicians are those who are commonly called evil-doers on account of the enormity of their crimes. They stir up the elements, disturb men's minds and without any poisonous potion they destroy by the mere force of incantation.

Isidore of Seville (7th century), *Etymologiae.*

Magic of Divine Origin

Nor for that reason ought anyone to believe that certain men can perform magic operations without the permission of God.

Rabanus Maurus (9th century), Abbot of Fulda. De *Magicis Artibus.*

Ambivalence of Magic Art

Aristotle, the Prince of Philosophers, saith in many places, that every science is of the kind of good things: But notwithstanding, the operation sometimes is good and sometime evill: as the science is changed unto a good or to an evill end, to that which it mayketh. Of the which saying, two things are concluded: the first is that the science of Magick is not evill, for by the knowledge of it, evill may bee eschewed, and good means thereof may be followed.

The second thing also is concluded, for so much as the effect is so praised and so happily esteemed for the end, and also the end of science is dispraised, when it is not ordained to good or to vertue. It followeth then that every science or facultie, as operation is sometime good and sometime evill.

[9]

Therefore, because the science of Magick is a good knowledge (as it is presupposed) and is somewhat evill in beholding of causes and natural things, as I have considered and perceived in very many ancient authors: yea and ALBERT my selfe have found out the truth in many things and I suppose or imagine the trueth to be in some part of the Booke of Chirander, and also the Booke of Alchorac.

Albertus Magnus (c. 1206-1280), *Secrets of Albertus Magnus.*

The Essence of Magic

A great part of Philosophers or Phisytions, have believed that al marvellousness of experience, and marvels, came from naturall things, when they be brought to light, by hot and colde, drie and moist, and they shewed these four qualities and put them to bee the rootes of all marvellous things. And mixtion of them is required to every marvellous thing. They verified that in their workes; and when they found experiences of Philosophers they might not verifie those things by hot and colde, but rather by his contrary.

Therefore Plato said for a good cause that he which is not very cunning in logicke and wise in the vertues of naturall things likewise the aspects of the starres, shall not see the causes of marvellous things, nor know them, nor participate of the treasures of the Philosophers.

Albertus Magnus, *Book of the Marvels of the World.*

Power of Sorcery

Witchcraft is so enduring that it admits of no remedy by human operation.

St. Thomas Aquinas (13th century), *Sententiae.*

Eyewitness to Image Magic

We saw with our own eyes one of these individuals making the image of a person he wished to bewitch. These images are composed of things, the qualities of which bear a certain relation to the intentions and the projects of the operator, and which represent by means of symbols the names and the qualities of the unfortunate victim. The magician afterwards pronounces some words over the image which he has just placed before him, and which is a real or symbolical representation of the person whom he wishes to bewitch; then he blows and emits from his mouth a little saliva which had collected there, and at the same time makes those organs vibrate which are used in the utterance of this malevolent formula: next he holds over this symbolical image a cord which he has prepared with this intention, making a knot in it to signify that he is acting with resolution and persistence, that at the moment when he spat he made a compact with the demon who acted as his associate in the operation. To these processes and malevolent words a wicked spirit is united, which comes forth from the operator's mouth covered with saliva. Many evil spirits then descend, and the result of all is that the

SYRIAN FERTILITY MAGIC
This male figure of clay, dating about 2500 B.C., is called "The Old Man of Germayir."
When invoked, he was believed to increase crops, cattle, and children.
British Museum, London.

SAINT PETER AND SIMON MAGUS

Simon Magus was a sorcerer who appears in *Acts of the Apostles,* 8: "But there was a certain man, called Simon, which beforetime in the same city used sorcery, and bewitched the people of Samaria." Legend credited Simon Magus with the power of levitation. Levitation is the ability to raise one's own body, and also objects, into the air, contrary to the laws of gravity. This power was attributed to many thaumaturgists. St. Joseph of Copertino, an Italian monk of the seventeenth century, was credited with this ability, as are certain Tibetan priests in our own day.

(Tempera on wood painting by Benozzo Gozzoli, a 15th century Italian artist)

Courtesy of The Metropolitan Museum of Art.

AMULET SELLER

Amulets were objects usually worn on the person as a protection against black magic and its malefic effects. They were in use from the earliest times, especially among the Chaldeans, Egyptians, Greeks, and Romans. Roman matrons often used such amulets or talismans as love charms.

(Painting by H. Siemeradzki)

PHILO IUDAEUS

An ancient Greco-Jewish philosopher and religious mystic. He initiated new philosophic concepts of the cosmos.

magician causes the victim to be attacked by the desired evil.

Ibn Khaldun (14th century), Arab historian. He is here describing the practices of the Nabatean sorcerers who dwelt on the Lower Euphrates.

Academic Magic in Spain

This city of Toledo used to cultivate the study of necromancy. Men skilled in the magic art publicly taught pyromancy; and there was always geomancy too, and many an experiment in hydromancy.

Luigi Pulci (15th century), *Morgante Maggiore.*

Actuality of Witchcraft

To assert that acts of witchcraft are impossible is an erroneous belief.

Institor and Sprenger (15th century), *Malleus Maleficarum.*

Praise of Magic

The Metaphisicks of Magitians,
And Negromantick bookes are heavenly,
Lines, Circles, Letters, Characters.
O these are those that Faustus most desires.
O what a world of profite and delight,
Of power, of honour, and omnipotence,
Is promised to the Studious Artizan?
. . .
A sound Magitian is a Demi-god.

Christopher Marlowe (1564-1593), English dramatist. Author of *Dr. Faustus.*

Definition of Sorcery

Sorcerers, of both sexes, are those who by evil spells, dire curses, and the sending of foul spirits, by potions prepared by the Devil, or through illicit arts from corpses of hanged men, harm and destroy the health and lives of men and beasts. For witches are wont to concoct many things relating to magic from the flesh and bones of hanged men and to use them in magic sorceries.

Johann Georg Godelmann. *De Magis, Veneficiis et Lamiis recte Cognoscendis et Puniendis.* Frankfurt, 1591.

Belief in Spirits

Millions of spiritual creatures walk the earth
Unseen, both when we wake and when we sleep.

John Milton (1608-1674), English poet. Author of epic *Paradise Lost.*

Definition of Witchcraft

Since magic that is harmful to another is called witchcraft, for that reason witchcraft is the force and power of harming others in accordance with an expressed or tacit pact with a demon.

Giovanni Alberghini. *Manual,* 1671.

Hand of Glory

Wherever that terrible light shall burn,
Vainly the sleeper may toss and turn;

His leaden eyes shall he ne'r unclose
So long as that magical taper glows,
Life and treasure shall he command
Who knoweth the charm of the glorious
   Hand!

Thomas   Ingoldsby   (1788-1845),
Ingoldsby Legends.

MAGICAL TAPER: the Dead Man's Candle. A candle, placed between the fingers of the hand; made with wick of dead man's hair, from murderer's fat.
HAND: the Hand of Glory. Right hand of executed murderer. It was severed from the wrist during eclipse of moon. Dried and steeped in various salts, the hand was used in spells.

The Power of Evil

The Principle of Evil, and the Principle of Good, the God of Light and the God of Darkness, two streams contend for our soul, at least that is clear. At the present time, it is quite evident that the God of Good is in eclipse, that Evil reigns over the world, as master.

J-K Huysmans (1848-1907), French novelist. Author of *Là-Bas,* novel on Satanism.

How to Acquire Magic Power

Hearken,
And assist me;
I am taking this boat to the saints of
   God,
And I desire to ask for a little magic.
                    Malay Invocation.

Before this invocation, which is addressed to the ghost of a murdered man, the neophyte must meet this ghost and perform certain rites at the grave.

Chapter II

Magic techniques,
Spells, conjurations, incantations,
periapts, formulas

Chapter 2

MAGIC TECHNIQUES

SPELLS — CONJURATIONS — INCANTATIONS

PERIAPTS — FORMULAS

Introduction

The magic incantation was an occult formula, known only to the ancient priest-magician, or to the witch-doctor, or to the practicing adept, whose purpose was to summon an infernal power, to bewitch an enemy, to produce a phenomenon not arising from normal causes.

Night is the appropriate time for such spells, and, to increase efficacy, the words were usually whispered. The Roman Apuleius, who produced a fantastic novel pervaded by magic transformations and all the apparatus of witchcraft, speaks of "magic whispering." At times the formula, instead of being uttered, was inscribed on leaves or fruit and then swallowed in a liquid.

Talismans, amulets, charms, periapts—these variant terms all had as their objective the enlisting of demoniac aid or warding off the malefic operations of such forces. An amulet, carried or worn about the person, could protect against incubi and nightmare, against the evil eye, personal calamity, or black magic. Some amulets had geometric designs, or mystic formulas, inscribed on them. Or the amulet might be a lizard, or a gem, a chameleon, or a key, a knot, a scorpion, the tail of a fox. Actorius, for instance, a stone worn round the neck, conferred courage on the owner. Heliotrope, a magic herb, reputedly endowed the possessor with invisibility. Other herbs that were efficacious in exorcising haunted cattle, recovering stolen property, banishing sickness, or understanding the language of birds, included: sage, malaxis, christianwort, and forest manna. Garlic was used in the Middle Ages as a specific against fascinatio, the Evil Eye. Lubin was a fish whose heart drove off demons. The triskelion, a symbol consisting of three legs bent at the knee and joined at the thigh, protected against fascinatio. The triskelion was known in Mediterranean countries as early as the fifth century B.C. An Egyptian charm, the Nefer amulet, shaped like a musical instrument, brought good luck. Sam, another Egyptian periapt, was of phallic shape, and attracted amorous relationships. In Madagascar, sanaves are pieces of aromatic wood wrapped in cloth, suspended from the neck or wrist, and protect against magicians. Among the ancient Druids of Gaul, the serpent's egg—putatively of monstrous reptilian biological origin—was worn, suspended from the neck, by the Druids, the priest-magicians, themselves.

The story is not ended. It continues, without abatement, into the contemporary scene, as is the case with so much of traditional wizardry. In the south of England, in Devon, a rabbit's foot was recently used as a love charm to win back a disinterested lover. In the Black Forest, in Germany, dragon's blood, a red gum, was similarly and potently used. In Northern England, fern seed, gathered on the Eve of St. John's Day, reputedly produces equally effective results. Some love-sick girls scatter hemp seed in a churchyard, in the dark of the moon, while they chant a spell as old as the spells of ancient love-enthralled Greek maidens. So, too, charms, designed for apotropaic purposes, have multiplied and become more prevalent than ever, in Italy and France, among rustics and literates: double walnuts to ward off headaches, charm rings, potatoes, pieces of coal, a variety of "mascots," beads, leaks, and "witch balls."

Magic Symbolism

Life subsists on two planes. One existence is material, palpable, visible. The other is intangible, impalpable, no less real in its fundamental basis, a mystic zone wherein strange concepts are born, and esoteric cults breed among startling realities that have their own mores, their own laws.

This darker undercurrent of subtleties, running like a murmurous motif through the coarser strata of the material cosmos, has always been most manifest in the antique Asian cultures, that probed into the arcana of the cosmic scheme and discovered mystic relationships between men and things, between the heavens and the physical life, between form and thought.

Thus a consistent stream of symbolism permeates all Asiatic thought. Numbers acquire Kabalistic connotations. The beasts and creatures of the fields, plants and geometric shapes, colors and sounds imply esoteric conjunctions, cryptic forebodings, and life and death, fame and sickness, health and longevity, beauty and turmoil can all be deciphered in the vast multiple design of the orderly universe. What is required to achieve this knowledgeable state is the key, the code to the cryptic metaphysics.

There is in fact such a code, such a key, in the religious chants, in the numerology, in the art of Asia, in the elaborate ink and brush strokes of the ancient Chinese artists, in the pictorial depiction of birds and flowers, animals and objects in the sequence of Japanese kakemonos, in the intricate mosaics of the Iranians, in the monstrous Elephantine and Ajanta cave carvings of the Hindus, in the Sumerian and Akkadian pictographs still visible on the crumbling pillars of temples, on Mauryan palace murals, on the forlorn Persian Gulf island of Bender-Bushir.

The East reads a meaning into the soft rustle of leaves, into the shape of a water plant, into the configuration of an artistic design, the color of cloth, the aroma of herbs, the timeless recitative of sacred formulas. And of all such formulas that have had their most dominant, most deep-rooted impact on Asian culture, the Sanskrit Om Mani Padme Hum—Hail, O Jewel in the flower of the lotus—has been the most significant. It is the fundament of Buddhism, addressed to Avalokita, god of compassion, and the mere articulation of the formula is considered, by the devout Buddhist, sufficiently effective to transport him to his paradise, to the ultimate state of Nirvana, the zone of eternal contemplative blissful perfection.

In the Hindu Pantheon, the member deities are invariably associated with distinctive objects, with symbolic divine periapts. Thus the rosary, the lotus, a vessel of water, a lustral spoon are all tokens of Brahma. Vishnu is sensitive to the conch shell, a club, a quoit. The heraldic arms of Siva are the trident, the drum, the noose, and the antelope, while Rama, whose adventures are so gloriously related in the Ramayana, is identified primarily with the bow and arrow.

In Chinese art, in which the symbolic elements are most evident, the symbolism has religious and philosophical interpretations, embracing Buddhist and

Taoist features and folk elements of an apotropaic nature or intended as auspicious talismans: because the folkways are basically pragmatic, and symbolism becomes, among the vast inarticulate hordes, not a metaphysical concept, but a factual means of averting ill fortune or inviting favor. Among such symbols, then, are animal heads, bird forms, diagrammatic figures, the Yang and Yin —the male and female characteristics represented as red and black hemispheres. There are, further, the eight trigrams associated with divination: animals of the Zodiac: the blue-black tortoise, the Dark Warrior, encircled by a snake, who rules the North: the blue-green dragon of the East: the red bird, Feng Huang, the phoenix, of the South: the white tiger or the unicorn of the West: while the centre is symbolized by the yellow dragon. Thus the four Cardinal Points of the Universe are under the control of creatures that must be appeased, placated by mystic formulas, by appealing incantations.

Likewise, in Japan, luck symbols are grouped together under the name of takara—mono, treasure things. They include, of course, Chinese symbols as well as indigenous elements derived from Japanese folkways. Such symbols are: the mallet of Daikoku, one of the Seven Gods of Luck, and the magic feather cloak, hagoromo. Plant life is a common motif in a wider, more cultural direction, and the paulownia, the maple, and the wisteria all have their beneficent, propitious implication. The paulownia, in fact, is the crest of the Japanese Empress.

The protean forms of the ancient classical Pantheon, or Tibetan or Assyrian cults, were most frequently made manifest in animals. Thus, among the Hindus as well, the most sacred animal is the cow, humble catalyst toward the pilgrimage to perfection. The multiple Hindu divinities are constantly linked, in religious ritual and art symbolism, with various creatures, some actual, others mythical. So the bull is the Siva identification. Garuda—half man, half bird, relates to Vishnu. The elephant alludes to Indra, the goose to Brahma. Agni affects the ram, while Kali or Durga, more violent, seeks the tiger. Kama has the parrot, Kartikkeya the peacock. The buffalo is associated with Yama, the rat with Ganesh.

The Tibetans too hold certain animals sacred; members, figuratively, of the divine family. They are the elephant, the horse, peacock, and lion. The gazelle is traditionally a Buddhist symbol, while in Japan the humble hare, instead of the Man as in Western lore, inhabits the Moon.

Some symbols, fish or plants, are specific though not always religious or metaphysical interpretations. They represent more earthy, more factual concepts. For instance, in Chinese art, the crane, the pine tree, the butterfly are all and equally equated with longevity; while in Tibet the folk symbol of longevity is the peach. A carp leaping through a dragon gate represents a successful Civil Service candidate. The bamboo and blossoming plum betoken constancy. The bat and the lotus mean happiness. Coral is an indication of prospective wealth, while the badger is a useful creature to depict, as, like the fox, it is endowed with magic potency. A lunar symbol is the water buffalo. The elephant portends fecundity, as does the pomegranate. The Japanese bird, the hoo, commonly identified with the phoenix, foretells favorable issues. The snake, so sinister in Western European cultures, is, in Chinese art, a symbol of fertility.

The Buddhist eight-spoked Wheel of the Law, on the other hand, has a purely spiritual connotation, denoting the eightfold path of Buddha's teaching. There was an ironical touch, in all probability, in identifying the Chinese hsieh-chai, the horned lion, with the lesser nobles and the court censors.

The dragon, in Western legend and folklore, has always been related to sinister deeds, cataclysms and assault, death and devastation. But in China the dragon, the spirit of rain, was always beneficently linked traditionally with Imperial distinction. The throne was the dragon's throne. The dragon robe was the Imperial dress. Under the Manchus the national flag bore a dragon on a yellow ground. A dragon's head is the motif of Chinese temple decoration. Mystically, the dragon is the Taoist symbol of cosmic vitality, while in Chinese legend the Emperor Yao was the offspring of a mortal mother and a dragon.

Color, too, plays its part in Asian mysticism. In ancient China, anything colored red was considered auspicious for weddings and similar festivities; while colorless objects, of solid black or white, were shunned. For repelling demons, the scarlet peony was thought to be efficacious. In Tibetan Buddhism, color is symbolic of certain lamaistic sects. Monks of the Red Sect are represented by Black Hats. The White Sect has, as an official badge, both red and black hats. The Yellow Sect is the Reformed Church of Tibet. The Multi-colored Sect and the White Sect are Semi-Reformed.

Among all nations, numbers have had, from proto-historic eras, sacred or mystic meanings. Seven was such a number, being associated with the planets. Five too had its significance as the number of fingers on the hand. Among the Greeks, the dead and the gods were invoked thrice. Similarly, incantations were repeated thrice. Nine, as a multiple of three, was also of magical significance. The god Apollo, who, among other functions, presided over the art of prophecy, was associated with seven, while thirteen, being outside the 'round' number twelve, acquired an occult identity of its own.

In Asiatic cultures, too, as in Pythagorean speculations, numbers have metaphysical, cosmological, and religious implications. In China, there are the five canons of the Confucian classics—the Book of Changes, the Book of History, Spring and Autumn, the Book of Poetry, the Canon of Rites; the three kingdoms, the eight Trigrams, the four forms. In Tibet, among other numerical groupings, there are the three precious things— Buddha, faith, community; the seven gems; the ten space directions. Three is a frequent figure in oriental mores. In Chinese art, the three friends of winter were the pine, the bamboo, and the blossoming plum, the only plants that display their colors against the snow; and hence symbols of constancy. The three religions, again, refer to Confucianism, Taoism, and Buddhism. In art, the three motifs are Lei wen—the thunder cloud, Kuei—a stylized animal form, prototype of the dragon; and T'ao-Tieh—the horror mask. The ethical teachings of Buddha, arranged by a special council of elders into a threefold corpus are called the Three Baskets, or the Tripitaka. The three rituals are three ancient Chinese compilations of ceremonials and doctrines of Confucianism, in relation to kingly duties as affected by astronomical and astrological conditions. In Chinese art, the three masters are the landscape painters Tuan Yuan, Li Ch'eng, and Fan K'uan, all of the tenth century. In Vedic India, the establishment of the three sacred fires, the Agnihotra, the new-moon sacrifices, and the full-moon sacrifices are associated with Vedic religious practices. In Japanese art, the plum, symbolizing beauty, and the bamboo and the pine-tree, that represent longevity, form a triad. For a Japanese woman, the three obediences are: to father, husband, and, if a widow, to a son. A creature popular in Japanese legend is the Three-eyed Friar. The Tibetans designate Buddha, Lamaism, and the Law as the Three Gems. Four is a number connected with the attributes of the Chinese scholar: a book, a scroll, a lute, and a chess-board. The Four Books of the Confucian classics are dominant in Korea. The Four Noble Truths are the Buddhist principles that offer surcease from the misery of material existence. In painting, the four gentlemen are: the plum, orchid, chrysanthemum, and bamboo.

In Japan, five refers to the major national seaports. In the art of China, the five poisons are five loathsome creatures—the spider, lizard, centipede, snake, and toad—that express the evil forces of Yin, the female element in the cosmos and the source of darkness, cold, and death. Paradoxically, the five poisons also had apotropaic powers to ward off the Yin influence. The five canons of Confucianism are of beneficent import, as are the five duties. In ancient India, the number five hundred, like six hundred among the Romans or a thousand among the Greeks, was the equivalent of numberless.

The Buddhist six senses were the eyes, nose, ears, heart, tongue, body. The Tibetan six good things are cloves, sandalwood, saffron, nutmeg, camphor, and cardamon. In India, the Seven Holy Hindu Cities are: Hardwar, Mathura, Benares, Dwarka, Conjeeveram, Ajodhya, Ujjain. Just as in the West the number seven is associated with luck and games of chance, so in Japan the Seven Gods of Luck are: Daikoku, linked with rice and hence with wealth: Ebisu—associated with toil: Hotei, symbol of contentment: Fukurokuju, representing wisdom and longevity: Benten, goddess of luck: Jurojin, a counterpart of Fukorokuju: Bishamon, typifying war. This concept of the seven gods stems from Brahman, Buddhist, Taoist, and Shinto sources. Yet the number seven, in Japan, and numbers containing a seven, are held to be unlucky.

The number eight, has, to the Japanese, an esoteric meaning. In Chinese art, the eight Buddhist symbols are: the Wheel of the Law, the lotus, the vase, the conch shell, the twin fish, the endless knot, the royal canopy, the state umbrella. These were originally Indian symbols of remote antiquity, long before

IAMBLICHUS

Iamblichus (c. 250-325 A.D.) was a Neoplatonic philosopher and the author of a defense of ritual magic entitled *The Mysteries of the Egyptians, Chaldeans, and Assyrians,* that is still extant.

The illustration depicts a divinatory procedure known as alectryomancy. The cock is picking up grains that form the Greek letters for THEOD, prophesying that THEOD-(ORUS), a high-ranking court official, would be the future Emperor. A detailed description of the practice occurs in Thornton Wilder's *The Ides of March.*

WITCH PREPARING A PHILTRE
Notice the familiar, the Satanic spirit that attends her in animal form, crouching at
her feet.
(By an Unknown Master of the Flemish School, middle 15th century)
Leipsig Museum.

WITCHES

An artist's conception of the three witches in Shakespeare's Macbeth, Act I, Scene I.
(Nineteenth century engraving)

FORTUNE TELLING

David Teniers has his wife's fortune told. Fortune telling by the hand, as in the illustration, is called chiromancy.

(After David Teniers, 17th century Dutch artist)

Courtesy of The Metropolitan Museum of Art,
N. Y. Dick Fund, 1953.

the advent of Buddhism. In China, however, they rapidly degenerated into mere lucky charms, only the wheel and the lotus retaining a special spiritual significance. In religious history, again, the number eight refers to the Taoist Immortals, who achieved that state by esoteric practices. Each of them was identified in art by one or two attributes —a flower basket, a gourd and crutch, a bamboo rattle, a lotus, fan, flute, sword, and castanets. In the course of time the attributes were painted, instead of the persons represented, and finally the Chinese believed that the symbolic attributes had thaumaturgic powers in themselves. Thus the symbols of the eight Taoist Immortals became identifications of good luck. There are, in Tibetan lamaism, eight glorious emblems: the wheel of the law, the vase of ambrosia, the lotus of immortality, the golden fish, the victorious flag, the umbrella, the conch shell trumpet of victory, the lucky diagram. So that, in effect, the East is knit together, in its religious and spiritual life, by designs and figures, emblems and numbers, all corresponding to inner cryptic significances that can be unraveled by life itself, by the ultimate rhythmic consistency of the cosmos.

Royal Enchanter

King Manasseh used enchantments and dealt with familiar spirits and wizards.

II Kings, 21.6.

Incantation against Noxious Animals

Come to me, O Lord of Gods!
Drive far from me the lions coming from the earth, the crocodiles issuing from the river, the mouth of all biting reptiles coming out of their holes!
Stop, crocodile Mako, son of Set!
Do not wave thy tail:
Do not work thy two arms:
Do not open thy mouth.
May water become as a burning fire before thee!
The spear of the seventy-seven gods is on thine eyes:
The arm of the seventy-seven gods is on thine eye:
Thou who wast fastened with metal claws to the bark of Ra,
Stop, crocodile Mako, son of Set!

Egyptian magic tablet.

MAKO: a mystic crocodile.
SET: Egyptian deity.
RA: Egyptian prototype of man.

Egyptian Invocation

O Oualbpaga!
O Kammara!
O Kamalo!
O Karhenmon!
O Amagaaa!

The series of names refers to magically transfigured names of the gods Osiris and Seth.

Chaldean Incantation

He who forges the image, he who enchants—

[21]

The spiteful face, the evil eye,
The mischievous mouth, the mischievous
tongue,
The mischievous lips, the mischievous
words,
Spirit of the Sky, remember!
Spirit of the Earth, remember!

This incantation involves image or sympathetic magic, fascinatio or the Evil Eye, and the casting of spells.
The oldest magic texts are Akkadian-Chaldean inscriptions, belonging to the royal library at Nineveh, and dating in the second millennium B.C.

Babylonian Invocation

I, son of . . . , whose god is . . . , whose
goddess is . . . ,
In the evil of an eclipse of the Moon,
which in . . . month and on . . . day
has taken place
In the evil of the powers, of the portents,
evil and not good, which are in my
palace and my land,
Have turned toward thee! I have established thee!
Listen to the incantation! Before Nabu
thy spouse, the lord, the prince, the
first-born son of Isagila, intercede for
me!
May he hearken to my cry at the word of
thy mouth.
May he remove my sighing, may he learn
my supplication!
At his mighty word may god and goddess deal graciously with me!
May the sickness of my body be torn
away!
May the groaning of my flesh be consumed!

May the consumption of my muscles be
removed!
May the poisons that are upon me be
loosened!
May the ban be torn away!

> Babylonian Magic Invocation.

Invocation to goddess Tasmitu, to remove sickness and enchantments.

Babylonian Incantation

Incantation. Bright oil, pure oil, shining
oil, the purifying oil of the gods, oil
which softens the sinews of man.
With the oil of the incantation of Ea,
with the oil of the incantation of Marduk
I have made thee drip; with the oil of
softening which Ea has given for
soothing
I have anointed thee; the oil of life I
have put on thee.

> Babylonian Magic Text.

EA; MARDUK: Babylonian gods of magic.

Incantation against Malefic Demons

They are seven, they are seven.
In the valley of the abyss, they are seven.
In the numberless stars of heaven, they
are seven.
In the abyss, in the depths, they grow in
power.
They are not male, they are not female.
They dry up the moistness of the waves.
They do not love women, they have not
begotten offspring.
They scorn consideration and justice.

[22]

They hearken to neither request nor prayer.

Like the horses of the mountains, they are big.

They are the enemies of En-Kin, the God.

They who have revolted cause the gods to tremble.

They spread terror over the highways, and advance with whistling roar.

They are evil, they are evil.

They are seven, they are seven, and again they are twice seven.

Spirit of the Sky, remember them!

Spirit of the Earth, remember them!

Conjure them!

Conjure these evil spirits, spirit of Ramanu, King of the luminous Word, conjure them.

Spirit of Samas, King of Justice, conjure them!

Spirit of Annunas, mighty god, conjure them.

Incantations of these evil spirits.

Chaldean Text, Bilingual Tablet, British Museum.

SEVEN: this number, in occult rites, possessed mystic implications.

Incantation against Disease

The wicked god, the wicked demon, the demon of the desert, the demon of the mountain, the demon of the sea, the demon of the marsh,

Spirit of the heavens, conjure it! Spirit of the earth, conjure it!

Akkadian magic tablet.

Conjuration against Seven Subterranean Demons

They are seven! They are seven!

In the depths of the ocean, they are seven!

In the brilliancy of the heavens, they are seven!

They proceed from the ocean depths, from the hidden retreat.

They are neither male nor female, those which stretch themselves out like chains, they have no spouse, they do not produce children; they are strangers to benevolence.

The enemies! The enemies!

They are seven! They are seven! They are twice seven!

Spirit of the heavens, may they be conjured!

Spirit of the earth, may they be conjured!   Akkadian magic tablet.

The seven demons are known as Maskim. The number seven has special significance in magic ritual; while repetition is the essence of conjuration.

Incantation on Periapt

Incantation. Wicked demon, malignant plague, the Spirit of the earth had made you leave his body.

May the favorable genius, the good giant, the favorable demon, come with the Spirit of the earth.

Incantation of the powerful, powerful, powerful god. Amen.

Akkadian magic tablet.

Used for apotropaic purpose in case of person who was cured of plague once.
POWERFUL: triple repetition is characteristic of magic ritual.

Spell for Keeping the Apshait away from the Dead

Depart from me, O thou that hast lips which gnaw, for I am Khnemu, the lord of Peshennu, and I bring words of the gods to Ra, and I report my message to the lord thereof.

The Book of the Dead, Egyptian funeral ritual.

The apshait was a kind of beetle.

An Egyptian Mummy Asks for Magical Formulae to Enable It to Carry out Its Wishes

I am Tem-Khepera, who brought himself into being upon the thigh of his divine mother. Those who are in Nu are made wolves, and those who are among the sovereign princes are become hyenas. Behold, I gather together the charm from every place where it is, and from every man with whom it is, swifter than greyhounds and quicker than light. Hail, thou who towest along the Makhent boat of Ra, the stays of thy sails up the Pool of Fire in the underworld. Behold, thou gatherest together the charm from every place where he is, and from every man with whom it is, swifter than greyhounds and quicker than light, the charm which created the forms of being from the mother, and which either createth the gods or maketh them to be silent, and which giveth the heat of fire unto the gods. Behold, the charm is given unto me, from wherever it is and from him with whom it is, swifter than

greyhounds and quicker than light, or, as others say, quicker than a shadow.

The Book of the Dead, Egyptian funeral ritual.

Getting Rid of Ulcers

That which does not go away, that which is not propitious,
That which grows up, ulcers of a bad kind,
Poignant ulcers, enlarged ulcers, excoriated ulcers, ulcers,
Ulcers which spread, malignant ulcers,
Spirit of the heavens, conjure it!
Spirit of the earth, conjure it!

Akkadian incantation.

Conjuration against Disease

The seven gods of the vast heavens,
the seven gods of the great earth,
the seven gods of the igneous spheres,
these are the seven gods, the seven malevolent gods, the seven malevolent phantoms.
Spirit of the heavens, conjure!
Spirit of the earth, conjure it!

Akkadian magic tablet.

The number seven is significant in magic ritual.

Babylonian Exorcism

May the wicked demon depart. May the demons seize one another. The pro-

pitious demon, the propitious giant, may they penetrate his body.
Spirit of the heavens, conjure it!
Spirit of the earth, conjure it!

Tablet of Assurbanipal.

Babylonian Incantation

Hearken to my prayer. Free me from my bewitchment. Loosen my sin. Let there be turned aside whatever evil may come to cut off my life.

Tablet of Assurbanipal.

Talisman against Entrance of Demons into House

Talisman, talisman, boundary that cannot be taken away, boundary that the gods cannot pass, barrier immovable, which is opposed to malevolence! whether it be a wicked Utuq, a wicked Alal, a wicked Gigim, a wicked god, a wicked Maskim, a phantom, a spectre, a vampire, an incubus, a succubus, a nightmare, may the barrier of the god Ea stop him!

Chaldean magic tablet.

UTUQ, ALAL, GIGIM, MASKIM: demons.
VAMPIRE: ghost or human being that sucks blood.
INCUBUS: demon that copulates with human females.
SUCCUBUS: female demon that copulates with human males.
EA: Chaldean deity.

Assyrian Spell

The man of Ea am I,
The man of Damkina am I,

The messenger of Marduk am I,
My spell is the spell of Ea,
My incantation is the incantation of Marduk,
The circle of Ea is in my hand,
The tamarisk, the powerful weapon of Anu,
In my hand I hold,
The date-spathe, mighty in decision,
In my hand I hold.

This is an exorcism recited over sick people. Marduk, Ea, Damkina, Anu are ancient Assyrian deities: Ea being the god of wisdom, Marduk the son of Ea, and Damkina the consort of Marduk.

Remedy against Headache

Knot on the right and arrange flat in regular bands, on the left a woman's diadem:

divide it twice in seven little bands;
gird the head of the invalid with it:
gird the seat of life with it:
gird his hands and his feet:
seat him on his bed:
pour on him enchanted waters.

Chaldean magic formula.

Polyglot Invocation

I call upon thee that didst create the earth and bones, and all flesh and all spirit, that didst establish the sea and that shakest the heavens, that didst divide the light from the darkness, the great regulative mind, that disposeth everything, eye of the world, spirit of spirits, god of gods, the lord of the spirits, lord of spirits, the immovable Aeon, Iaoouei, hear my voice.

[25]

I call upon thee, the ruler of the gods, high-thundering Zeus, Zeus, king, Adonai, lord, Iaoouee. I am he that invokes thee in the Syrian tongue, the great god, Zaalaer, Iphphou, do thou not disregard the Hebrew appellation, Ablanthanalb, Abrasiloa.

For I am Silthakhookh, Lailam, Blasaloth, Iao, Ieo, Nebouth, Sabiothar, Both, Arbathiao, Iaoth, Sabaoth, Patoure, Zagoure, Baroukh Adonai, Eloai, Iabraam, Barbarauo, Nau, Siph.

Graeco-Egyptian magical manuscript.

This powerful spell, uttered in Greek, Hebrew, and Syriac, is particularly binding on the spirit invoked.

Magic Terms

Sacred terms that Hermes Trismegistus wrote in Heliopolis in hieroglyphic form:

arbakoriph
obaob
abniob
baiax
chenor
ora
oresion
ousiri
pneuamousiri.

Magic Papyrus.

HERMES TRISMEGISTUS: Hermes three times the Greatest. The Egyptian god Thoth, reputed originator of books on magic.

Egyptian Spell

Flow out, thou poison, come forth upon the ground. Horus conjures thee,

he cuts thee off, he spits thee out, and thou risest not up but fallest down. Thou art weak and not strong, a coward and dost not fight, blind and dost not see. Thou liftest not thy face. Thou art turned back and findest not thy way. Thou mournest and dost not rejoice. Thou creepest away and dost not appear. So speaketh Horus, efficacious of magic! The poison which was rejoicing, the hearts of multitudes grieve for it; Horus has slain it by his magic. He who mourned is in joy. Stand up, thou who wast prostrate. Horus has restored thee to life. He who came as one carried is gone forth of himself: Horus has overcome his bites. All men, when they behold Re, praise the son of Osiris. Turn back, thou snake, conjured is thy poison which was in any limb of N the son of N. Behold, the magic of Horus is powerful against thee. Flow out, thou poison, come forth upon the ground.

Egyptian Papyrus.

This spell to be recited over a hawk with two feathers on head, made of isy-wood and painted. Open its mouth and offer it bread and beer and incense. Place it on the face of one suffering from the bite of any snake and recite from beginning to end. It will repel the poison. A successful specific.

HORUS: Egyptian deity, son of Osiris. Magicians often claimed that they were the 'servants of Horus.'

RE: Egyptian sun-god: associated with magic.

OSIRIS: Egyptian deity.

N: i.e., Nomen, the name. The name of person affected by spell was here inserted.

Egyptian Spell

Thou hast carried thy hands into the house of eternity, thou art made perfect in gold, thou dost shine brightly in sun metal, and thy fingers shine in the dwelling of Osiris, in the sanctuary of Horus himself.

Egyptian Book of the Dead.

Address to deceased. The object is to make all the good features of the spell happen to the dead.

OSIRIS: Egyptian deity.
HORUS: Egyptian deity, son of Osiris. Magicians often claimed that they were the 'servants of Horus.'

Love Knots

You take a band of linen of sixteen threads, four of white, four of green, four of blue, four of red, and make them into one band, and stain them with the blood of a hoopoe, and you bind it with a scarab in its attitude of the sun-god, drowned, being wrapped in byssus, and you bind it to the body of the boy who has the vessel and it will work magic quickly.

Demotic Magical Papyrus—Griffith and Thompson.

Invocation to Great Bear

I invoke you, holy ones, mighty, majestic, glorious luminaries, holy and earth-born, mighty arch demons: dwellers in Chaos, Erebus, and the unfathomable abyss . . . guardians of secrets, captains of the hosts of hell . . . omnipotent, holy, invincible, perform my commands.

Greek magical papyrus.

CHAOS: confusion, the most ancient of the Greek gods.
EREBUS: The Lower Regions.

Invocation of Spirits of Dead

I place this charm down beside you, subterranean gods, Kore Persephone, Ereschigal and Adonis, Hermes, the subterranean, Thoth and the strong Anubis, who hold the keys of those in Hades, the gods of the underworld and the demons, those untimely carried off, men, women, youths and maidens, year by year, month by month, day by day, hour by hour. I conjure you, all demons assembled here, to assist this demon. And awaken at my command, whoever you may be, whether male or female. Betake yourself to that place and that street and that house and bring her hither, and bind her.

Greek magical papyrus.

The ritual was accompanied by image magic on the grave of the person affected.

Spell Inscribed on Weapon

I wield the large sword of Heaven to cut down spectres in their five shapes; one stroke of this divine blade disperses a myriad of these beings.

Ancient Chinese spell inscribed on sword.

Chinese Invocation

Heart of Heaven, eyes of Heaven, core of Heavenly light, defeat the spiritually powerful light of the earth, sun and moon, produce your light; quick, quick, let the Law and the command of the Five Emperors be obeyed.

This Chinese spell is repeated seven times to intensify its efficacy.

[27]

Kabalistic Formula for Invoking Demons

A G L A

This mystic term was formed from the initial Hebrew letters of the expression: Aieth Gadol Leolam Adonai—God will be great forever.

Talisman against Sickness

Ananisapta

A mystic Kabalistic term that was inscribed on parchment as an apotropaic assurance against disease.

Demoniac Formula

Xilka, Xilka, Besa, Besa

This ancient formula was a means of invoking malefic demons.

Spell to Banish Fever

Ochnotinos
Chnotinos
Notinos
Tinos
Inos
Nos
Os

Ancient Hebraic incantation.

As the demon's name was uttered in diminishing size, the fever disappeared correspondingly.

Ancient Hebraic Spell

Shabriri
Briri
Riri
Iri
Ri

With the decrease in size, the demon Shabriri shrank correspondingly.

Oracle of Delphi

The oracle of Apollo, ancient Greek god of prophecy, had a traditionally strange origin. While a goatherd tended his flock on the slopes of Mount Parnassus, the wandering animals approached a long, deep chasm that appeared in the rock. A vapour issued from the chasm. The goats, inhaling the fumes, began to play and frisk about. The goatherd, anxious to discover the cause, bent his head over the chasm. The rising fumes made him assume various strange attitudes, while he uttered words meaningless to himself but of prophetic significance.

On this spot a temple of Apollo was erected. The apartments of the oracle were immediately over the chasm. A priestess, called Pythia, delivered the responses. She sat on a tripod, over the seat of the vapours. After some time, her figure became enlarged, her hair stood on end, and her voice grew more than human. In this condition she uttered wild, incoherent phrases that were considered divinely inspired. The questions of visitants were then proposed to her, and her answers were taken down by a priest, who arranged them in metrical form. The priestess-prophetess could be consulted on one day in every month.

In the course of time, the oracular utterances, obscurely worded and often ambivalent, acquired such a widespread reputation in the ancient world that no expedition, no major activity was undertaken, no important decision made, without consultation of the oracle.

A Healing Incantation

Then Odysseus aimed well and smote him on his right shoulder, so that the point of the bright spear went clean through, and the boar fell in the dust with a cry, and his life passed from him. Then the dear sons of Autolycus began to busy them with the carcase, and as for the wound of the noble godlike Odysseus, they bound it up skilfully, and stayed the black blood with a song of healing.

Homer's *Odyssey*, Book 19.

The 'song of healing' was a chanted spell.

Invocation to Hell

Awake, ye powers of Hell! the wandering ghost
That once was Clytemnestra calls—Arise!

Aeschylus (525-456 B.C.). Greek poet. Author of *The Eumenides*.

The speaker is the ghost of Clytemnestra, slain by her son Orestes.

Spell for Banishing Demon

Lofaham,
Solomon,
Iyouel,
Iyosenaoui.

Incantation used by King Solomon, who was traditionally known as an arch magician, when the king of the demons sent infernal beings to extract human hearts.

The Spell
Simaetha, a Greek Maiden, Tries
to Win back Delphis's Love by
Magic Means

Where are my laurel leaves? Come, bring them, Thestylis; and where are the love charms? Wreath the bowl with bright-red wool, that I may knit the witch-knots against my grievous lover, who for twelve days, oh cruel, has never come hither, nor knows whether I am alive or dead, nor has once knocked at my door, unkind that he is! Hath Love flown off with his light desires by some other path—Love and Aphrodite? To-morrow I will go to the wrestling school of Timagetus, to see my love and to reproach him with all the wrong he is doing me. But now I will bewitch him with my enchantments! So thou, Selene, shine clear and fair, for softly, Goddess, to thee will I sing, and to Hecate of Hell. The very whelps shiver before her as she fares through black blood and across the barrows of the dead.

Hail, awful Hecate! To the end be thou of our company, and make this medicine of mine no weaker than the

[29]

spells of Circe, or of Medea, or of Perimede of the golden hair.

My magic wheel, draw home to me the man I love!

Lo, how the barley grain first smoulders in the fire,—nay, toss on the barley, Thestylis! Miserable maid, where are thy wits wandering? Even to thee, wretched that I am, have I become a laughing-stock, even to thee? Scatter the grain, and cry thus the while, ' 'Tis the bones of Delphis I am scattering!'

My magic wheel, draw home to me the man I love!

Delphis troubled me, and I against Delphis am burning this laurel; and even as it crackles loudly when it has caught the flame, and suddenly is burned up, and we see not even the dust thereof, lo, even thus may the flesh of Delphis waste in the burning!

My magic wheel, draw home to me the man I love!

Even as I melt this wax, with the god to aid, so speedily may he my love be molten, the Myndian Delphis! And as whirls this brazen wheel, so restless, under Aphrodite's spell, may he turn and turn about my doors.

My magic wheel, draw home to me the man I love!

Now will I burn the husks, and thou, O Artemis, hast power to move hell's adamantine gates, and all else that is as stubborn. Thestylis, hark, 'tis so; the hounds are baying up and down the town! The Goddess stands where the three ways meet! Hasten, and clash the brazen cymbals.

My magic wheel, draw home to me the man I love!

Lo, silent is the deep, and silent the winds, but never silent the torment in my breast. Nay, I am all on fire for him that made me, miserable, no wife but a shameful thing, a girl no more a maiden.

My magic wheel, draw home to me the man I love!

Three times do I pour libation, and thrice, my Lady Moon, I speak this spell: Be it with a friend that he lingers, be it with a leman he lies, may he as clean forget them as Theseus, of old, in Dia—so legends tell—did utterly forget the fair-tressed Ariadne.

My magic wheel, draw home to me the man I love!

Coltsfoot is an Arcadian weed that maddens, on the hills, the young stallions and fleet-footed mares. Ah! even as these may I see Delphis; and to this house of mine, may he speed like a madman, leaving the bright palaestra.

My magic wheel, draw home to me the man I love! This fringe from his cloak Delphis lost; that now I shred and cast into the cruel flames. Ah, ah, thou torturing love, why clingest thou to me like a leech to the fen, and drainest all the black blood from my body? My magic wheel, draw home to me the man I love.

Lo, I will crush an eft, and a venomous draught to-morrow I will bring thee!

But now. Thestylis, take these magic herbs and secretly smear the juice on the jambs of his gate whereat, even now, my heart is captive, though nothing he recks of me, and spit and whisper, ' 'Tis the bones of Delphis that I smear.'

THE CONJURER

A milder, innocuous form of mass deception not unknown in contemporary society.
(Painting by Hieronymus Bosch, 15th century German artist)
Courtesy of the Musée Municipal, Saint Germain-en-Laye, France.

ST. ANTHONY TORMENTED BY DEMONS

In all ages and countries demons were believed to assume human or partly human form
in order to torment or tempt mortals.
(Tempera on wood painting by Stefano de Giovanni Sassetta, medieval Italian artist)
Courtesy of Yale University Art Gallery.

SABBAT OR THE GATHERING OF SORCERERS

In the Middle Ages, witches were believed to meet at specified seasons on mountain sides, isolated valleys, or ruined castles, to pay homage to their Master Satan. Satan was represented in goat form. In the illustration a witch is offering a child as a human sacrifice to the Arch Demon.

(Painting by Goya, 18th century Spanish artist)

Courtesy of the Museo Lazaro Galdiano, Madrid.

THE WITCH OF MALLEGHEM

The witch, with the help of attendants, is engaged in healing a procession of sick and maimed peasants and others. Note the creature in the background, a familiar. Scattered around are pills, phials, and similar evidences of her occult art.

(After Pieter Brueghel, 16th century Flemish painter)

Courtesy of The Metropolitan Museum of Art,
N. Y. Dick Fund, 1930.

My magic wheel, draw home to me the man I love!

And now that I am alone, whence shall I begin to bewail my love? Whence shall I take up the tale: who brought on me this sorrow?

The maiden-bearer of the mystic vessel came our way, Anaxo, daughter of Eubulus, to the grove of Artemis; and behold, she had many other wild beasts paraded for that time, in the sacred show, and among them a lioness.

Bethink thee of my love, and whence it came, my Lady Moon!

And the Thracian servant of Thauchar-idas—my nurse that is but lately dead, and who then dwelt at our doors—besought me and implored me to come and see the show. And I went with her, wretched woman that I am, clad about in a fair and sweeping linen stole, over which I had thrown the holiday dress of Clearista.

Bethink thee of my love, and whence it came, my Lady Moon!

Lo! I was now come to the mid-point of the highway, near the dwelling of Lycon, and there I saw Delphis and Eudamippus walking together. Their beards were more golden than the golden flower of the ivy; their breasts (they coming fresh from the glorious wrestler's toil) were brighter of sheen than thyself, Selene!

Bethink thee of my love and whence it came, my Lady Moon!

Even as I looked I loved, loved madly, and all my heart was wounded, woe is me, and my beauty began to wane. No more heed took I of that show, and how I came home I know not; but some parching fever utterly overthrew me, and I lay a-bed ten days and ten nights.

Bethink thee of my love, and whence it came, my Lady Moon!

And oftentimes my skin waxed wan as the colour of boxwood, and all my hair was falling from my head, and what was left of me was but skin and bones. Was there a wizard to whom I did not seek, or a crone to whose house I did not resort, of them that have art magical? But this was no light malady, and the time went fleeting on.

Bethink thee of my love, and whence it came, my Lady Moon!

Thus I told the true story to my maiden, and said, "Go, Thestylis, and find me some remedy for this sore disease. Ah me, the Myndian possesses me, body and soul! Nay, depart, and watch by the wrestling-ground of Timagetus, for there is his resort, and there he loves to loiter."

Bethink thee of my love, and whence it came, my Lady Moon!

"And when thou art sure he is alone, nod to him secretly, and say, 'Simaetha bids thee to come to her,' and lead him hither privily."

So I spoke; and she went and brought the bright-limbed Delphis to my house. But I, when I beheld him just crossing the threshold of the door, with his light step—

Bethink thee of my love, and whence it came, my Lady Moon!

Grew colder all than snow, and the sweat streamed from my brow like the dank dews, and I had no strength to speak, nay, nor to utter as much as children murmur in their slumber, calling to their mother dear: and all my fair body turned stiff as a puppet of wax.

Bethink thee of my love, and whence it came, my Lady Moon!

Then when he had gazed on me, he that knows not love, he fixed his eyes on the ground, and sat down on my bed, and spake as he sat him down: "Truly, Simaetha, thou didst by no more outrun mine own coming hither, when thou badst me to thy roof, than of late I outran in the race the beautiful Philinus:

Bethink thee of my love, and whence it came, my Lady Moon! "For I should have come: yea, my sweet Love, I should have come, with friends of mine, two or three, as soon as night drew on, bearing in my breast the apples of Dionysus, and on my head silvery poplar leaves, the holy boughs of Heracles, all twined with bands of purple."

Bethink thee of my love, and whence it came, my Lady Moon!

And if you had received me, they would have taken it well, for among all the youths unwed I have a name for beauty and speed of foot. With one kiss of thy lovely mouth I had been content; but an if ye had thrust me forth, and the door had been fastened with the bar, then truly should the torch and axe have broken in upon you.

Bethink thee of my love, and whence it came, my Lady Moon! And now to Cypris first, methinks, my thanks are due, and after Cypris it is thou that hast caught me, lady, from the burning, in that thou badst me come to this thy house, half consumed as I am! Yea, Love, 'tis plain, lights oft a fiercer blaze than Hephaestus the God of Lipara.

Bethink thee of my love, and whence it came, my Lady Moon! 'With his madness dire, he scares both the maiden from her bower and the bride from the bridal bed, yet warm with the body of her lord!'

So he spake, and I, that was easy to win, took his hand, and drew him down on the soft bed beside me. And immediately body from body caught fire, and our faces glowed as they had not done, and sweetly we murmured. And now, dear Selene, to tell thee no long tale, the great rites were accomplished, and we twain came to our desire. Faultless was I in his sight, till yesterday, and he, again, in mine. But there came to me the mother of Philista, my flute player, and the mother of Melixo, today, when the horses of the Sun were climbing the sky, bearing Dawn of the rosy arms from the ocean stream. Many another thing she told me; and chiefly this, that Delphis is a lover, and whom he loves she vowed she knew not surely, but this only, that ever he filled up his cup with the unmixed wine, to drink a toast to his dearest. And at last he went off hastily, saying that he would cover with garlands the dwelling of his love.

This news my visitor told me, and she speaks the truth. For indeed, at other seasons, he would come to me thrice, or four times, in the day, and often would leave with me his Dorian oil flask. But now it is the twelfth day since I have even looked on him! Can it be that he has not some other delight, and has forgotten me? Now with magic rites I will strive to bind him, but if still he vexes me, he shall beat, by the Fates I vow it, at the gate of Hell. Such evil medicines I store against him in a certain coffer, the use whereof, my lady, an Assyrian stranger taught me.

But do thou farewell, and turn thy steeds to Ocean, Lady, and my pain I will bear, as even till now I have endured it. Farewell, Selene bright and fair, farewell ye other stars, that follow the wheels of quiet Night.

> Theocritus (c. 310-c. 250 B.C.), Greek poet, born in Syracuse, Sicily. Author of a series of thirty bucolic Idyls, of which this is the Second Idyl.

Charm against Evil

Get thee a feather of the wide-feathered bird Varenjana, O Spitama Zarathustra. With that feather thou shalt rub thy body: with that feather thou shalt curse back thine enemy. He who hath a bone of the mighty bird or a feather of the mighty bird gaineth divine favor. No one, however magnificent, smiteth him or turneth him to flight.

> *Avesta*, sacred Persian texts.

ZARATHUSTRA: also known as Zoroaster, ancient Persian founder of religious cult.

Spell to Banish Pain

On a paper hung round the neck:
"An ant has no blood nor bile: flee, uvula, lest a crab eat you."

> Ancient Roman formula.

Magic Betting:
Curse against Opponents' Horses

I summon you demon and hand over to you these horses to keep them and bind them so that they cannot move.

> Roman magic tablet.

Incantation for Dislocated Bone

Huat hanat huat
Ista pista sista
Domiabo damnaustra

> Cato (234-149 B.C.), Roman statesman and writer. Author of *De Agri Cultura*.

Carna Uses a Charm to Banish Harpies

Forthwith she touched the lintels with arbutus leaf, thrice, in sequence. Thrice she marked the thresholds with arbutus, and sprinkled water on the entrance—for water is potent—and examined the fresh organs of a two-month-old sow.

> Ovid (43 B.C.-17 A.D.), Roman Poet, *Fasti*.

The goddess Carna used this ritual to drive away the monstrous creatures, half bird, half woman, known in ancient times as harpies.

The number three, in magic ritual, is a significant number. Among the ancients, the Egyptians and the Hebrews dwelt on the occult properties of numbers. Odd numbers were lucky: even numbers instigated demoniac attacks from the infernal powers. Three was effective in incantations. Similarly, seven, nine, and multiples of these numbers possessed thaumaturgic potency. In Pythagorean philosophy, which had mystic phases, the number ten indicated the god Atlas, who upholds the cosmos. Justice is symbolized by the number five, while one is equated with primal chaos.

umphant, and let thy strength be his strength. Thy members, O Ra, are established by this Chapter.

The Book of the Dead, Egyptian funeral ritual.

Spell Written on Strip of Byssus and Placed round the Neck of Deceased. Address to Ra

O thou that cleavest the water as thou comest forth from the stream and dost sit upon thy place in thy boat, sit thou upon thy place in thy boat as thou goest forth to thy station of yesterday, and do thou join the Osiris, the overseer of the house of the overseer of the seal, Nu, triumphant, the perfect Khu, unto thy mariners, and let thy strength be his strength. Hail, Ra, in thy name of Ra, if thou dost pass by the eye of seven cubits, which hath a pupil of three cubits, then verily do thou strengthen the Osiris Nu, triumphant, the perfect Khu, and let him be among thy mariners, and let thy strength be his strength. Hail, Ra, in thy name of Ra, if thou dost pass by those who are overturned in death then verily do thou make the Osiris Nu, triumphant, the perfect soul, to stand up upon his feet, and may thy strength be his strength. Hail, Ra, in thy name of Ra, if the hidden things of the underworld are opened unto thee and thou dost gratify the heart of the cycle of thy gods, then verily do thou grant joy of heart unto the overseer of the house of the overseer of the seal, Nu, tri-

How to Become Immortal

Immortality be upon this one! He is a sharer of the Sun's everlasting life. Indra and Agni have blessed him, and have taken him into immortality.
Bhaga and Soma are with him, carrying him high, to prolong his days.

There will now be no danger of death.
This world will keep you, forever, rise up!
The Sun, the Wind, the Rain, are all with thee!

Thy body shall be strong and unaffected by any disease.
Life will be thine, I promise it; enter this ascending
Never-perishing, age-old chariot.

Savitar, the Saver, will guard thee, taking into converse
The great Vayu, of the living, Indra; and strength and
Breath shall be with thee; the spirit of life will
Ever remain. No illness shall touch thee; all Powers are on Thy side.

Spell from *Atharva Veda,* Hindu manual of magic. Sacred Books of the East, Bloomfield. London, 1892.

[34]

How to Arouse a Woman's Passion

With the all-powerful arrow of Love do I pierce thy heart, O woman! Love, love that causes unease, that will overcome thee, love for me!

That arrow, flying true and straight, will cause in thee burning desire. It has the point of my love, its shaft is my determination to possess thee!

Yea, thy heart is pierced. The arrow has struck home. I have overcome by these arts thy reluctance, thou art changed! Come to me, submissive, without pride, as I have no pride, but only longing! Thy mother will be powerless to prevent thy coming, neither shall thy father be able to prevent thee! Thou are completely in my power.

O Mitra, O Varuna, strip her of will power! I, I alone, wield power over the heart and mind of my beloved!

Atharva Veda, Sanskrit magic text.

How to Gain a Man's Love

I am possessed by burning love for this man: and this love comes to me from Apsaras, who is victorious ever. Let the man yearn for me, desire me, let his desire burn for me! Let this love come forth from the spirit, and enter him.

Let him desire me as nothing has been desired before! I love him, want him: he must feel this same desire for me!

O Maruts, let him become filled with love. O Spirit of the Air, fill him with love. O Agni, let him burn with love for me!

Atharva Veda, Sanskrit magic text.

How to Gain a Man's Love

By the power and Laws of Varuna I invoke the burning force of love, in thee, for thee. The desire, the potent love-spirit which all the gods have created in the waters, this I invoke, this I employ, to secure thy love for me!

Indrani has magnetized the waters with this love-force.

And it is that, by Varuna's Laws, that I cause to burn!

Thou wilt love me, with a burning desire.

Atharva Veda, Sanskrit magic text.

Invocation to Magic Herbs

We invoke brown, white, speckled, colored and black plants. They are to protect this person from ills sent by the gods: their father is the sky, mother the earth, root the ocean. Heavenly plants drive forth sinful disease.

The plants that spread forth, plants that are bushy, some with a single sheath, and those that are creepers; these do I invoke. I call the plants that have roots, plants that have stalks, those that cause their limbs to be divided, those that have been made by the gods, strong ones that give life to man.

With the might that is yours, ye mighty ones, with the power and the force that is yours, with that do ye, O Plants, rescue this man from his ill-health! I am now making the remedy.

The plants givala, naghrisha, givanti, and the plant arundhati, which takes away ills is flowering, and I call upon them to help him.

[35]

The wise plants are to come here, they understand what I am saying, and we may come together to bring this man safely to good health.

They are the food of the fire, the children of the water, they grow and regrow, strong, healing plants, with a thousand names, brought all together here.

Prickly plants, thrust aside evil. Plants that act against witchcraft, shall come here, plants which have been bought, which protect animals and men, they shall come.

The tops, the ends, the middles of all these plants are steeped in honey, and they shall all, even unto thousands, aid against death and suffering.

The talisman made of plants is like a tiger; it will protect against hostility, it will drive off all disease.

Diseases will flow away along the rivers.

Atharva Veda, Sanskrit magic text.

How to Acquire a Husband

I seek a husband. Sitting here, my hair flowing loose, I am like one positioned before a giant procession, searching for a husband for this woman without a spouse.

O Aryaman! This woman cannot longer bear to attend the marriages of other women. Now, having performed this rite, other women will come to the wedding-feast of hers!

The Creator hold up the Earth, the planets, the Heavens.

O Creator, produce for me a suitor, a husband!

Atharva Veda, Sanskrit magic text.

Spell to Acquire Virility

Thou art the plant which Varuna had dug up for him by Gandharva, thou potent and lusty herb, which we have uprooted.

Ushas, Surya, Pragapati, all are with me; all will give me the potent force I seek! O Indra, give this material power; it has heat like that of the fire. Like the he-antelope, O Herb, thou hast all the force there is, as the brother of the great Soma.

Atharva Veda, Sanskrit magic text.

Talisman of Invulnerability

Bound upon the owner this charm is all-powerful. It makes the possessor strong and brave, kills enemies, brings fortune to him who has it. It is potent, too, against all magic. This is the charm used by Indra to kill Vritra. He smashed the Asuras and became master of heaven and earth, and with its aid he overcame the four spheres of space. Yes, this talisman, is an attacking and victorious one. It will destroy the enemy, and will protect us from him.

This is what Agni and Soma have said, Indra, Brihaspati and Savitar, all concur in this. Those who attack me will be repelled, and the same force as they use shall rebound upon them: by the force of this talisman!

Heaven, Earth, the Sun, the Ages, all shall stand between me and the enemy. Their force shall rebound upon them: by the force of this talisman!

This talisman is to me and other users

as is an all-powerful armour. It ascends the spheres like the Sun rising into Heaven, destroys all magic against me. It is a potent force, and the Rashas will fall before it!

Indra, Vishnu, Savitar, Rudra, Agni, Prajapati, Parameshthin, Viraj, Vaysvanara, all of them, the powerful spirits, shall stand behind the amulet, which is affixed to the wearer, as a powerful armour.

O most potent tree, potent like a leader amongst beasts, thou art my guardian and my help, such did I need, such have I found. And I, wearing this charm am like a tiger, like a bull, like unto a lion: nothing can touch me, wearer of this charm. He who wears it can command all, and be their ruler.

Produced and made by Kassyapa, worn by Indra in his battles, surely he is a vanquisher. It is the power of the spirits that makes this amulet one of power multiplied a thousandfold. O Indra, with a whip of a hundred lightning-flashes, strike him who would seek to strike me, by virtue of this charm!

And this great and powerful talisman does strike to victory wherever it is used. It produces children, fecundity, security, fortunes!

Those who are against us in the north, in the south, in the west, in the east, uproot them, O Indra!

My protection, like an armour, is the sun, the day and the night, the heavens and the earth. My protection is Indra, and Agni. Dhatar will give me that protection. Every spirit that there is cannot pierce the defenses of Indra and Agni: this is the strength that I have between me and the enemy. O spirits! Let me

become old and not be cut off in my youth!

Nothing can happen to the wearer of this amulet. It is the very talisman of invulnerability!

Atharva Veda, Sanskrit magic text.

This spell is pronounced in connection with a talisman made from Sraktya wood.

Invocation to Magic Herbs

We invoke and address the magical plants: plants that are red, those that are white, and the brown and black herbs: all these do we invoke! Verily the spirits are in control of the infirmities. Herbs, rooted in the seas, mothered by the lands, fathered by the sky!

Plants and herbs of the Heavens! Illness and maladies coming from sinfulness do you exorcise! I call upon the creepers, upon those plants that bear luxurious foliage. These are herbs that give us life: they multiply by division, they are vigorous, they have strong roots.

O plants and herbs! You have the power to rescue this sufferer! I call upon and adjure you to make the remedy that I shall prepare powerful and effective.

Atharva Veda, Sanskrit magic text.

Charm against Illness

The seers, while speaking the name of Indra, gave to man the Gangida. It had been made a remedy by the gods from the beginning, and a destroyer of the Vishkandha.

Protect us, Gangida, for we look after

his treasures, verily the gods and the Brahmanas made him a protection that nullifies evil forces!

I have approached the evil eye of the inimical: O thousand-eyed one, destroy all these! Gangida, thou art our refuge.

The Gangida will protect me from the heavens, from the earth, from plants, from the air; and from the past, and from the future. I am to be protected in every direction!

May the all-powerful, protective Gangida render all the magic of gods and men weak and powerless!

Atharva Veda, Sanskrit magic text.

Spell chanted in connection with talisman made from Gangida wood.

How to Acquire a Wife

I take upon myself strength, strength of a hundred men. I take up this power in the name of the spirit that comes here, that is coming, that has come. O Indra, give me that strength!

As the Asvins took Surya, the child of Savitar, to be a bride, so has destiny said that here shall come a wife for this man! Indra, with that hook of gold, of power, bring here a wife for him that desires a wife.

Atharva Veda, Sanskrit magic text.

Spell to Banish Evil

Release me, evil power; please release me, the unfortunate victim of your malice! Let me escape this evil thing, and be happy again!

If you do not release me, then I will abandon you at the next crossroads; and you will follow and possess another!

Go, follow another: join the man who is my enemy, strike him!

Atharva Veda, Sanskrit magic text.

The Sanskrit term veda means *divine knowledge*. The Vedas are Hindu scriptural literature, dating in the second millennium B.C. They are divided into four collections covering hymns to the gods, priestly chants, sacrificial formulas, magical incantations. These four Vedas are: Rig Veda, Yajur Veda, Sama Veda, Atharva Veda.

Apotropaic Spell

Hring, may the Adya protect my head;
Shring, may Kali protect my face;
Kring, may the Supreme Shakti protect my heart;
May She Who is the Supreme of the Supreme protect my throat;
May Jagaddhatri protect my two eyes;
May Shamkari protect my two ears;
May Mahamaya protect my power of smell;
May Sarva-mamgala protect my taste;
May Kaumari protect my teeth;
May Kamalalaya protect my cheeks;
May Kshama protect my upper and lower lips;
May Charu-hasini protect my chin;
May Kuleshani protect my throat;
May Kripa-mayi protect the nape of my neck;
May Bahuda protect my two arms;
May Kaivalya-dayini protect my two hands;
May Kapardini protect my shoulders;
May Trailokya-tarini protect my back;

May Aparna protect my two sides;
May Kamathasana protect my hips;
May Vishalakshi protect my navel;
May Prabha-vati protect my organ of generation;
May Kalyani protect my thighs;
May Parvati protect my feet;
May Jaya-durga protect my vital breaths;
And Sarva-siddhi-da protect all parts of my body.

Tantra.

The Hindu Tantras, written in Sanskrit, constitute an encyclopedic corpus of esoteric knowledge, traditionally assumed to have been expounded in form of dialogue between deity Siva and wife Parvata. The Tantric themes, the scriptures of this fourth or present age, are: creation, worship of gods, spiritual exercise, rituals, six magical powers, meditation.
Hring, Shring, Kring, etc.: Hindu deities.

Charm for Gout

Touch the earth, spit downward, and chant twenty-seven times, fasting:

O Earth, keep the pain,
and health with me remain
in my feet.

Varro (116-27 B.C.), Roman author of *De Agri Cultura*.

Evil Eye on Cattle

Some eye or other casts an evil spell on my young lambs.
Vergil (70-19 B.C.), Roman poet. *Eclogues*.

Lover's Lament

Thrice I with Sulphur purified you round,
And thrice the Rite, with Songs th' Enchantress bound:
The Cake, by me thrice sprinkled, put to flight
The death-denouncing Phantoms of the Night,
And I next have, in linen Garb array'd,
In silent Night, nine Times to Trivia pray'd.

Tibullus (c. 48-19 B.C.), Roman elegiac poet. Translated by J. Grainger, 1759.

The poem is addressed to Delia, who scorned the poet's love.
THRICE: in magic rites, three was an effective number in incantations.
SULPHUR: regularly associated with magic rites.
CAKE: compounded of flour and salt, made three times a year by the Vestal Virgins, Roman priestesses.
NINE: a magic number.
TRIVIA: a variant name for Hecate, goddess of the Lower Regions and patroness of witchcraft.

Invocation of Medea

O night, faithful preserver of mysteries, and ye bright stars, whose golden beams with the moon succeed the fires of day; thou three—formed Hecate, who knowest our undertakings and comest to our aid: ye spells and arts that the wise men use; and thou, O Earth, who dost provide the wise men with thy potent herbs; ye breezes and winds, ye mountains and streams and pools; all ye gods of the groves, all ye gods of the night;

[39]

be with me now. With your help I stir up the calm seas by my spell; I break the jaws of serpents with my incantations. I bid ghosts to come forth from their tombs. Now I have need of juices by whose aid old age may be renewed and may turn back to the bloom of youth and regain its earthly years.

> Ovid (43 B.C.-17 A.D.), Roman poet. Author of *Metamorphoses*, Loeb Classical Library.

Roman Charm against Fascinatio

A grandmother or a superstitious aunt has taken the baby from the cradle and is charming its forehead and slobbering lips against mischief by the action of her middle finger and her purifying spittle: for she is skilled in checking the evil eye.

> Persius (34-62 A.D.), Roman satirist. Satire 2.

Magic Curse

We are all afraid of being nailed by spells and dire curses.

> Pliny the Elder (23-79 A.D.), Roman Encyclopedist. Author of *Natural History*.

Doomed person's name was inscribed on a lead tablet, through which a nail was driven.

A Man's head as a Talisman

Olenus Calenus (who was reputed the most famous diviner and prophet of all the Tuscans) foreseeing the great felicity it imported, intended by a subtle interrogation to translate the benefit thereof to his own native country of Tuscany. So having first described with a staff the outline of a temple on the ground before him he questioned the Roman ambassadors in this wily manner. 'Is it so, Romans, as you say? Are these your words, that there must be a temple of Jupiter here, where we have lighted on a man's head?' Unto which interrogation the Roman ambassadors, according to the instructions they have received, answered in this manner. 'No, not here in this very place, but at Rome (we say) the head was found.' Indeed, our ancient Chronicles constantly affirm that, had they not been forewarned what to say, the fortune of the Roman State and Empire had gone quite away to the Tuscans and been established among them.

> Pliny the Elder (23-79 A.D.). Roman encyclopedist, author of voluminous *Natural History*. Translated by Philemon Holland, 1601.

When the foundations of a temple to Jupiter were being dug in Rome, the Romans found a man's head, a portent that was duly interpreted by Tuscan soothsayers.

Getting Rid of an Emperor by Magic

A discovery was made of a singular nature. Under the floor and in the cavities of the walls, a collection of human bones was found, with charms and magic verses and incantations. The

LABORATORY OF THE ALCHEMIST

Alchemy, developing from the second century onward, reached its height in the Middle Ages. It was considered a branch of the occult arts. One of its aims was the transmutation of base metals into gold. Note, in the illustration, the furnace, crucibles and alembics and other apparatus that were virtually the foundation of the modern chemical laboraory.

(After P. Brueghel, 16th century Flemish painter)

Courtesy of The Metropolitan Museum of Art, N. Y.

THE MAGIC MIRROR

In occult practice magic mirrors were used to foretell future events. Such a scene is here depicted. Note the cabalistic and alchemical formulas on the wall.

(Miniature from *La Très Sainte Trinosophie*, attributed to the Comte de Saint-Germain: 18th century)

Courtesy of the Bibliothèque de Troyes, France.

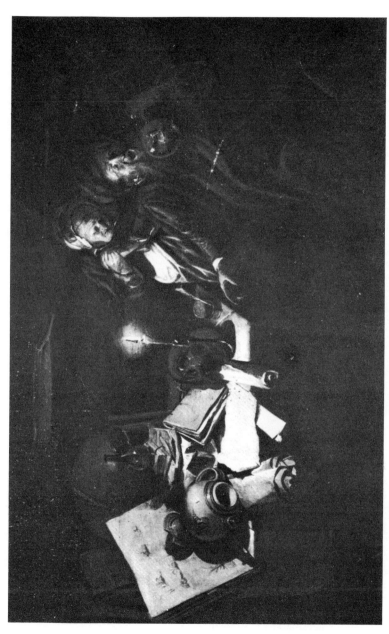

CREATION OF AN ANDROID

Medieval alchemists, in the course of their operations in the transmutation of metals, were also believed to practice the occult arts. Here is the alchemist amazed at having produced, in the glass vessel, life in embryo by magic skill.

(Painting by Rijckaert David, Antwerp, 1612-1661)

Courtesy of the Museum of Mannheim, Germany.

THE ALCHEMIST

Notice, among the alchemist's properties, the human skull and the hourglass. In the background, one assistant is preparing a concoction with mortar and pestle, while the alchemist himself consults an occult work.

(After David Teniers, 17th century Dutch painter)

Courtesy of the Bibliothèque de Troyes, France.

name of Germanicus was engraved on plates of lead; fragments of human bodies, not quite consumed to ashes, were discovered in a putrid condition, with a variety of those magic spells which, according to the vulgar opinion, are of potency to devote the souls of the living to the infernal gods.

Tacitus (c. 55-c. 116 A.D.), Roman historian. Author of *Annals.* Translated by A. Murphy.

Germanicus (15 B.C.-19 A.D.): Roman Emperor.

Spell on Crops

The magic you speak of, as far as I hear, is proscribed by law. It was long ago interdicted, in ancient times, by the Twelve Tables, on account of the incredible spells cast on crops. Hence magic is secretive and foul and horrible, usually practiced at night and shrouded in darkness.

Apuleius (2nd century A.D.), Roman novelist. Author of *Apologia,* in which he refutes charges of witchcraft.

TWELVE TABLES: ancient Roman Laws that proscribed magic practices detrimental to the state.

Apotropaic Love Spells

Mopsus: What does it benefit me that the mother of rustic Amyntas has purified me thrice with fillets, thrice with a sacred bough, thrice with the vapour of frankincense, burning the crackling laurels with live sulphur, and pours the ashes out into the stream with averted

face, when thus wretched I am every way inflamed for Meroë?

Lycidas: These same things the many-coloured threads have done for me, and Mycale has carried round me a thousand unknown herbs. She has chanted the charm, by which the moon swells, by which the snake is burst, the rocks run and standing corn removes, and a tree is plucked up. Lo! My handsome Iollas is nevertheless more, is more to me.

Nemesianus (3rd century A.D.), Roman poet. Author of *Eclogues.* Translated by J. J. Mooney.

To Banish a Spell

I take refuge with the Lord
of the Daybreak from the evil
of the blowers upon knots
and from the evil of the
envious one when he envies.

Al Koran.

BLOWERS UPON KNOTS: in Moslem demonology, enchanters who cast spells by blowing on knots to affect their victims.
The knot was so commonly associated with magic that "tying knots" or "binding" was synonymous with magic.
Such knots, consisting of multicolored threads, animal hair, plain stems, were used to remove spells or cure sickness. In Egyptian talismans the knot was a frequent design. Petronius, the Roman novelist who flourished in the reign of Nero, describes the use of multicolored twisted threads to free a person from a spell.

Demoniac Conjuration

I invoke and command thee, O Spirit, by all the resplendent and potent Names of the Great and unparalleled Jehovam Sabaoth, our Lord, to come here to this place instanter! Come, from whichever place in the world thou art. And give answer to my questions: answers that shall be true and reasonable. Come, then, in visible form, come and speak pleasantly, and that I may understand thy words!

I conjure thee, and thou art invoked, by all the Names that have been spoken! And by the Seven Secret Names wherewith Solomon, the King, son of David, did compel thee and thy fellow spirits in the brazen Vessel. And these are thus:

By Adonai, by Prerai, by Tetragrammaton, by Anexhexeton, by Inessesensatoal, by Pathumaton, and by Itemon!

Come, visibly, before this Circle, obedient in every way to my desires! If thou dost come not, or disobey in any way, I will curse thee, and will cause thee to be stripped of thy powers, and consigned to the bottomless Pit, where thou wilt remain until the Day of Judgement!

I will cause thee to be bound to the Waters of Everlasting Flame, Fire and Brimstone! Come, then, and appear before this Circle, to obey me utterly!

And otherwise thou art cursed in the Name of the Most Powerful Lord! In the Name Eye, the Name Saray, the Name Primematum, the Supreme Power of all Heaven! And in the Name of the Lord who created the entire World, all within it, in the space of six days!

Come, then, through the virtue of the Most Holy and Efficacious Names Adonai, Sabaoth, Amioram!

Come, in the Name of Adonai!

Lemegeton, a medieval grimoire.

Invocation to Make Magic Carpet

Agla, Agla, Agla, Agla! O Almighty God, Thou art the Life of the Universe, and rulest over the four parts of that immense area, through the power of Thy Holy Name Tetragrammaton: Yod, He, Vau, He! Bless this carpet in Thy Name, as Thou blessed the cloak of Elijah in the hands of Elijah; so that, with Thy wings, I may be able to be protected against all: He shall hide thee under His wings and under His feathers thou shalt trust, and His truth shall be thy protection.

Key of Solomon, medieval grimoire.

The carpet, made of new wool during the full moon, produces oracular utterances.

Charm for Securing Husband

Ojala
Ojal
Oja
Oj
O

Spell of Spanish—Moorish origin.

The expression stems from the Arabic Allah —God.

Invocation for Finding Treasure

Adonai, Elohim, El, Eheieh, Asher Eheieh: King of Kings, Existence of all Existences, be merciful to me, and look upon me Thy servant, who calls Thee with humility, and begs by Thy most holy name Tetragrammaton to be benefited.

[42]

Order Thy Angels and planetary spirits to come and be here: O Angels and planetary spirits! O all of you, spirits, I conjure you: I, the deputed of God! let God order you to come, that I ask most fervently and most humbly. Amen.

Key of Solomon, medieval grimoire.

Curse

O commanders and friends, I conjure and command you to obey this order without hesitation: consecrate this figure in the name of [victim] and the one is against the other. Thus they are henceforth irreconcilable.

Key of Solomon, medieval grimoire.

The curse involves image of victim left in a dish of burning fumes.

Charm against Witches

Black-luggie, hammer-head,
Rowan-tree, and red thread
Put the warlocks to their speed
                    Old English charm.

Rowan-tree: reputed to have protective powers against demons.

License of Demon to Depart

O Spirit, because thou hast diligently answered my demands, I do hereby license thee to depart, without injury to man or beast. Depart, I say, and be thou willing and ready to come, whensoever duly exorcised and conjured by the Sacred Rites of Magic. I conjure thee to withdraw peaceably and quietly, and may the peace of God continue for ever between me and thee. Amen.

Medieval grimoire.

Mosaic Invocation

I conjure you, Azliel called X: I conjure you, Arel called X, Ta'aniel called X, Tafel called X, and the most glorious of these Yofiel Mittron called X, the glory from above. With the permission of my king I conjure Yadiel called X, Ra'asiel called X, Haniel called X, Asrael called X, Yisriel called X, A'shael called X, Amuhael called X, and Asrael called X, that you attach yourselves to me and surrender the 'Sword' to me, so that I may use it according to my desire, and that I find shelter under the shadow of our Lord in heaven in the glorious Name, the mighty and awe-inspiring X, the twenty-four letters from the Crown; that you deliver unto me with this 'Sword' the secrets from above and below, the mysteries from above and below, and my wish be fulfilled and my words harkened unto, and my prayers received through the conjuration with the Ineffable name of God which is glorified in the world.

Sword of Moses. An ancient book of magic first published by Dr. M. Gaster. London, 1896.

NAME: ineffable name: i.e., the Tetragrammaton, the Kabalistic term for the four-letter name of God.

Conjuration against an Enemy

I call thee, evil spirit, cruel spirit, merciless spirit. I call thee, bad spirit, who sittest in the cemetery and takes away healing from man. Go and place a knot in N's head, in his eyes, in his mouth, in his tongue, in his throat, in his windpipe: put poisonous water in his belly. If you do not go and put poisonous water in his belly, I will send you the evil angels Puziel, Guziel, Psdiel, Prziel. I call thee and those six knots that you go quickly to N and put poisonous water in his belly and kill N because I wish it. Amen. Amen. Selah.

Sword of Moses. An ancient book of magic first published, from a unique manuscript, by Dr. M. Gaster. London, 1896.

KNOT: knots are regularly associated with spell-binding.
N: i.e. Nomen—the name of the victim is here inserted. The efficacy of a curse is normally confirmed by minute listing of all parts of the victim's body affected by the spell.

Creation by Spell

Sang a dog with pointed muzzle
Sang a golden-breasted marten
By his spells a hen created
Thereupon a hawk created.

The *Kalevala*, Finnish epic.

SANG: that is, produced by means of occult incantations.

Creation by Spell

But the mighty son of Poja
By his spells a wolf created
and upon the floor he sang him
To devour the fleshy bullock.

The *Kalevala*, Finnish epic.

HE SANG HIM: that is, he induced him, by means of incantations.

Casting of Spell

"Noble dame, Creation's daughter,
Noble one, as gold all lustrous,
Thou the oldest of all women,
Thou the first of all mothers,
Knee-deep in the lake descend thou,
To thy waist among the billows,
From the perch the slime obtain thou,
And the slime from creeping creatures,
Do thou smear with this the gateway,
And upon the sides anoint it,
Free the damsel of her burden,
And the woman from her sufferings,
Free her from this grievous torment,
And release her from her sufferings.
"But if this is not sufficient,
Ukko, thou of Gods, the highest,
Hither come where thou art needed,
Come thou at our supplication.
Here there is a girl in childbed,
And a woman suffering greatly,
Her amid the bathroom's vapour,
Brought into the village bathroom.
"Do thou take thy club all golden,
In thy right hand do thou take it,
Each impediment remove thou,
And the door-posts move asunder,
Bend thou the Creator's castles,
Break thou all the bars asunder,
Push the large ones and the small ones,
Even to the very smallest."

Kalevala, Finnish epic.

The woman Louhi is casting a spell on a pregnant woman.

Spells against Evil

Then the aged Vainamoinen,
He the great primeval sorcerer,
Went to drive away the evil,

And his people's lives to succour,
Forth he went to war with Tuoni,
And against disease to struggle.

Thereupon he warmed the bathroom,
And the stones prepared to heat it,
And the finest wood provided,
Faggotts too he laid in water;
Water brought in covered vessels,
Bath-whisks also, well-protected,
Warmed the bath-whisks to perfection,
And the hundred twigs he softened.

Then he raised a warmth like honey,
Raised a heat as sweet as honey,
From the heated stones he raised it,
From the glowing stones he raised it,
And he spoke the words which follow,
And in words like these expressed him:

"Now the bath approach, O Jumala,
To the warmth, O heavenly Father,
Healthfulness again to grant us,
And our peace again secure us.
Drive away these foul diseases,
From these dread diseases save us,
Calm thou down this heat excessive,
Drive away this heat so evil,
That it may not burn thy children,
Neither may destroy thy offspring.

"Therefore will I sprinkle water,
On the glowing stones I cast it,
Let it now be changed to honey,
May it trickle down like honey,
Let it flow a stream like honey,
Flowing to a lake like honey,
As it flows along the hearthstones,
Flowing through the mossy bathroom,

"Do not let us guiltless perish,
Nor be overcome by sickness,
'Gainst the great Creator's mandate,
When sends Jumala our death not.

"Bring me now a sword of fire,
Bring me now a flashing sword blade,
That I may oppose these evils,

Quite subdue these frightful evils,
On the wind's path drive our sufferings,
Drive them far amid the deserts.

"Thence I'll drive these sorcerers' torments,
Thence these sufferings will I banish,
Far away to rocky caverns."

Kalevala, Finnish epic.

The aged Vainamoinen, through sorcery, dispelled evils, and lifted burdens from his people.

Conjuration

I conjure you that you forthwith appear, and show yourself unto me, before this circle in a fair and human shape without any deformity or ugly shape, and without delay.

I conjure you by him to whom all creatures are obedient: and by this ineffable Name Tetragrammaton Jehovah, which being heard the Elements are overturned, the air is shaken, the sea runs back, the fire is quenched, the earth trembles.

Therefore come you in the name Adonaij-Zabaoth, Adonaij Amiorem.

Come, come, why stay you. Hasten, Adonay Saday the King of Kings commands you.

Lemegeton, medieval grimoire.

The exorcist who utters this conjuration has fasted one month, observed chastity during that time, is clad in white, and is girdled with a lion's skin.

TETRAGRAMMATON: Kabalistic term for the four-letter name of God. It involved mystic combinations of letters and of multiple lettered names of attributes, some consisting of seventy-two elements.

[45]

Magic Power of Evil

"Whence the life he gave unto it?
Life he brought from Hiisi's coal heap.
Whence was then its heart created?
Out of Syojatar's own heartstrings.
Whence the brains for this foul creature?
From a mighty torrent's foaming.
Whence a head, this foul enchantment?
From the bean, a bean all rotten.
Whence then were its eyes created?
From the seed of flax of Lempo.
Whence were the toad's ears created?
From the leaves of Lempo's birch tree.
Whence was then its mouth constructed?
Syojatar's own mouth supplied it.
Whence the tongue in mouth so evil?
From the spear of Keitolainen.
Teeth for such an evil creature?
From the beard of Tuoni's barley.
Whence its filthy gums created?
From the gums of Kalma's maiden.
Whence was then its back constructed?
Of the coals of fire of Hiisi.
Whence its wriggling tail constructed?
From the plaits of Pahalainen.
Whence its entrails were constructed?
These were drawn from Death's own
  girdle."

Kalevala, Finnish epic.

This passage refers to the origin of a serpent, created by Hiisi, a giant, representing
power of Evil.

Spell to Banish Mists

With his sword he clove the water,
In the lake his sword plunged deeply,
Mead along his blade was flowing,
Honey from his sword was dropping,
Then the fog to heaven ascended,

And the cloud in air rose upward,
From the lake the mist ascended,
And the vapour from the lake-waves,
And the lake extended widely,
Wider spread the whole horizon.

Kalevala, Finnish epic.

This passage refers to the aged Vainamoinen, son of Creatrix of World, Ilmatar.

Kaukomieli Creates by Incantation

I'll create by songs of magic
Both a man and horse of alder
And a man of snow I'll sing me
Made of frozen snow a hero.

Kaukomieli, a character in the
Kalevala, the epic of Finland.

Charm against Eagle Attack

Took the feathers of the blackfowl
Leisurely he rubbed the feathers
. . . . .
And a flock of grouse created.

This is the work of the sorcerer Lemminkäinen, a character in the *Kalevala*.

Incantation for Banishing Sickness

Ofano, Oblamo, Ospergo.
Hola Noa Massa.
Light, Beff, Cletemati, Adonai,
Cleona, Florit.
Pax Sax Sarax.
Afa Afca Nostra.
Cerum, Heaium, Lada Frium.

From the writings of Albertus Magnus (1206-1280), theologian, philosopher, and occultist.

[46]

Arabian Enchantments

Then she stood up; and pronouncing some words to me unintelligible, she said: "By virtue of my necromancy, become thou half stone and half man . . ."

And the citizens she transformed by her enchantments into fishes.

Arabian Nights.

Talisman for Acquiring Knowledge of All Minerals and All Remedies

This talisman and this ring will give you knowledge of all minerals and all vegetables, their virtues and properties, and you will possess universal medicine. There is no sickness that you will not be able to cure, no remedy that you cannot successfully undertake. Aesculapius and Hippocrates will be but schoolboys compared with you.

Just pronounce these words: Reterrem, Salibat, Cratares, Hisater, and when you are at a sick bedside, carry the talisman on your stomach and the ring attached to a red ribbon round your neck.

The Black Hen, a medieval grimoire or manual of magic.

Talisman for Achieving Invisibility

"This talisman and this ring will make you invisible, even to spirits. You will be able to traverse the bosom of the seas, the bowels of the earth. Likewise you will be able to sweep through the air, nor will any human act be hidden from you.

"Say only: Benatir, Caracrau, Dedos, Etinarmi."

The Black Hen.

The Black Hen is a mediaeval grimoire.

Incantation Stops Flow of Blood

Listen, o blood, instead of flowing,
  instead of pouring forth thy warm
  stream.
Stop, o blood, like a wall,
Stop like a hedge.
Stop like a reef in the sea:
  like stiff sedge in the moss,
  like a boulder in the field,
  like the pine in the wood.

Kalevala, Finnish epic.

Incantation against Sickness

O malady, disappear into the heavens: pain, rise up to the clouds: inflamed vapour, fly into the air, in order that the wind may take thee away, that the tempest may chase thee to distant regions, where neither sun nor moon give their light, where the warm wind does not inflame the flesh.

Kalevala, Finnish epic.

Spell-Bound Musicians

And Lemminkäinen began his spells.

He sang, and the most accomplished singers only brought forth ridiculous sounds.

Their hands became covered with

stone gloves, masses of stone bent their backs, a stone hat crushed their heads, stone collars squeezed their necks.

Kalevala, Finnish epic.

LEMMINKAINEN: a sorcerer.

Deities Subject to Sorcery

The Laplander cannot hurt me with his spells, for I hold in my hands the celestial wand, and he who hates me, and would bring evil upon me, does not possess it.

Kalevala, Finnish epic.

The speaker is the god Wäinämöinen, threatened by a sorceress of Lapland. The celestial wand acts as a divine apotropaic talisman.

Magic Ritual

Let him choose a holy place, undefiled, hidden, remote from noise, and let him be observed by no one, and let him consecrate this spot and exorcise it; and let him have in this spot either a table or a little altar covered with pure white linen, facing the East, and on two sides two lighted candles of pure wax, burning continuously all these days. In the centre of the altar, the sacred chart is placed, covered with white silk, that is not to be taken away until the end of the fast. Have materials for fumigations, and consecrated oil; likewise a censer placed at the head of the altar, that will remain lit by the sacred fire during the entire period of your supplication. Wear a long robe, of white linen, closed in front and behind, to cover you to your feet, girt with a girdle. On your head place a band or ribbon, on which will be inscribed in gold the name Tetragrammaton.

Peter of Abano (13th century). *The Heptameron.*

Procedure in Summoning Spirits

If you would call any evil Spirit to the Circle it first behooveth us to consider and to know his nature, to which of the planets he agreeth, and what offices are distributed to him from the planet.

This being known, let there be sought out a place fit and proper for his invocation, according to the nature of the planet, and the quality of the offices of the same Spirit, as near as the same may be done.

For example, if his power be over the sea, rivers or floods, then let a place be chosen on the shore, and so of the rest.

In like manner, let there be chosen a convenient time, both for the quality of the air—which should be serene, quiet and fitting for the Spirits to assume bodies—and for the quality and nature of the planet, and so, too, of the Spirit: to wit, on his day, noting the time wherein he ruleth, whether it be fortunate or unfortunate, day or night, as the stars and Spirits do require.

These things being considered, let there be a circle framed at the place elected, as well for the defence of the invocant as for the confirmation of the Spirit. In the Circle itself there are to be written the general Divine names, and those things which do yield defence unto us; the Divine names which do rule the said planet, with the offices of the Spirit himself; and the names, finally of the Spirits which bear rule and are able to bind and constrain the Spirit which we intend to call.

Agrippa (1486-1533) *Occult Philosophy.* Translated by Turner (18th century).

Charm for Toothache

Galbes, galbat, galdes, galdat

Johann Weyer, *De Praestigiis Daemonum et Incantationibus ac Veneficiis,* 1568.

Charm for Curing Hydrophobia

A piece of apple inscribed with
hax, pax, max,
Deus adimax

Johann Weyer, *De Praestigiis Daemonum et Incantationibus ac Veneficiis,* 1568.

Charm for Hydrophobia

A piece of bread inscribed with these words:

Irioni khirioni, effer
khuder fere

Johann Weyer, *De Praestigiis Daemonum et Incantationibus ac Veneficiis,* 1568.

Magic in Manuals

He opens the manuals, or reads all that are open:
How to write arcane spells:
How to compel love;
How a husband can find out his wife's adultery;
How virginal maiden can be forced to love;
How to make a hated husband impotent.

Girolamo Folengo. *Maccaronea,* 1519.

Faust Invokes Satan

Now that the gloomy shadow of the night,
Longing to view Orions drisling looke,
Leaps from th'Antarticke world unto the skie,
And dymns the Welkin, with her pitchy breathe:
Faustus, begin thine Incantations,
And try if devils will obey thy Hest,
Seeing thou has pray'd and sacrificed to them.
Within this circle is Iehova's Name,
Forward and backward, Anagramatis'd:
Th' abreviated names of holy Saints,
Figures of every adjunct to the heavens,
And Characters of Signes, and evening Starres,
By which the spirits are inforc'd to rise:
Then feare not Faustus to be resolute
And try the utmost Magicke can performe.
Thunder. May the gods of Acheron be propitious to me. Away with the triple divine power of Jehovah. Fires

of the air, spirits of the water, hail! Beelzebub Prince of the East, monarch and demogorgon of flaming hell, we propitiate you, that Mephistopheles may appear and rise. By Jehovah, Gehenna, and the consecrated water which I now sprinkle; and the sign of the cross which I now make and by our vows may Mephistopheles himself now appear to us.

Christopher Marlowe (1563-1594), English dramatist. Author of *Dr. Faustus.*

CIRCLE: the circle that the magician draws on the ground, to enforce demons to appear.
IEHOVA'S NAME: the reference is to the Tetragrammaton, the Kabalistic term for the four-letter name of God.

Wolf Charm

In some countries they nail a wolf's head to the door, to prevent and cure all mischiefs by charms and witchcrafts.

Reginald Scot, *The Discovery of Witchcraft,* 1665.

Incantation to Stop Hemorrhage

The snakhar squeezes the wound and recites three times, in one breath: In the Ocean-sea, on the isle of Buyan a fair maiden was weaving silk: she did not leave off weaving silk: the blood ceased flowing.

Slavic Incantation.

SNAKHAR: Slavic term for sorcerer.

To Cure Cripples

You, O Red Woman, you have caused it. You have put the intruder under him.

Ha! now you have come from the Sun Land. You have brought the small red seats with your feet resting upon them.

Ha! now they have swiftly moved away from you. Relief is accomplished.

Mooney, *Sacred Formulas of the Cherokee.*

An invocation of Cherokee shaman.

Operatic Sorcery

Mr. Wells: We practise Necromancy in all its branches. We've a choice assortment of wishing-caps, divining rods, amulets, charms, and counter-charms. We can cast you a nativity at a low figure, and we have a horoscope at three-and-six that we can guarantee. Our Abudah chests, each containing a patent Hag who comes out and prophesies disasters, with spring complete, are strongly recommended. Our Aladdin lamps are very chaster, and our Prophetic Tablets foretelling everything— from a change of Ministry down to a rise in Unified—are much enquired for. Our penny Curse—one of the cheapest things in the trade—is considered infallible. We have some very superior Blessings, too, but they're very little asked for. We've only sold one since Christmas—to a gentleman who bought it to send to his mother-in-law—but it turned out that he was afflicted in the head, and it's been returned on our

CHRISTIAN'S COMBAT WITH APOLLYON
Apollyon, the Destroyer: one of the numerous names of Satan.
(A nineteenth century illustration for John Bunyan's *Pilgrim's Progress*)
Courtesy of the Museum of Mannheim, Germany.

WITCHES ASSEMBLED
(Medieval woodcut)

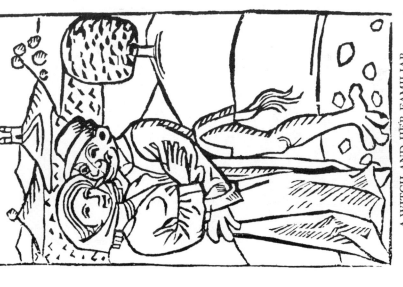

TRANSVECTION OF WITCHES

Transvection or levitation was believed in the Middle Ages to be a regular practice of witches. Frequently the witch, as here, changed into animal form and was thus carried on a broomstick to her assignation with his Satanic Majesty.

(A medieval conception)

A WITCH AND HER FAMILIAR

A familiar was an attendant demon attached to a witch: sometimes assuming animal shape, but also at times appearing in almost human form. Note in the illustration the demon's tail and animal feet.

(A medieval conception)

THE SABBAT

The Sabbat, or Sabbath, was a Satanic gathering of witches to do homage to the Arch-fiend. Note in the foreground the strange elemental spirits and the familiars of the witches: cats, lizards, and toads. The upper part of the picture shows witches riding the air on monstrous creatures. In the foreground St. James the Elder is seen combating a magician's malefic operations.

(Painting by Brueghel the Elder, 16th century Flemish artist) hands. But our sale of penny curses, especially on Saturday nights, is tremendous. We can't turn 'em out fast enough.

Song—Mr. Wells

Oh! My name is John Wellington Wells,
I'm a dealer in magic and spells,
 In blessings and curses
 And ever-filled purses,
In prophecies, witches, and knells.
If you want a proud foe to "make tracks"—
If you'd melt a rich uncle in wax—
 You've but to look in
 On our resident Djinn,
Number Seventy, Simmery Axe!

We've a first-class assortment of magic;
 And for raising a posthumous shade
With effects that are comic or tragic,
 There's no cheaper house in the trade.
Love-philtre—we've quantities of it;
 And for knowledge if any one burns,
We keep an extremely small prophet, a prophet
 Who brings in unbounded returns:

 For he can prophesy
 With a wink of his eye,
 Peep with security
 Into futurity,
 Sum up your history,
 Clear up a mystery,
 Humour proclivity
 For a nativity—for a nativity;
 With mirrors so magical,
 Tetrapods tragical,
 Bogies spectacular,
 Answers oracular,
 Facts astronomical,

 Solemn or comical,

And, if you want it, he
Makes a reduction on taking a quantity!
 Oh!
If any one anything lacks,
He'll find it all ready in stacks,
 If he'll only look in
 On the resident Djinn,
Number seventy, Simmery Axe!

He can raise you hosts
 Of ghosts,
And that without reflectors;
 And creepy things
 With wings,
And gaunt and grisly spectres.
He can fill you crowds
 Of shrouds,
And horrify you vastly;
 He can rack your brains
 With chains,
And gibberings grim and ghastly!

Then, if you plan it, he
Changes organity,
With an urbanity,
Full of Satanity,
Vexes humanity
With an inanity
Fatal to vanity—
Driving your foes to the verge of insanity!

Barring tautology,
In demonology,
'Lectro-biology,
Mystic nosology,
Spirit philology,
High-class astrology,
Such is his knowledge, he
Isn't the man to require an apology!
 Oh!

[51]

My name is John Wellington Wells,
I'm a dealer in magic and spells,
> In blessings and curses
> And ever-filled purses,
In prophecies, witches, and knells.

If any one anything lacks,
He'll find it all ready in stacks,
> If he'll only look in
> On the resident Djinn,
Number seventy, Simmery Axe!

Alexis: I have sent for you to consult you on a very important matter. I believe you advertise a Patent Oxy-Hydrogen Love-at-first-sight Philtre?

Mr. Wells: Sir, it is our leading article. (*Producing a phial.*)

Alexis: Now I want to know if you can confidently guarantee it as possessing all the qualities you claim for it in your advertisement?

Mr. Wells: Sir, we are not in the habit of puffing our goods. Ours is an old-established house with a large family connection, and every assurance held out in the advertisement is fully realised. (*Hurt.*)

Aline (aside): Oh, Alexis, don't offend him! He'll change us into something dreadful—I know he will!

Alexis: I am anxious from purely philanthropical motives to distribute this philtre, secretly, among the inhabitants of this village. I shall of course require a quantity. How do you sell it?

Mr. Wells: In buying a quantity, sir, we should strongly advise you taking it in the wood, and drawing it off as you happen to want it. We have it in four-and-a-half and nine gallon casks—also in pipes and hogsheads for laying down,

and we deduct 10 per cent for prompt cash.

Alexis: I should mention that I am a Member of the Army and Navy Stores.

Mr. Wells: In that case we deduct 25 per cent.

Alexis: Aline, the villagers will assemble to carouse in a few minutes. Go and fetch the tea-pot.

Aline: But, Alexis—

Alexis: My dear, you must obey me, if you please. Go and fetch the tea-pot.

Aline (*going*): I'm sure Dr. Daly would disapprove of it.
> (*Exit Aline.*)

Alexis: And how soon does it take effect?

Mr. Wells: In twelve hours. Whoever drinks of it loses consciousness for that period, and on waking falls in love, as a matter of course, with the first lady he meets who has also tasted it, and his affection is at once returned. One trial will prove the fact.

> *Enter* Aline *with large tea-pot.*

Alexis: Good: then, Mr. Wells, I shall feel obliged if you will at once pour as much philtre into this tea-pot as will suffice to affect the whole village.

Aline: But bless me, Alexis, many of the villagers are married people!

Mr. Wells: Madam, this philtre is compounded on the strictest principles. On married people it has no effect whatever. But are you quite sure that you have nerve enough to carry you through the fearful ordeal?

Alexis: In the good cause I fear nothing.

Mr. Wells: Very good, then, we will proceed at once to the Incantation.
> (*The stage grows dark.*)

Incantation

Mr. Wells: Sprites of earth and air—
  Fiends of flame and fire—
  Demon souls,
  Come here in shoals,
  This dreadful deed
   inspire!
  Appear, appear,
   appear.
Male Voices: Good master, we are here!
Mr. Wells: Noisome hags of night—
  Imps of deadly shade—
  Pallid ghosts,
  Arise in hosts,
  And lend me all your aid.
  Appear, appear, appear!
Female Voices: Good master, we are
  here!
Alexis (aside): Hark, they assemble,
  These fiends of the night!
Aline (aside): Oh, Alexis, I tremble,
  Seek safety in flight!

Aria—Aline

Let us fly to a far-off land,
 Where peace and plenty dwell—
Where the sigh of the silver strand
 Is echoed in every shell
To the joy that land will give,
 On the wings of Love we'll fly;
In innocence there to live—
 In innocence there to die!

Chorus of Spirits

Too late—too late
It may not be!
That happy fate
Is not for thee!

Alexis, Aline and Mr. Wells

Too late—too late,
 That may not be!
That happy fate
 Is not for { me!
     { thee!
Mr. Wells: Now shrivelled hags, with
  poison bags,
  Discharge your loathsome
   loads!
  Spit flame and fire, unholy
   choir!
  Belch forth your venom,
   toads!
  Ye demons fell, with yelp
   and yell,
  Shed curses far afield—
  Ye fiends of night, your filthy
   blight
  In noisome plenty yield!

Gilbert and Sullivan, *The Sorcerer.*

In this laughable burlesque of magic practice, the authors preserve the techniques
and idiom of the Black Arts.

ABUDAH: a reference to a Bagdad merchant,
in Tales of the Genii, by James Ridley
(1736-1765). Abudah is haunted by a
witch until he seeks the talisman of
Oromanes.

DJINN: in Moslem demonology, spirits endowed with magic powers.

IN WAX: a reference to the image of the
victim in sympathetic magic.

TETRAPODS: four-footed stools. An imitation
of tripod, the three-footed brazier associated with magic rites.

Love Charm

Waiting on Matsuo's shore
This quiet Evening
For you who do not come,

I burn with longing:
Fierce as the fire of the salt-pans.

Japanese spell, repeated thrice. J.
E. De Becker, *Nightless City.* 1905.

Charm for Sickness: pronounced over embers

If you are at one with me, rise toward
   me, O smoke:
If you are not at one with me, rise
   athwart me, O smoke,
Either to right or left.

Malay charm.

Charm is preceded by preparations involving magic accessories—incense, three kinds
of rice, three wax tapers.

Charm for Fever

Jembalang Jembali, Demon of the Earth,
Accept this portion as your payment
And restore (name of person sick).
But if you do not restore him
I shall curse you with the saying
'There is no god but God.'

Malay charm.

Initial preparations require seven cigarettes,
seven betel leaf chews, seven bananas,
parched rice, an egg—rolled up in banana
leaf and placed at triple crossroads.

Malayan Incantaton

Zabur Hijau is your name, O incense,
Zabur Bajang the name of your Mother,
Zabur Puteh the name of your Fumes.
May you fumigate the Seven Tiers of the
   Earth,
May you fumigate the Seven Tiers of the
   Sky

And serve as a summons to all spirits,
To those that have magic power.

This invocation is addressed to the Spirit
of Incense. In Malayan witchcraft, each
type of incense is potent in exorcising a
particular demon. The incenses, and their
ingredients, include ammoniac, sulphur,
euphorbia, and bdellium.

Charm to Cure Small Pox

Good folk! I know your beginning,
Ye did dwell formless in the depths of
   hell,
And issuing from the depths of hell did
   visit the children of Adam and take on
   visible form.
Seven brothers were ye in all,
Born of black exudings, of black pores,
   of black skin,
Of black flesh, blood, veins, and sinews,
   of black bones,
Not mine this charm but that of the
   Dewa Sang Samba,
Not mine this charm but that of the
   Dewa Betara Narada,
Not mine this charm but that of the very
   dregs of hell.
Well versed am I in all poisons,
And can quench fiery pains.
Poison do I charm away, fiery pains I
   quench,
Efficacious am I, yea successful by my
   teacher's help.

J. D. Gimlette, *Malay Poisons and
charm Cures.* London, J. and A.
Churchill, 1923.

Recited by Malay medicine—man over
draught of water, which sick person drinks.
SEVEN: in magic ritual, a number of potency.

[54]

Love Charm — Pacific Style

Mr. Hair—of—his—head, Mr. Hair—of—
his—head,

Go you to him, to Taratake!

Whisper my name when he dreams,
when he wakes,

When he walks among the women.

Draw him by the hand,

Draw him by the foot,

Draw him by the heart and entrails to
me.

He thinks only of me;

He dies for love of me;

There is no woman for him but me, no
love but mine, no love-making but
mine.

He comes to me, he comes, he is here
with me,

With me, Laughter—of—Waves—o—o—o!

Return to the Islands, by Arthur
Grimble. London, John Murray,
1957.

Taratake is the love-sick girl. There is a
striking similarity to the procedure described in the passage from Theocritus.

Charm against Evil Spirits

Off with you, spirits of fear, spirits of
death!

Give way to the sun and the moon,

For this is a sanctuary,

This is a place made safe.

Blessings and peace upon us,

Blessings and peace.

This charm is accompanied with certain rituals:

It only remained to provide against the
spirits of the sea, sky and underworld.
The sign of a magic solar cross, stepped
out without the circle, easily did that.
Intoning his powerful spell as he went,
the old man strode first, from north to
south and back again, himself the sun
in its yearly course from solstice to sol-
tice; then from east to west and back
again, the sun this time in his daily
rising and setting. And behold! (as he
said to me afterwards) a roof of safety
and a floor of protection for the sanctuary were complete.

The scene is the Gilbert Islands, the
time, after World War I. *Return to
the Islands,* by Arthur Grimble. London, John Murray, 1957.

Chapter III

Operations of magic,
Sympathetic magic, Herb lore,
Magic instruments, Potions,
Wands, Magic circles, Pentacles

Chapter 3

OPERATIONS OF MAGIC

SYMPATHETIC MAGIC

HERB LORE — MAGIC INSTRUMENTS — POTIONS

WANDS — MAGIC CIRCLES — PENTACLES

Introduction

At her disposal the witch has a formidable battery of apparatus, objects fashioned with occult secrecy, numbers and formulas, herbs and brews, rare juices and liquids, mandrake, blood, and milk: mystic diagrams and geometric figures, circles and pentacles. Reinforced by such aids, she can consummate invisibility and rejuvenation, transformations, alterations in weather conditions—especially the downfall of rain.

An essential feature in the prospective efficacy of a magic procedure was scrupulous adherence to the formalities: involving the right time and place, the proper instruments—fresh or new, the right intonation in the incantations, and, above all, the exact formation of the figures. The pentacle, the five-pointed figure, contained mystic symbols, used especially in divination and the conjuration of spirits, but also a concomitant of thaumaturgic technique in a wide sense. The pentalpha, a design formed by interlacing five A's, was also in similar use. To summon demoniac help, the pentagram was fashioned: a five-pointed geometric figure.

[59]

The most frequently used diagram was the magic circle. It was drawn around an object or person that was to be subjected to a magic operation. This circle, described with a new sword around the karcist, symbolized the frontier separating the wizard from the infernal powers. Within this circle, the warlock performed his thaumaturgy. In this regard, the name of Honi Ha Me'agel, a Hebrew magician of the first century A.D., is particularly recorded. Standing within the magic circle, he used to produce rain so frequently that he was known as the circle-drawer.

The occult circle was used for apotropaic purposes in ancient Assyria to ward off evil spirits and sickness; in India, to ease childbirth. And in the Middle Ages, woodcuts and paintings always depict the practicing magician as having ready at hand, under any circumstance, the potent circle.

THE GRIMOIRE OF HIPPOCRATES

A grimoire was a magician's manual. In the Middle Ages, grimoires were anachronistically attributed to King Solomon, Alexander the Great, and the ancient Greek physician Hippocrates. Here, in an alchemical laboratory, a grimoire is being consulted for the purpose of preparing a magic potion.

(After David Teniers, 17th century Dutch artist)

Courtesy of The Metropolitan Museum of Art, N.Y.

FAUST IN HIS STUDY
Dr. Johannes Faustus, in medieval legend, was a German occultist, considered the greatest necromancer of his age. Christopher Marlowe's play *Dr. Faustus* presents a revealing picture of the man and his work. Here Faustus is engaged in a magic operation. The central diagram consists of occult formulas.
(Painting by Rembrandt)
Courtesy of The Metropolitan Museum of Art, N. Y.

THE ALCHEMIST
Alchemy, a branch of the occult arts, reached its height in the Middle Ages. One of its
aims was the transmutation of base metals into gold.
(Painting by Quinten Matsijs, 16th century Flemish artist)

THE WITCH'S CAVE

An old woodcut depicting a young traveler consulting a witch in her cave. Note the familiars, the spirits that attend the witch in the form of cats, mice, bats. She is engaged in brewing a gruesome potion in her cauldron. At her feet lie fortune-telling cards and dice.

Origin of Magic

They balmed as victim on the grass
    Purusha born in earliest time.
With him the deities sacrificed.
From that great general sacrifice the
    dripping fat was gathered up.
He formed the creatures of the air, and
    animals both wild and tame.
Therefrom were spells and charms pro-
    duced.

Purusha Sukta—Hymn of Man.
From Rigveda—a collection of 1017
Sanskrit religious hymns, dating in
the second millennium B.C., filled
with magical incantations and invocations.

PURUSHA IS THE SOUL: man.

Magic Transformation

And he cried unto the Lord; and the
Lord shewed him a tree, which when he
had cast into the waters, the waters were
made sweet.
               Exodus, 15.25.

Magic Transformation

Behold, I will stand before thee there
upon the rock in Horeb; and thou shalt
smite the rock, and there shall come
water out of it, that the people may
drink. And Moses did so in the sight of
the elders of Israel.
               Exodus, 17.6.

Blood Used in Magic Rite

Speak unto the children of Israel that
they bring there a red heifer without
spot, wherein is no blemish and upon
which never came yoke, and ye shall
give her unto Eleazar the priest . . . and
one shall slay her before his face: and
Eleazar the priest shall take of her blood
with his finger, and sprinkle of her
blood toward the front of the tent.
               Numbers, 19.1.

The blood was used for purification purposes.

Mandrake for Love

And Reuben went in the days of
wheat harvest, and found mandrakes in
the field, and brought them unto his
mother, Leah. Then Rachel said to Leah,
Give me, I pray thee, of thy son's mandrakes.

And she said unto her, Is it a matter
that thou hast taken my husband? and
wouldest thou take away my son's mandrakes also? And Rachel said, Therefore
he shall lie with thee tonight for thy
son's mandrakes.   *Genesis*, 30. 14-15.

The mandrake, mandragora officinarum, is
a plant of the potato family: also known as
mandragore. It was a frequent ingredient in
love-philtres, and was also called the plant
of Circe—since the witch-brew of Circe,
the ancient Homeric sorceress, were traditionally believed to contain infusions of
mandrake.

Consecration of Magic Circle

Ban! Ban! Barrier that none can pass,
Barrier of the gods, that none may break,
Barrier of heaven and earth that none
    can change,

Which no god may annul,
Nor god nor man can loose,
A snare without escape, set for evil,
A net whence none can issue forth,
  spread for evil.
Whether it be evil Spirit, or evil Demon,
  or evil Ghost,
Or evil Devil, or evil God, or evil Fiend,
Or Hag-demon, or Ghoul, or Robber-
  sprite,
Or Phantom, or Night-wraith, or Hand-
  maid of the Phantom,
Or evil Plague, or Fever sickness, or
  Unclean Disease,
Which hath attacked the shining waters
  of Ea,
May the snare of Ea catch it;
Or which hath assailed the meal of
  Nisaba,
May the net of Nisaba entrap it;
Or which hath broken the barrier,
Let not the barrier of the gods,
The barrier of heaven and earth, let it go
  free;
Or which reverenceth not the great gods,
May the great gods entrap it,
May the great gods curse it;
Or which attacketh the house,
Into a closed dwelling may they cause it
  to enter;
Or which circleth round about,
Into a place without escape may they
  bring it;
Or which is shut in by the house door,
Into a house without exit may they
  cause it to enter;
Or that which passeth the door and bolt,
With door and bolt, a bar immovable,
  may they withhold it;
Or which bloweth in at the threshold
  and hinge,

Or which forceth a way through bar and
  latch,
Like water may they pour it out,
Like a goblet may they dash it in pieces,
Like a tile may they break it;
Or which passeth over the wall,
Its wing may they cut off;
Or which (lieth) in a chamber,
Its throat may they cut;
Or which looketh in at a side chamber,
Its face may they smite;
Or which muttereth in a chamber,
Its mouth may they shut;
Or which roameth loose in an upper
  chamber,
With a basin without opening may they
  cover it;
Or which at dawn is darkened,
At dawn to a place of sunrise may they
  take it.

  Assyrian tablet.

Death by Magic

Put a two-tailed lizard into oil and
cook it, and anoint the man with it, and
then he dies.

  Ancient magic papyrus.

To Overpower a Dragon

If you would destroy Apep, say this
chapter over an image of Apep, which
has been drawn in green color on a
sheet of new papyrus, and over a wax
figure of Apep on which his name has
been cut and inlaid in green color: and

lay them on the fire, to consume the enemy of Ra.

Book of Overthrowing Apep, ancient Egyptian manual.

APEP: in Egyptian demonology, a monstrous human-shaped dragon, or crocodile-shaped demon: led other demons in an assault on the Sun.

RA: i.e., Amen-ha. Egyptian god.

Winning Love by Magic

Not of my philtres thy lord hateth thee,
But that thy nature is no mate for his.
That is the love-charm: woman, 'tis not
  beauty
That witcheth bridegrooms, nay, but
  nobleness.

Euripides (c. 485-406 B.C.), Greek dramatic poet. Author of *Andromache,* translated by A. S. Way.

Andromache was charged by Hermione, wife of Neoptolemus, with winning his affections by the use of philtres.

Socrates and Magic

"Do you know such arts, Socrates?" asked Theodota.

"Through what other influence," replied the philosopher, "do you think that Apollodorus and Antisthenes stay with me, and Cebes and Simmias come to me from Thebes? I do not accomplish this without many love-charms, incantations, and magic wheels."

Xenophon (c. 430-c. 354 B.C.), Greek historian. Author of *Memorabilia,* dealing with life of the philosopher Socrates.

Love Philtres

"They say," replied Socrates, "that there are certain incantations which those who know them chant to whomsoever they please, and thus make them their friends; and that there are also love potions which those who know them minister to whomso they will; and are in consequence loved by them."

Xenophon (c. 430-c. 354 B.C.), Greek historian. Author of *Memorabilia.*

Roman Charm

Chant thrice, spit thrice after uttering the incantations.

Tibullus (c. 48-19 B.C.), Roman poet.

THRICE: in magic rites, the number three had a special potency.

Magic Use of Milk

Now with magic howlings she keeps the swarms of the grave before her: now she sprinkles them with milk and bids them retreat.

Tibullus (c. 48-19 B.C.), Roman poet.

Roman Charms

Here herbs are of no avail, nor nocturnal Cytaeis, nor grasses brewed by the hand of Perimede.

Propertius (c. 48-c. 16 B.C.), Roman elegiac poet.

CYTAEIS: i.e., the witch Medea.
PERIMEDE: a witch whom Homer calls Agamede.

Pharmaceutria

The pastoral muse that inspired Damon and Alphesiboeus, at whose contention the heifer stood wondering and forgot to graze, whose strains held lynxes spell-bound, and made rivers suffer change, and arrest their flow—the Muse that inspired Damon and Alphesiboeus shall be our song.

But thou, whether my heart is with thee as thou art surmounting the rocks of mighty Timavus or coasting the shore of the Illyrian sea, will that day ever come that will find me free to tell of thy deeds? Shall I ever be free to publish the whole world through those strains of thine, alone worthy of Sophocles' tragic march? From thee is my beginning, for thee shall be the end. Accept these strains commenced at thy bidding, and suffer this ivy to wind itself round thy brows among thy triumphal bays.

Scarce had night's cold shade parted from the sky, just at the time that the dew on the tender grass is sweetest to the cattle, when leaning on his smooth olive wand Damon thus began:

Rise, Lucifer, and usher in the day, the genial day, while I, deluded by a bridegroom's unworthy passion for my Nisa, make my complaint, and turning myself to the gods, little as their witness has stood me in stead, address them nevertheless, a dying man, at this very last hour. Take up with me, my pipe, the song of Maenalus.

Maenalus it is whose forests are ever tuneful, and his pines ever vocal; he is ever listening to the loves of shepherds, and to Pan, the first who would not have the reeds left unemployed. Take up with me, my pipe, the song of Maenalus.

Mopsus has Nisa given him: what may not we lovers expect to see? Matches will be made by this between griffins and horses, and in the age to come hounds will accompany timid does to their draught. Mopsus, cut fresh brands for to-night; it is to you they are bringing home a wife. Fling about nuts as a bridegroom should; it is for you that Hesperus is leaving his rest on Oeta. Take up with me, my pipe, the song of Maenalus.

O worthy mate of a worthy lord! There as you look down on all the world, and are disgusted at my pipe and my goats, and my shaggy brow, and this beard that I let grow, and do not believe that any god cares aught for the things of men. Take up with me, my pipe, the song of Maenalus.

It was in our enclosure I saw you gathering apples with the dew on them. I myself showed you the way, in company with my mother—my twelfth year had just bidden me enter on it. I could just reach from the ground to the boughs that snapped so easily. What a sight! what ruin to me! what a fatal frenzy swept me away! Take up with me, my pipe, the song of Maenalus.

Now know I what love is; it is among savage rocks that he is produced by Tmarus or Rhodope, or the Garamantes at earth's end; no child of lineage or blood like ours. Take up with me, my pipe, the song of Maenalus.

Love, the cruel one, taught the mother to embrue her hands in her children's blood; hard too was thy heart, mother. Was the mother's heart harder,

[64]

or the boy god's malice more wanton? Wanton was the boy god's malice; hard too thy heart, mother. Take up with me, my pipe, the song of Maenalus.

Aye, now let the wolf even run away from the sheep; let golden apples grow out of the tough heart of oak; let narcissus blossom on the alder; let the tamarisk's bark sweat rich drops of amber; rivalry let there be between swans and screech-owls; let Tityrus become Orpheus—Orpheus in the woodland, Arion among the dolphins. Take up with me, my pipe, the song of Maenalus.

Nay, let all be changed to the deep sea. Farewell, ye woods! Headlong from the airy mountain's watchtower I will plunge into the waves; let this come to her as the last gift of the dying. Cease, my pipe, cease at length the song of Maenalus.

Thus far Damon; for the reply of Alphesiboeus, do ye recite it, Pierian maids; it is not for all of us to have command of all.

Bring out water and bind the altars here with a soft woollen fillet, and burn twigs full of sap and male frankincense, that I may try the effect of magic rites in turning my husband's mind from its soberness; there is nothing but charms wanting here. Bring me home from the town, my charms, bring me my Daphnis.

Charms have power even to draw the moon down from heaven; by charms Circe transformed the companions of Ulysses; the cold snake as he lies in the fields is burst asunder by chanting charms. Bring me home from the town, my charms, bring me my Daphnis.

These three threads distinct with three colours I wind round thee first, and

thrice draw the image round the altar thus; heaven delights in an uneven number. Twine in three knots, Amaryllis, the three colours; twine them, Amaryllis, do, and say, 'I am twining the bonds of Love.' Bring me home from the town, my charms, bring me my Daphnis.

Just as this clay is hardened, and this wax melted, by one and the same fire, so may my love act doubly on Daphnis. Crumble the salt cake, and kindle the crackling bay leaves with bitumen. Daphnis, the wretch, is setting me on fire; I am setting this bay on fire about Daphnis. Bring me home from the town, my charms, bring me my Daphnis.

May such be Daphnis' passion, like a heifer's, when, weary of looking for her mate through groves and tall forests, she throws herself down by a stream of water on the green sedge, all undone, and forgets to rise and make way for the fargone night—may such be his enthralling passion, nor let me have a mind to relieve it. Bring me home from the town, my charms, bring me my Daphnis.

These cast-off relics that faithless one left me days ago, precious pledges for himself, them I now entrust to thee, Earth, burying them even on the threshold; they are bound as pledges to give me back Daphnis. Bring me home from the town, my charms, bring me my Daphnis.

These plants and these poisons culled from Pontus I had from Moeris' own hand. They grow in plenty at Pontus. By the strength of these often I have seen Moeris turn to a wolf and plunge into the forest, often call up spirits from the bottom of the tomb, and remove standing crops from one field to another. Bring me home from the town, my charms, bring me my Daphnis.

Carry the embers out of doors, Amaryl- lis, and fling them into the running stream over your head; and do not look behind you. This shall be my device against Daphnis. As for gods or charms, he cares for none of them. Bring me home from the town, my charms, bring me my Daphnis.

Look, look! the flickering flame has caught the altar of its own accord, shot up from the embers, before I have had time to take them up, all of themselves. Good luck, I trust! . . . Yes, there is something, I am sure . . . and Hylax is barking at the gate. Can I trust myself? Or is it that lovers make their own dreams? Stop, he is coming from town; stop now, charms, my Daphnis!

Vergil (70-19 B.C.), Roman poet. *The Poems of Vergil,* translated by John Conington.

Similar magic techniques are mentioned in the sketch by Theocritus.
MADE RIVERS SUFFER CHANGE: changing or arresting the course of rivers was a charac- teristic feature in witchcraft.
THREE THREADS: the number three had a magic force, according to the ancient writers Theocritus, Ovid, Tibullus, Horace. The three colors were white, rose-red, black.
UNEVEN NUMBER: there was an ancient be- lief that odd numbers were immortal, be- cause they could not be divided into two equal parts.
THESE PLANTS AND THESE POISONS: the references are to lycanthropy, necromancy, and the casting of spells on crops. Pontus anciently had a reputation for witchcraft, and for poisons, particularly the poison plant aconite.

Love Philtre Made from Human Heart

"What, O ye gods, who from the sky
Rule earth and human destiny,
What means this coil? And wherefore be
These cruel looks all bent on me?
Thee by thy children I conjure
If at their birth Lucina pure
Stood by; thee by this vain array
Of purple, thee by Jove I pray,
Who views with anger deeds so foul,
Why thus on me like stepdame scowl,
Or like some wild beast, that doth glare
Upon the hunter from its lair?"

As thus the boy in wild distress
Bewail'd, of bulla stripp'd and dress,
So fair, that ruthless breasts of Thrace
Had melted to behold his face,
Canidia, with dishevell'd hair
And short crisp vipers coiling there,
Beside a fire of Colchos stands,
And her attendant hag commands
To feed the flames with fig-trees torn
From dead men's sepulchres forlorn,
With dismal cypress, eggs rubb'd o'er
With filthy toads' envenom'd gore,
With sceech-owl's plumes, and herbs of bane,
From far Iolchos fetch'd and Spain,
And fleshless bones by beldam witch
Snatch'd from the jaws of famish'd bitch.
And Sagana, the while, with gown
Tucked to the knees, stalks up and down,
Sprinkling in room and hall and stair
Her magic hell-drops, with her hair
Bristling on end, like furious boar,
Or some sea-urchin wash'd on shore;
Whilst Veia, by remorse unstay'd,
Groans at her toil, as she with spade
That flags not digs a pit, wherein
The boy imbedded to his chin,

With nothing seen save head and throat,
Like those who in the water float,
Shall dainties see before him set,
A maddening appetite to whet,
Then snatch'd away before his eyes,
Till famish'd in despair he dies;
That when his glazing eyeballs should
Have closed on the untasted food,
His sapless marrow and dry spleen
May drug a philtre-draught obscene.
Nor were these all the hideous crew,
But Ariminian Folia, too,
Who with unsatiate lewdness swells,
And drags by her Thessalian spells
The moon and stars down from the sky,
Ease-loving Naples' vows, was by;
And every hamlet round about
Declares she was, beyond a doubt.

　　Now forth the fierce Canidia sprang,
And still she gnaw'd with rotten fang
Her long sharp unpared thumb-nail.
　　What
Then said she? Yea, what said she not?
　　"O Night and Dian, who with true
And friendly eyes my purpose view,
And guardian silence keep, whilst I
My secret orgies safely ply,
Assist me now, now on my foes
With all your wrath celestial close!
Whilst, stretch'd in soothing sleep, amid
Their forests grim the beasts lie hid,
May all Suburra's mongrels bark
At yon old wretch, who through the dark
Doth to his lewd encounters crawl,
And on him draw the jeers of all!
He's with an ointment smear'd, that is
My masterpiece. But what is this?
Why, why should poisons brew'd by me
Less potent than Medea's be,
By which, for love betray'd, beguiled,
On mighty Creon's haughty child

She wreaked her vengeance sure and
　　swift,
And vanish'd, when the robe, her gift,
In deadliest venom steep'd and dyed,
Swept off in flames the new-made bride?
No herb there is, nor root in spot
However wild, that I have not;
Yet every common harlot's bed
Seems with some rare Nepenthe spread,
For there he lives in swinish drowse,
Of me oblivious, and his vows!
He is, aha! protected well
By some more skilful witch's spell!
But, Varus, thou, (doom'd soon to know
The rack of many a pain and woe!)
By potions never used before
Shalt to my feet be brought once more.
And 'tis no Marsian charm shall be
The spell that brings thee back to me!
A draught I'll brew more strong, more
　　sure,
Thy wandering appetite to cure;
And sooner 'neath the sea the sky
Shall sink, and earth upon them lie,
Than thou not burn with fierce desire
For me, like pitch in sooty fire!"
　　On this the boy by gentle tones
No more essay'd to move the crones,
But wildly forth with frenzied tongue
These curses Thyestean flung.
"Your sorceries, and spells, and charms
To man may compass deadly harms,
But heaven's great law of Wrong and
　　Right
Will never bend before their might.
My curse shall haunt you, and my hate
No victim's blood shall expiate.
But when at your behests I die,
Like the Fury of the Night will I
From Hades come, a phantom sprite—
Such is the Manes' awful might.
With crooked nails your cheeks I'll tear

[67]

And, squatting on your bosoms, scare
With hideous fears your sleep away!
Then shall the mob, some future day,
Pelt you from street to street with stones,
Till falling dead, ye filthy crones,
The dogs and wolves and carrion fowl,
That make the Esquiline their prowl,
In banquet horrible and grim
Shall tear your bodies limb from limb,
Nor shall my parents fail to see
That sight—alas, surviving me!"

> Horace (65 B.C.-8 B.C.), Roman
> poet. *Satires.*

Nocturnal Witchery

Under the wandering moon, bare-footed and hair dishevelled, Canidia and Sagana, pale of face, gather bones and poisonous herbs in the cemetery: then start whooping a witch-chant. With their nails they scratch the ground and tear a black lamb to pieces. The blood is poured into a pit, to conjure the spirits of the dead. There is an image made of wool, representing Canidia: another one, of wax, representing the victim. The waxen image stands suppliant, destined to perish. Hecate, goddess of Hell, and Tisiphone, one of the Furies, are invoked. Snakes and hounds of hell appear. Ghosts utter shrill, forlorn cries. The waxen image, thrown into the fire, makes a blaze.

> Horace (65 B.C.-8 B.C.), Roman
> poet. *Satires* 2.8.

Canidia and Sagana are practicing sympathetic magic.
Sympathetic—or image—magic was directed toward the injury or destruction of an enemy by making a figurine in the victim's likeness. The image might be made of clay, wax, wool, bitumen, wood, or tallow. The effigy was then punctured with thorns, pins, or needles, or flint darts. The dissolution of the figurine coincided with the dissolution of the original. The device was known to the Egyptians, in the reign of Rameses II, in the twelfth century B.C. An Assyrian cuneiform tablet mentions an image fashioned by a witch. Among the Greeks and Romans, and in the Middle East, the procedure was well known. Celtic witches, in later centuries, called the images 'pictures', while in Scotland they were termed 'clay bodies'. In Scotland, in the seventh century, a certain King Duffus had his effigy melted by witches bent on his death. In 1066 Bishop Eberhard, of Trèves, accused the Jewish population of image magic. In 1560, in London, an image of Queen Elizabeth of England was discovered, with a pin piercing her breast.

The practice is even now far from obsolescent; it is a regular feature among the witch-doctors of Malaya, and became notably prevalent during the Second World War.

Medea at Work

With dishevelled locks she roams over the graves and gathers bones from the still warm tombs. She puts a curse on the absent ones, and shapes the waxen images and sticks sharp pins into the poor liver.

> Ovid (43 B.C.-c. 17 A.D.). Roman
> poet. Author of *Heroides.*

The reference is to the Roman witch Medea, who is here practicing sympathetic magic.

Rejuvenation by Magic

"By my skill we shall try to renew the old age of my father-in-law. Only let the triple goddess aid me and by her presence favor my bold enterprise."

Three nights passed, for the horns of the moon to meet and form a circle. After it shone in its plenitude and gazed upon the earth with its entire image, Medea came forth, her robe ungirt, bare of foot, her unbound locks sweeping over her shoulders.

Unaccompanied, she stepped uncertainly through the still silence of midnight. Deep slumber had relaxed men and birds and wild beasts. Without a sound, the hedges, the motionless branches lay still. The dewy air was still. Lonely, the stars glimmered. Thrice extending her arms, she turned toward them. Thrice, taking some water, she copiously bedewed her locks. Thrice she uttered howls from her lips. Then, on bent knee, touching the hard ground, she said:

"O night, most propitious for mysteries, and you, golden stars, that, along with the moon, follow the fiery day, and you, triple Hecate, who, aware of our undertaking, come forth to help in incantation and magic art, and you, Earth, who teach magicians the potency of herbs, and you, zephyrs and winds and hills and streams and lakes, and all you gods of the groves, and all you gods of the night, be my aid. By your aid, when I so willed, the streams returned to their springs to the astonishment of the river banks, and by your aid I stay the upturned waters and upheave the stagnant straits by spells, and I drive away the clouds and bring them back, and banish and summon the winds and break the jaws of snakes with my words and spells, and move natural rocks and trees uprooted from the ground and forests and I bid the mountains tremble and the

ground rumble, and the spirits of the dead arise from the tomb. You also, O Moon, I draw down, and Helios' chariot too pales at my incantation. The Dawn grows pale with my poisons. All of you have quenched the flames of the oxen for me and pressed their necks, reluctant for the task, under the crooked plough. You brought wars upon the serpent-born warriors and sleep upon the grim guardian.

"Now there is need of juices whereby old age revived may bloom once more, and regain its former years. And you deities will grant this request—for not in vain is the chariot at hand, drawn by winged dragons."

There was the chariot, sent from high heaven. No sooner had she mounted and soothed the frenzied necks of the dragons and shaken the reins lightly with her hands than she was whisked off aloft, and beheld the herbs growing on Mount Ossa and lofty Pelion and Othrys and Pindus and Olympus greater than Pindus. She plucked out suitable herbs by the root, and some she cut away with the curved blade of a bronze sickle. The herbs that grew thick on the banks of the Apidanus caught her fancy too and those on the banks of the Amphrysus. Nor were you overlooked, Enipeus: and the Peneus and the waters of the Spercheus contributed their quota, and the reedy banks of the Boebeis. Medea gathered too the sturdy grasses in Euboean Anthedon. And now when the ninth day and the ninth night had seen her traversing all the fields in her winged-dragon chariot, she returned.

As she advanced, she halted at the threshold and the gate, and stood under the sky. And she shunned contacts with men: and set up two altars of turf, on the right of Hecate, on the left of Youth. After she had wreathed them with vervain and wild foliage, close by she made a sanctuary by means of two ditches, and pierced the throat of a black ram with the sacrificial knife, and soaked the wide ditches in the blood.

Then she poured over it a beaker of flowing wine and a bronze beaker of warm milk and at the same time murmured words over it, and called upon the divinities of the earth, and begged the King of the Lower Regions and his stolen wife not to hasten to rob the limbs of the aged soul.

When she had propitiated them with prayer and many a chant, she bade that the exhausted body of Aeson be carried out of doors, and on the strewn herbs she extended the lifeless shape, relaxed by incantation in deep slumber. She bade Aeson's son stand clear away, and the attendants too, and she admonished them to withdraw their profane sight from the mysteries. So bidden, they scattered in different directions. With disheveled hair, like a Bacchante, Medea encircled the blazing altars. She dipped finely split torches in the dark pool of gore, and lighted the bloody brands on the two altars. Thrice she encircled the aged body with fire, thrice with water, thrice with sulphur.

Meanwhile the potent drug boiled in the bronze kettle and leapt and whitened in the swelling froth. She threw in roots cut in Thessalian valley and seeds and blossoms and pungent juices. She added pebbles secured from the remote East and sands washed by the refluent Ocean

stream. She added too the frost caught in the full moon and the baleful wings of a screech-owl together with the flesh itself, and the entrails of a werewolf wont to change its animal form into a man. Nor was there lacking the scaly skin of a water-serpent, the liver of a living stag. In addition, she threw in the head of a crow nine centuries old. By these and a thousand other unspeakable means she planned to delay the destined function of Tartarus. With a dry twig of long softened olive she stirred all the ingredients together, turning them over from top to bottom.

Behold now the old twig stirring in the boiling kettle first turned green, and presently put forth leaves, and suddenly became loaded with heavy olives. But wherever the fire belched out foam from the hollow kettle and the drops fell hot on the ground, the soil grew fresh, and flowers and soft grass sprang up.

As soon as she beheld this sight, with drawn sword Medea pierced the aged man's throat and, allowing the old blood to exude, filled the spot with juices. After Aeson had drunk them, either with his lips or through his wound, his beard and hair, shedding their greyness, quickly assumed a dark color. The emaciation vanished, and the pallor and decay disappeared, and the hollow wrinkles were filled up in the fresh body, and the limbs grew rapidly.

Aeson stood amazed, recalling that this was how he was forty years back.

Metamorphoses, by Ovid (43 B.C.-17 A.D.), Roman poet.

Medea, anciently famed for her magic powers, is addressing her lover Jason, Aeson's son.

THE REIGN OF ANTICHRIST

In the Middle Ages witchcraft was believed to be a survival of pagan rites. Hence all those who were reputedly associated with occult practices were pursued with active enmity by the Church as followers of the Antichrist, the Satanic Archfiend. The illustration depicts an ecclesiastical council confronted by demoniac challenges. In the upper part of the picture, note the forms of fiends battling against righteousness.

NECROMANCY IN A GRAVEYARD

Edward Kelly, a magician of the sixteenth century, is performing a necromantic act in a graveyard. His companion is Dr. John Dee, also a reputed magician. Note the magic circle within which the occultists stand. The magic circle contains the names of spirits and demons: Raphael, Rael, Miraton, Tarmiel, Rex. Kelly holds the magic wand and reads the Black Book, while Dr. Dee raises the burning torch.

WITCHES AND FAMILIARS

Familiars were attendant demons attached to a witch. They assumed various shapes, sometimes human, but more frequently those of animals: goats, apes, lizards, ferrets, moles, birds. In the corpus of demonological writings, familiars are identified by names: Zewuiel, Robin, Phrin, Rapho, and by pet endearments such as dandriprat, bunn, little master, puckril, naumet.

Agrippa von Nettesheim, a sixteenth century occultist, had a black dog, whom he called Monsieur, as a familiar. Josaphat was another familiar, attached to Jehanneret Regnal-le-Boiteux, a French fifteenth century warlock. Oliver Cromwell, who reputedly was interested in the Black Arts, had a familiar called Grimoald.

BESTIAL SHAPES

A fantastic scene characteristic of Goya's absorption in the Black Arts. A witch is con-
sorting with bestial-shaped elemental spirits.

(Painting by Goya, 18th century Spanish artist)

Courtesy of The Metropolitan Museum of Art, N. Y.

TRIPLE GODDESS: Hecate, associated with the Lower Regions. She is also Luna, the Moon goddess, and Diana, the huntress.
THRICE: the number three, and multiples of three, had occult significance.
HELIOS' CHARIOT: the Chariot of the Sun.
STOLEN WIFE: that is, Proserpina, whom her uncle Pluto kidnapped and made queen of the Lower Regions.
BACCHANTE: a female devotee of the god Bacchus: associated with wild orgies.

Magic Number Three

Thrice she purifies the old man with flame, thrice with water, thrice with sulphur.

Ovid (43 B.C.-c. 17 A.D.), Roman poet. Author of *Metamorphoses*.

Thrice she caressed him with her hand, thrice she uttered spells.

Ovid.

A Victim of Witchcraft

Does my body languish doomed by a Thessalian drug? Does a charm or herb injure me, poor wretch? Or has a witch nailed down my name in Punic wax, or driven fine needles into my very liver?

Ovid (43 B.C.-c. 17 A.D.), Roman poet. Author of *Amores*.

THESSALIAN: Thessaly, a region in Greece, was anciently notorious for witchcraft.
NAILED DOWN MY NAME: a reference to the practice of defixio.
DRIVEN FINE NEEDLES: a reference to the magic practice of fashioning images to represent the victim.

Image Magic

She dooms the absent victims and fashions waxen images, and thrusts thin needles into the wretched livers.

Ovid (43 B.C.-17 A.D.), Roman poet. *Heroides* 6.91.

As the image is pierced, the victim suffers corresponding agonies.

Recovering Virility by Witchcraft

When Chrysis found I had read the reproach, "This is the custom, Sir," said she, "and chiefly of this City, where the women are skill'd in Magick-charms, enough to make the Moon confess their power, therefore the recovery of any useful Instrument of Love becomes their care; 'tis only writing some soft tender things to my Lady, and you make her happy in a kind return. For 'tis confest, since her Disappointment, she has not been her self." I readily consented, and calling for Paper, thus addrest myself.:
" 'Tis confest, Madam, I have often sinned, for I'm not only a Man, but a very young one, yet never left the Field so dishonourably before. You have at your Feet a confessing Criminal, that deserves whatever you inflict: I have cut a Throat, betray'd my Country, committed Sacrilege; if a punishment for any of these will serve, I am ready to receive sentence. If you fancy my death, I wait you with my Sword; but if a beating will content you, I fly naked to your Arms. Only remember, that 'twas not the Workman, but his Instruments that fail'd: I was ready to engage, but

wanted Arms. Who rob'd me of them I know not; perhaps my eager mind outrun my body; or while with an unhappy haste I aim'd at all; I was cheated with Abortive joys. I only know I don't know what I've done: You bid me fear a Palsie, as if the Disease cou'd do greater that has already rob'd me of that, by which I shou'd have purchas'd you. All I have to say for my self, is this, that I will certainly pay with interest the Arrears of Love, if you allow me time to repair my misfortune.

Having sent back Chrysis with this Answer, to encourage my jaded Body, after the Bath and Strengthening Oyles, had a little rais'd me, I apply'd my self to strong meats, such as strong Broths and Eggs, using Wine very moderately; upon which to settle my self, I took a little Walk, and returning to my Chamber, slept that night without Gito; so great was my care to acquit my self honourably with my Mistress, that I was afraid he might have tempted my constancy, by tickling my Side.

The next day rising without prejudice, either to my body or spirits, I went, tho' I fear'd the place was ominous, to the same Walk, and expected Chrysis to conduct me to her Mistress; I had not been long there, e're she came to me, and with her a little Old Woman. After she had saluted me, "What, my nice Sir Courtly," said she, "does your Stomach begin to come to you?"

At what time, the Old Woman, drawing from her bosome, a wreath of many colours, bound my Neck; and having mixt spittle and dust, she dipt her finger in't, and markt my Fore-head, whether I wou'd or not.

When this part of the Charm was over, she made me spit thrice, and as often prest to my bosom Enchanted Stones, that she had wrapt in purple.

Petronius Arbiter (1st Century A.D.), Roman novelist. Author of *The Satyricon*; translated by Burnaby, 1694.

Effect of Love Philtre

Caligula is believed to have drunk a love philtre administered by his wife Caesonia and to have been driven mad.
Suetonius (c. 69-c. 140 A.D.), Roman biographer.

CALIGULA (12-41 A.D.): Roman Emperor

Thessalian Magic

The cities of Thessaly were for a long time associated with magic.
Pliny the Elder (1st. century A.D.), Roman encyclopedist. Author of *Natural History*.

THESSALY: a region in Greece, noted for witchcraft. Reputedly, the home of magic arts.

Sacrifice to Hecate

The Greeks sacrifice a bitch to Hecate. Plutarch (46-120 A.D.), Greek biographer. Author of *Roman Questions,* a treatise on Roman religious practices.

HECATE: in Greek and Roman mythology, witch-goddess who presided over Underworld.

Early Italian Magic

Two demigods, Picus and Faunus, are said to have used powerful drugs and practiced clever incantations.

Plutarch (46-c. 120 A.D.), Greek biographer. Author of *Lives of Greeks and Romans.*

Thessalian Magic

The central regions of Thessaly, universally known for magic incantations.

Apuleius (2nd. century A.D.), Roman novelist. Author of novel, *Metamorphoses,* pervaded by occult adventures.

THESSALY: a region in Greece, noted for witchcraft.

Magic Ingredients

They dig out all kinds of philtres from everywhere:
they search for the agent that arouses mutual love:
pills and nails and threads,
roots and herbs and shoots,
the two-tailed lizard, and
charms from mares.

Quoted from old Latin poet by Apuleius (2nd. century A.D.), Roman novelist. Author of *De Magia.*

Power of Love Philtres

He said that I was the only one found capable of defiling her widowhood, as if it were virginity, by my incantations and love-philtres.

Apuleius (2nd century A.D.). Roman novelist. Accused of marrying Pudentilla, wealthy widow, by magic practices.

King Solomon's Power over Winds

And to Solomon we taught the use of blowing winds that moved with his command.

Al Koran.

Hecate's Circle

Hecate's Circle is a golden sphere, enclosing a sapphire in the centre, turned by a thong of bull's hide, and having characters through the whole of it. They made conjurations by turning this: and they are wont to call such things wheels, whether they have a spherical or triangular or any other shape whatsoever. Shaking these, they uttered unintelligible or beastlike sounds, laughing, and striking the bronze. It accordingly teaches the operations of the rite, or the motion of such a circle, as possessing secret power and it is called 'Hecate's' as being dedicated to Hecate: and Hecate is a divinity among the Chaldeans.

Michael Constantius Psellus (1020-c. 1079 A.D.), Greek philosopher and scholar. Wrote on alchemy and demonology.

HECATE: goddess known to Greeks and Romans as patroness of witchcraft.
CHALDEANS: a generic name for adepts in the Black Arts.

Curse

Where are you, Soignatore, Usore, Dilapidatore, Dentore, Concisore, Divoratore, Seductore, Seminatore?

O ye, makers of hatred and prolongers of enmity: I conjure you by Who has created you for this work, I conjure you to complete this work, so that when (the victim) eats this food, or when (the victim) places a hand to it in any way, he shall never rest.

Key of Solomon, medieval grimoire.

This curse is associated with bewitched food to which the victim is exposed.

How to Separate Husband and Wife

Write upon a new-laid egg in a Nazarene cemetery:

"I conjure you, luminaries of heaven and earth, as the heavens are separated from the earth, so separate and divide N from his wife N, and separate them from one another, as life is separated from death, and sea from dry land, and water from fire, and mountain from vale, and night from day, and light from darkness, and the sun from the moon; thus separate N from N's wife, and separate them from one another in the name of the twelve hours of the day and the three watches of the night, and the seven days of the week, and the thirty days of the month, aand the seven years of Shemittah, and the fifty years of Jubilee, on every day, in the name of the evil angel Imsmael, and in the name of the angel Iabiel, and in the name of the angel Drmiel, and in the name of the angel Zahbuk, and in the name of the angel Ataf, and in the name of the angel Zhsmael, and in the name of the angel Zsniel, who preside over pains, sharp pains, inflammation, and dropsy, and separate N from his wife N, make them depart from one another, and that they should not comfort one another, swiftly and quickly."

Sword of Moses. An ancient book of magic, containing mystical names, formulas and recipes, and eschatological doctrines. First published from a unique manuscript by Dr. M. Gaster, London, 1896.

N: the name of the person affected is here inserted.
SEVEN YEARS OF SHEMITTAH: ancient Hebraic agricultural regulations.
FIFTY YEARS OF JUBILEE: ancient Hebraic land regulations.

Magician's Wand

I beg thee, O Great Adonai, Eloim, Ariel, Jehovam, exert Thy beneficence towards me, and give to this rod as I cut it the power and the virtue of the rods of Jacob, of Moses, and of Joshua the powerful!

I beg Thee, O Great Adonai, Eloim, Ariel, Jehovam, to place in this wand the entire strength of Samson, the anger of Amanuel, and the blasting power of the mighty Zariatnatmik, he who will revenge against sin on the Day of Judgement. Amen.

True Grimoire, medieval magic manual.

How to Consecrate Pentacles

O Adonai, Omnipotent, El, all-powerful, Agla, holiest, On, most righteous, Aleph and Tau, the Beginning and the End! O thou that hast caused everything through thy knowledge! Thou, who elected Abraham as thy servitor, and who promised that all the nations shall be blessed by his progeny; and thou who hast manifested thyself to thy slave Moses as a flame in the Burning Bush; who enabled him to walk dryshod through the Red Sea! Thou, who gavest him the Law upon Sinai, thou, who gave to thy servant Solomon these Pentacles, of thy mercy unequalled, that souls and bodies might be saved!

We with humility beg and implore thee, Majestic and Holiest One, to cause the consecration of these Pentacles, through thy power: that they may be made potent against all the Spirits: through thee, Adonai, Most Holy, for ever and ever.

Key of Solomon, medieval grimoire.

How to Make a Pentacle

In these pentacles he will find the great and holiest names of God, written by him on the tablets of Moses. These I, Solomon, learned through the services of an angel. And I have collected and consecrated them, for the good of all humanity, and for the defence of the body and the soul.

The pentacles are to be made on the day of Mercury, and in its hour. The Moon is to be in a sign of air or earth, and waxing, and her days shall be the same as those of the Sun.

Retire to a specially prepared room or other place, set aside for this purpose, with your companions. It is to be censed and perfumed with magical incense and fragrances.

Key of Solomon, medieval grimoire.

The Magician Enters the Magic Circle

May all devils flee, and particularly those who are inimical to this operation! When we enter herein we call with humility that God the Almighty entering this Circle will cast down divine pleasure and prosperity and joy and charity and greeting.

May the Angels of Peace help and defend this Circle, may discord disappear from it!

Help and magnify us, O Lord. Thy Most Holy Name bless our meeting and our speech. O Lord our God, bless our entry into this Circle, for Thou art blessed for Ever and Ever!

Key of Solomon, medieval grimoire.

Note that the magician here enlists beneficent powers: a frequent characteristic in mediaeval grimoires.

Creation by Magic

And he took some ewe's wool from it
And until t'was soft, he rubbed it
'Twixt his fingers . . .
Ewes ran bleating forth

This is the work of the sorcerer Lemminkainen, a character in the Finnish *Kalevala.*

[75]

A Magic Serpent

Of the slime of toad disgusting
From Syojatur's filthy spittle
Formed from this a twisting serpent.

This is the work of Hiisi, a character in the Finnish epic *Kalevala*.

The Cabalistic Circle

You will begin by making a circle with the goatskin, as previously indicated, nailing down the skin with four nails. Then you will take your blood stone and trace a triangle inside the circle, beginning with the direction of the east; and you will also trace with the blood stone the great A, the small E, the small A and the small J, along with the holy name of Jesus, between two crosses, to prevent the spirits from attacking you in the rear.

After which, the karcist will gather his assistants into the circle, each in his own place, as indicated, and he will enter it himself without fear, whatever sounds he may hear; placing the two candlesticks with the two verbena wreaths on the right and the left of the inner triangle.

This done, you will begin to light your two candles, and you will have a brand new vase before you, that is, before the karcist, filled with charcoal made of willow, burnt the same day, that the karcist will light, throwing a drop of brandy on it, and a pinch of the incense and the camphor that you have, keeping the rest to maintain a constant fire, as the duration of the operation requires.

After all that has been previously mentioned has been performed, you will pronounce the following words:

"I offer you, O mighty Adonai, this purest incense, as I offer this charcoal made from the lightest wood. I offer it, O great and potent Adonai, Eloim, Ariel, and Jehovam, with all my soul and all my heart. Deign, O mighty Adonai, to accept it favorably."

Then you will also make sure not to have on your person any impure metal: only gold and silver to throw at the spirit, wrapping it in a piece of paper that you will throw at it, so that it may do you no injury when it presents itself before the circle.

While the spirit picks up the coin, you will begin the following prayer, fortifying yourself with courage, strength, and wisdom. Also see to it that only the karcist speaks. The others must maintain silence, even when the demon questions or threatens them:

"O mighty living Lord! In one and the same person, father, son, and holy spirit, I worship you with the greatest reverence, and submit to your holy and worthy protection in the deepest confidence. I believe, with the utmost faith, that you are my creator, my benefactor, my support and my master, and I declare to you that I have no other desire but to belong to you in all eternity."

The Great Grimoire.

Image Making

X made and fashioned two images of wax with lead from fishing nets: moulded the lead: collected flies, spiders, frogs, snake skin, and a great many other items and placed them under the images along with conjurations and invocations of the demons. Then he drew blood from some part of his own body and mixed it with the blood of the frog and offered or gave it to the invoked demons.

Bernardus Guidonis (1261-1331).

How to Acquire Invisibility

And if they came not at the first night, then do the same the second night, and so the third night, until they do come: for doubtless they will come, and lie thou in thy bed, and look thou have a fair silken kerchief bound about thy head, and be not afraid, they will do thee no harm. For there will come before thee three fair women, and all in white clothing, and one of them will put a Ring upon thy finger, wherewith thou shall go invisible. When thou hast this Ring on thy finger, look in a Glass, and thou shalt not see thyself.

Reginald Scot, *Discoverie of Witchcraft*, 1584.

THEY: three sister fairies—Milia, Sibylia, Achilia.

Suitable Place for Performing Exorcism

As for the places of Magical Circles, they are to be chosen melancholy, doleful, dark and lonely; either in Woods or Deserts, or in a place where three ways meet, or amongst ruins of Castles, Ab-beys, Monasteries, etc. or upon the Seashore when the Moon shines clear, or else in some large Parlor hung with black and the floor covered with the same, with doors and windows closely shut, and waxen candles lighted.

Reginald Scot, *Discoverie of Witchcraft*, 1584.

Witches' Brew

A cavern. In the middle, a boiling cauldron.
Thunder. Enter the Three Witches.

1 Witch: Thrice the brinded cat hath mew'd.
2 Witch: Thrice, and once the hedgepig whin'd.
3 Witch: Harpier cries; 'tis time, 'tis time.
1 Witch: Round about the cauldron go;
In the poison'd entrails throw.
Toad, that under cold stone
Days and nights has thirty-one
Swelter'd venom sleeping got,
Boil thou first i' the charmed pot.
All: Double, double toil and trouble;
Fire burn and cauldron bubble.
2 Witch: Fillet of a fenny snake,
In the cauldron boil and bake;
Eye of newt and toe of frog,
Wool of bat and tongue of dog,
Adder's fork and blind-worm's sting,
Lizard's leg and howlet's wing,
For a charm of powerful trouble,
Like a hell-broth boil and bubble.
All: Scale of dragon, tooth of wolf,
Witches' mummy, maw and gulf
Of the ravin'd salt-sea shark;
Root of hemlock digg'd i' the dark,

Liver of blaspheming Jew,
Gall of goat, and slips of yew
Sliver'd in the moon's eclipse,
Nose of Turk and Tartar's lips,
Finger of birth-strangled babe
Ditch-deliver'd by a drab,
Make the gruel thick and slab:
Add thereto a tiger's chaudron,
For th' ingredients of our cauldron.
All: Double, double toil and trouble;
Fire burn and cauldron bubble.
2 Witch: Cool it with a baboon's blood,
Then the charm is firm and good.
Enter Hecate to the other Three Witches
Hecate: O, well done! I commend your
    pains;
And every one shall share in th' gains:
And now about the cauldron sing,
Like elves and fairies in a ring,
Enchanting all that you put in.
    (*Music, and a Song, 'Black Spirits,'*
        etc.)
        (*Exit Hecate*)
2 Witch: By the pricking of my thumbs,
Something wicked this way comes:
Open, locks,
Whoever knocks!

William Shakespeare (1564-1616).
Macbeth Act 4, scene I.

HECATE: Goddess of Lower Regions and
patroness of witchcraft.

Concoction of Philtres

Black dust of tomb, venom of toad, flesh
of brigand, lung of ass, blood of blind
infant, corpses from graves, bile of ox.

Girolamo Folengo. *Maccaronea*,
1519.

Witch Ointment

Hemlock, water of aconite, poplar
leaves, soot.
Another concoction: Infant's fat, juice
of cowbane, aconite, cinquefoil, deadly
nightshade, soot.

Johannes Wierus (16th century),
demonographer.

Witches Make Rain

Witches can control not only rain and
hail and wind but even lightning, with
God's permission.

Francesco Guazzo. *Compendium
Maleficarum*, 1608.

Consecration of the Magic Circle

In the name of the holy, blessed, and
glorious Trinity, proceed we to our work
in these mysteries to accomplish that
which we desire; we therefore, in the
names aforesaid, consecrate this piece of
ground for our defence, so that no spirit
whatsoever shall be able to break these
boundaries, neither be able to cause
injury nor detriment to any of us here
assembled; but that they may be compelled to stand before the circle, and
answer truly our demands, so far as it
pleaseth Him who liveth for ever and
ever and who says, I am Alpha and
Omega, the Beginning and the End,
which is, and which was, and which is
to come, the Almighty; I am the First
and the Last, who am living and was
dead; and behold I live for ever and
ever; and I have the keys of death and

hell. Bless, O Lord! this creature of earth wherein we stand; confirm, O God! thy strength in us, so that neither the adversary nor any evil thing may cause us to fail.

> *The Magus,* by Francis Barrett, Professor of Chemistry, Natural and Occult Philosophy. Published in London, 1801.

Plighted Troth Magically Returned

Then she has taken a crystal wand,
And she has stroken her troth thereon:
She has given it him out at the shot window
Wi' many a sad sigh and heavy groan.

> Spencer and Gillen, *The Native Tribes of Central Australia.*

A ghost has asked his beloved to return its troth, which is done ritually.
WAND: the usual staff that is part of the magician's equipment: endowed with magic potency.

Summoning the Wind

Come hither, Sir, come hither, my Lord,
Let down your locks so long and flowing.

> Invocation of Malay magician.

Love-Philtres in Africa

I had known the dancers in the oasis for several months before I stumbled on a practice of theirs which I had not imagined still existed. Interwoven deeply into their lives were sorcery, black magic, and, most common of all, the use of love-philtres with which they believed they could enslave any man. In the pot of mint tea in Yacourte's room had been a philtre intended to help the erring lover to make up his mind.

> *Flute of Sand,* by Lawrence Morgan. London: Odhams Press, 1956.

Yacourte was an Ouled-Naïl public dancer.

Power of Rain Making

My adoption away back in 1918, into the Tarawa sect of the royal and priestly clan of Karongoa had given me the right to practice the magic of rain-making and rain-dismissing (incidentally also of eclipse-undoing) whenever the fancy took me.

> *Return to the Islands,* by Arthur Grimble. London: John Murray, 1957.

The reference is to the author's colonial service in the Gilbert Islands.

Charm to Stop Heavy Rain

Though the stem of the Meranti tree rocks to and fro
Let the Yam leaves be as thick as possible,
That Rain and Tempest may come to naught.

> Malay charm.

This is an invocation by a Malay pawang or witchdoctor. Usually, the invocation is directed toward the production of rain.

The modern scientist can now break a cloud over a specified area, producing rain almost at will. But what could primitive man do when drought threatened, when the fields lay parched, and the crops were on the point of shriveling into decay?

Primitive man did what modern man now does. He made the rains come. But he induced the rain not in accordance with the laws of the natural sciences, but by manipulation of dark forces, by appeal to the occult spirits summoned by the sorcerer.

The harnessing of the invisible, potent forces of the cosmos in the service of man dates back beyond historic times. In Biblical days the practice of rain making was already well established. Samuel, for instance, was able to produce a thunderstorm against the warring Philistines:

Is it not wheat harvest today?
I will call unto the Lord, and he shall send thunder and rain . . .
So Samuel called unto the Lord; and the Lord sent thunder and rain that day; and all the people greatly feared the Lord and Samuel.

That is, of course, rain making through what is called White Magic, through enlisting the Beneficent Divine Name. But most often the conjuration, the invocation for help, was addressed to Vercan or Belphegon or Asmodeus or the Satanic Majesty in his multiple ethnic variations, and to his numberless host of satellites.

By ritually prescribed sacrifices the wizard made his summons. By conjuration the dread but effective will of the secret beings was secured. So the thaumaturgist of the tribe, the witch-doctors and the diviners made the magic circle, inscribed the mystic pentacle, or concocted a brew that would achieve the required purpose. The ritual once completed, to the accompaniment of murmurous incantations, the demoniac powers came forward in manifest shape, swiftly, obediently. Tumultuous storms then broke out over the clamant land. The rains poured down upon the dying crops.

Each tribal group, each ethnic culture employed, in the succession of the ages, its own techniques of approach to the powerful spirits. Thus among the Semites of the first century B.C. there was a certain Judaic thaumaturgist, Honi Ha Ma'agel. Standing within the protective area of a magically circumscribed circle, he called down rain from the heavens. According to legend, he was so successful that he was called the Circle-Drawer.

Once there was drought in Rome. So the Roman matrons marched toward the Capitoline Hill, with hair loose and feet bare, to pray for rain to Jupiter, the dishevelled hair and bare feet being features of the rite. Among the Druids of Ancient Gaul, again, the priest-magicians and astrologers, endowed with arcane knowledge, frequently were called on to induce rain. The Druids performed a unique ritual, involving a nude maiden. They sprinkled water over her, and this device of sympathetic magic brought the rain clouds.

In the Middle Ages, the techniques became more varied and also more exact. For instance, among the Jewish communities of medieval Germany, steeped in mystic Kabalistic lore that demon-

[80]

THE SABBAT
The Sabbat, or Sabbath, was the seasonal assembly of witches in honor of the Archfiend.
The broomstick is the magic means of the witch's transvection or flight through the air.
Notice the cats, toads, and other familiars of the witch.

VOLAVERUNT

Volaverunt is the Latin for *They have flown away*: a reference to the young witch in the illustration who is flying by levitation, bearing three startled travelers with her.

(Painting by Goya, 18th century Spanish artist)

Courtesy of The Metropolitan Museum of Art, N. Y.

PRETTY TEACHER

A young witch, with an older companion, ride the traditional broomstick, on their way
to a Sabbat. Note the witch's familiar, the owl, flying near her.

(Painting by Goya, 18th century Spanish artist)

Courtesy of The Metropolitan Museum of Art, N. Y.

SORCERERS AT WORK
For their goetic operations, sorcerers bought still-born children. In the upper illustration,
the magician is performing a black rite with a dead body. The lower illustration depicts
young folk being killed for occult ceremonies. Note the skulls in the barrel.

strated the power of esoteric knowledge, of conjurations, spells, and incantations, it was a custom, during a drought, for the entire community to observe a fast. This was believed to be a means of inducing rain through crowd appeal.

Another medieval inducement to rain was to kill a white cock. After it was torn apart, the entrails were extracted. Then the carcase was filled with myrrh, white pepper, frankincense, milk, wine. The cock was now held toward the sun, while an incantation was chanted. Rain followed.

Still another method was to sprinkle milk, honey, and wine on the ground, seven times, and to utter the sacred name—the Tetragrammaton. Rain came at once.

In a print by the medieval artist Ulrich Molitor, which is the Latinized form of Miller, who flourished in the fifteenth century, two witches are depicted holding a cock over a blazing cauldron. They are performing a Black Magic rite. Above them a heavy shower of rain is already appearing, as the result of their rain-making operation.

Among Asian peoples local procedures have differed, but the purpose—to induce rain from reluctant skies—is the same. Among the natives of the Celebes a cat, tied to a chair, is carried around the parched fields. The mewing of the cat is the signal for an invocation: O Lord, may the rain come! In Java, the procedure is to bathe a cat and carry it round in procession. In Sumatra, the women wade in the river and throw a black cat into the water, forcing it to swim. In China, the Great Invocation to the Red Ti, to secure 'sweet rain,' was accompanied by sacrificial music, interspersed with wailing and imploring. Another Chinese method involved a wizard with three mouths, howling for rain and beseeching the spirits to open the heavens. Still another device was the burning of an image of a deformed person. The act would produce rain through divine pity. In Malaya, if a woman puts on her head an inverted pot and sets it on the ground and fills it with water and washes the cat in it until the cat is almost half drowned, heavy rains are assumed to follow.

Chapter IV

Raising the Devil - and the dead, Satan the Arch Fiend, Satanic Hierarchy, Satanic realms, Satanic pact, Rites, Exorcisms, Necromantic rites

RAISING THE DEVIL—AND THE DEAD

SATAN THE ARCH FIEND

SATANIC HIERARCHY

SATANIC REALMS — SATANIC PACT

RITES — EXORCISMS — NECROMANTIC RITES

Introduction

The cult of Satanism, implying necromantic rites, credence in the demoniac hierarchy, blasphemous and monstrous distortions of accepted beliefs, and a boundless faith in the potency of the infernal powers, can be traced at least as far back as the Manichean cult of ancient Persia, that predicated two cosmic forces—one evil and the other beneficent—in eternal conflict. The cult of Satanism, with local or ethnic variations, endured for centuries. In some instances, with the spread of Christianity, it went underground. But it did not disappear completely; and in contemporary times it has raised its sinister head in many quarters—as recently as the earlier decades of this century, under the macabre aegis of Aleister Crowley, and, more anonymously, in seclusive drawing rooms, in secretive clubs throughout the capitals of Europe.

In the fifteenth, sixteenth, and seventeenth centuries the belief in a material

Arch Fiend, apart altogether from religious doctrine, was so intense and prevalent throughout Europe, particularly in remote rural areas, that some fifty ecclesiastical and secular prohibitions were promulgated against Satanism. In consequence, hundreds of sorcerers were condemned to death by burning, hanging, or, in fewer cases, to banishment.

Satan is the supreme Arch-potentate, but he commands a vast military organization composed of subsidiary but tremendously potent demons. These demons are capable of assuming numberless forms, while their functions are equally varied. In ancient Chaldean magic, the demon was usually of multiple shape: the body of a man, head of a lion, eagle feet. Or the body was that of a dog, with lion claws, a scorpion tail, a skeleton head, horns of a goat, and four extended wings. The terrifying appearance of such creatures induced the karcist, in the course of his invocaton, to call upon the demon to come before him without monstrous or awesome shape.

Satanic Bill of Divorce

This is a bill of divorce to the Devil and to . . . and to Satan and to Nerig, and to Zachiah, and to Abitur of the mountain, and to . . . and to the night-monsters, commanding them to cease from Beheran in Batnaium, and from the country of the north, and from all who are tormented by them therein. Behold, I make the councils of these devils of no effect, and annul the power of the ruler of the night-monsters. I conjure you all, monsters both male and female, to go forth. I conjure you by the sceptre of the powerful one, who has power over the devils, and over the night-monsters, to quit these habitations. Behold, I now make you cease from troubling them, and make the influence of your presence cease in Beheran of Batnaium, and in their fields. In the same manner as the devils write bills of divorce and give them to their wives, and return not unto them again, receive ye your bill of divorce and take this written authority, and go forth, leave quietly, flee, and depart from Beheran in Batnaium in the name of the living, by the seal of the powerful one, and by this signet authority. Then will there flow rivers of water in that land, and there the parched ground will be water.

Inscribed on Babylonian earthen bowl (3rd century B.C.).

Functions of Demons

Demons have their own peculiarities, their physical distinctiveness, their functional activities. Some dwell in mines and forests, on mountain tops. Some copulate with humans. Some display beneficent attitudes to humans, teaching crafts, astrology, enchantments. Others have skill in herbs.

Book of Enoch.

Devils as Divine Agents

There are spirits that are created for vengeance, and in their fury they lay on grievous torments.

Ecclesiasticus, 39.33.

Power over Demons

And the seventy returned again with joy saying, "Lord, even the devils are subject to us through thy name."

Luke, 10.17.

Exorcism in Bible

In my name shall they cast out devils.

Luke, 16.17.

Invocation of Demon

Palas aron azinomas.

An ancient formula.

Invocation of Demon

Bagahi laca Bachabé.

An ancient formula.

[87]

First Mention of a Personal Devil

Beliar — Satan, Mastema, Sammael, Azazel.

Testaments of the Twelve Patriarchs (Apocrypha).

The names are synonymous.

Necromantic Invocation

In the presence of Atossa, widowed Empress of Persia, the chorus invokes the infernal gods to bring Darius, King of Persia, from the Tomb.
Chorus (chanting):
Yes, royal lady, Persia's honour'd grace,
To earth's dark chambers pour thy off'r-
ings: we
With choral hymns will supplicate the
powers
That guide the dead, to be propitious to
us.
And you, that o'er the realms of night
extend
Your sacred sway, thee mighty earth,
and thee
Hermes; thee chief, tremendous king,
whose throne
Awes with supreme dominion, I adjure;
Send, from your gloomy regions, send
his shade
Once more to visit this ethereal light;
That he alone, if aught of dread event
He sees yet threat'ning Persia, may
disclose
To us poor mortals Fate's extreme
decree.
Guide him as he takes his way,
And give him to the ethereal light of day.

Send then, monarch of the dead,
Such as Darius was, Darius' shade.

Aeschylus, Greek dramatic poet (525-456 B.C.), *The Persians*. Translated by R. Potter, 1777.

Roman Exorcism

Go hence, ghosts of my ancestors.
Old Roman Formula.

Recited nine times at the Lemuria, Roman festival held May 9 for exorcising spirits.

Necromantic Rite

They began to tear apart a black lamb.
Horace (65-8 B.C.), Roman poet. *Satires.*

THEY: witches.

Lilith

It is indiscreet for one to sleep in a house as the sole occupant, for Lilith will seize him.
Talmud.

LILITH: the night-visitor. Reputed to have been Adam's first wife: transferred into a destructive demon.

Devil's Number

According to Talmudic computation, the Devil's own number is four times four.

Satanic Nomenclature

Satan has his own individual national nomenclature, as follows:

Russian: Tchort
Persian: Dev
Syriac: Béherit
Welsh: Pwcca
Biblical: Asmodeus
Belial
Apollyon
Arabic: Sheitan
Egyptian: Set
Japanese: O Yama

Necromantic Rite

Then he summons the spirits of the dead and thee who rulest the spirits of the dead and him who guards the barriers of the stream of Lethe: and he repeats the magic spell and wildly, with frenzied lips, he chants a conjuration to appease or compel the fluttering ghosts. He pours a libation of blood on the altars and burns the sacrifices entire, and soaks the trench in pools of blood.

Seneca (4 B.C.-65 A.D.), Roman dramatist, author of *Oedipus*.

THEE: Pluto, king of the Underworld.
HIM: Cerberus, three-headed dog that guarded the entrance of Hell.
LETHE: Stream of forgetfulness in Hell.

The Oracle

Just as far removed from the western as from the eastern clime, Parnassus with its twofold summit reaches to the skies, a mountain sacred to Phoebus and to Bromius; on which, the Deities united, the Theban Bacchanals celebrate the triennial Delphic festival. This peak alone, when the deluge covered the earth, rose aloft and was the mid division of the sea and the stars. Thou even, Parnassus, raised above the sea, didst scarcely lift the top of thy rocks, and as to one ridge thou didst lie concealed. There, when her offspring extended her womb, did Paean, the avenger of his persecuted mother, lay Python prostrate, with his darts till then unused, when Themis was occupying the sway and the tripods. When Paean beheld that the vast chasms of the earth breathed forth divine truths, and that the ground exhaled prophetic winds, he enshrined himself in the sacred groves, and there, become prophetic, did Apollo abide in the inmost shrines.

Which of the Gods of heaven lies here concealed? What Deity, descended from the skies, deigns, enclosed, to inhabit the darkened caverns? What God of heaven puts up with the earth, preserving all the secrets of the eternal course of fate, and conscious of the future events of the world, and ready, himself, to disclose them to nations, and enduring the contact of mortals, both mighty and powerful, whether it is that he prophesies destiny, or whether it is that that becomes a destiny which by prophesying he commands? Perhaps a large portion of the entire Jove, pervading the earth by him to be swayed, which sustains the globe poised in the empty air, passes forth through the Cirrhaean caves, and is attracted, in unison with the aethera Thunder. When this divine in-

[89]

spiration has been conceived in the virgin's breast, coming in contact with the human spirit, it re-echoes, and opens the mouth of the prophetess, just as thus Sicilian peaks undulate when the flames press upon Aetna; or as Typhoeus, buried beneath the everlasting mass of Inarime, roaring aloud, heats the Campanian rocks.

This Deity, however, made manifest to all and denied to none, alone denies himself to the pollution of human criminality. Not there in silent whispers do they conceive impious wishes. For, prophesying what is destined and to be altered for no one, he forbids mortals to wish, and, benignant to the just, full oft has he assigned an abode to those quitting entire cities, as to the Tyrians; he has granted to drive back the threats of war, as the sea of Salamis remembers; he has removed the wrath of the earth when barren, the end of it being shown; he has cleared the air when generating pestilence. Our age is deprived of no greater blessing of the Deities, than that the Delphic seat has become silent, since monarchs have dreaded events to come, and have forbidden the Gods of heaven to speak. Nor yet, a voice denied them, do the Cirrhaean prophetesses mourn; they have the benefit of the cessation of the Temple's rites. For if the God enters any breast, a premature death is either the punishment of the Deity being received, or the reward; inasmuch as under the vehemence and the fitfulness of the frenzy the human frame sinks, and the impulses of the Gods shake the frail spirit.

Thus does Appius, an enquirer into the remotest secrets of the Hesperian destiny, make application to the tripods for a length of time unmoved, and the silence of the vast rocks. The priest, requested to open the dreaded seats, and to admit to the Gods a trembling prophetess, seizes Phemonoe, roving amid her wanderings around the streams of Castalia and the recesses of the groves, and compels her to burst open the doors of the Temple. The maid inspired by Phoebus, dreading to stand within the awful threshold, by a vain stratagem attempts to wean the chieftain from his ardent longing to know the future.

"Why, Roman," says she, "does an unbecoming hope of hearing the truth attract thee? Its chasms dumb, Parnassus holds its peace, and has silenced the God; whether it is that the spirit has forsaken these yawning clefts, and has turned its changed course towards the far regions of the world; or whether, when Python was consumed by the barbarian torch, the ashes entered the immense caverns, and obstructed the passage for Phoebus; or whether by the will of the Gods, Cirrha is silent, and it is sufficient that the secrets of future fate have been entrusted to yourselves in the lines of the aged Sibyl; or whether Paean, wont to drive out the guilty from his temples, finds not in our age mouths by which to disclose the Fates."

The deceit of the maiden is manifest, and, the Deities being denied, her very fear imparts confidence. Then does the wreathed fillet bind her locks in front, and her hair streaming down her back a white head-dress encircles with Phocaean laurel. She, dreading the fate-foretelling recess of the deep-seated

THE GOAT FIEND

A witch is sacrificing a human being to the Archfiend in goat form. Notice the broomstick, the vessel for the blood, and the cats that are the witch's familiars.

(Painting by Goya, 18th century Spanish artist)

Courtesy of the Metropolitan Museum of Art, N. Y.

PREPARING A CHARM
German witches are brewing a magic charm. The loathsome ingredients consisted of
poisonous herbs, animal organs, snakes and birds, human blood and heart.

DIVINING-ROD
Using the divining-rod in mining explorations.
(Medieval woodcut. Agricola, *De Re metallita*)

Witches were traditionally credited with the power of bringing down the moon, changing the courses of rivers, and creating storms. Olaus Magnus was a sixteenth century
Swedish chronicler.

In the Middle Ages, the belief in sorcery was so strong that mariners, setting out on a
voyage, bought favorable winds from warlocks. (Note three knots in the rope, in which
winds were allegedly tied.)

shrine, in the first part of the Temple, comes to a stop, and, feigning the inspiration of the God, utters from her breast, undisturbed beneath, fictitious words, testifying a spirit moved by no divine frenzy with no murmurs of a hurried voice, and not so much about to injure the chieftain to whom she is prophesying falsely, as the tripods and the credit of Phoebus.

Her words broken with no trembling sound, her voice not sufficing to fill the space of the capacious cavern, the laurels shaken off, with no standing of her hair on end, and the summits of the Temple without vibration, the grove, too, unshaken, all these betrayed that she dreaded to yield herself to Phoebus. Appius beheld the tripods unoccupied, and raging, exclaimed:

"Impious woman, thou shalt both pay the deserved penalty to me and to the Gods of heaven, whom thou art feigning as inspiring thee, unless thou art hidden in the caverns, and, consulted upon the tumults so vast of the trembling world, dost cease, thyself, to speak."

At length, the affrighted maiden flies for refuge to the tripods, and, led away within the vast caverns, there remains, and receives the Deity in her unaccustomed breast; who pours forth the spirit of the rock, now for so many ages unexhausted, into the prophetess; and at length having gained the Cirrhaean breast, never more fully did Paean enter into the limbs of female inspired by him; and he banishes her former mind, and throughout her whole breast bids the mortal give way to himself. Frantic, she rages throughout the cave, bearing her neck possessed, and, shaking from her

upright hair both the fillets of the God and the garlands of Phoebus, through the empty space of the Temple she whirls round with her neck shaking to and fro, and throws prostate the tripods that stand in her way as she roams along, and boils with mighty flames, enduring thee, Phoebus, raging with wrath.

Nor dost thou employ the lash alone and goads, flames, too, dost thou bury in her entrails; and the bridle she submits to; nor is it permitted the prophetess to disclose as much as to know. All time comes in a single mass; and ages so many press upon her afflicted breast. Such a vast chain of events is disclosed, and all the future struggles for the light of day; and fates are striving that demand utterance: not the first day, not the last of the world; not the laws of ocean, not the number of the sands, is wanting. Such did the Cumaean prophetess, in the Euboean retreat, indignant that her frenzy should be at the service of many nations, cull with proud hand the Roman from the heap of destinies so vast.

Thus does Phemonoe, filled with Phoebus, struggle, while thee, O Appius, consulter of the Deity hidden in the Castalian land, with difficulty she discovers, long amid fates so mighty seeking thee concealed. Then, first the foaming frenzy flows forth about her maddened lips, and groans and loud murmurs from her gasping mouth; then are there mournful yells in the vast caverns, and at last voices resound, the maiden now overcome:

"O Roman, thou dost escape from the vast threatenings of war, free from dangers so great; and alone shalt thou take thy rest in the wide valley of the Euboean quarter." The rest Apollo suppresses, and stops her speech.

Ye tripods, guardians of the Fates and ye secrets of the world, and thou, Paean, powerful in the truth, uninformed by the Gods of heaven of no day of the future, why dost thou hesitate to reveal the latest moments of the falling state, and the slaughtered chieftains, and the deaths of potentates, and nations so numerous falling amid Hesperian bloodshed? Is it that the Deities have not yet decreed mischief, and are destinies so numerous withheld, while the stars yet hesitate to doom the head of Pompey? Or art thou silent upon the crimes of the avenging sword and the penalties of civic frenzy and tyrannies falling to the avenging Bruti once again, that Fortune may fulfill her aim?

Then, smitten by the breast of the prophetess the doors open, and, hurried on, she leaps forth from the Temple. Her frantic fit still lasts; and the God whom as yet she has not expelled still remains in her not having said the whole. She still rolls her fierce eyes, and her looks wandering over the whole sky, now with timid, now stern, with threatening features; a fiery blush tints her face and her livid cheeks, and a paleness exists, not that which is wont to be in one who fears, but inspiring fear. Nor does her wearied heart find rest; but as the swelling sea after the hoarse blasts of Boreas moans, so do silent sighs relieve the prophetess. And while from the sacred light by which she has beheld the Fates she is being brought back to the sunbeams of ordinary day, shades, intervening, come on. Paean sends Stygian Lethe into her entrails, to snatch from her the secrets of the Gods. Then from her breast flies the truth, and the future returns to the tripods of Phoebus, and, hardly, come to herself, she falls to the ground.

Lucan (39-65 A.D.), Roman poet. Author of epic poem *Pharsalia*.

PHOEBUS: Apollo, ancient god of prophecy. BROMIUS: Dionysus, ancient god of tumultuous revels. BACCHANALS: women, inspired by Bacchus, god of wine; performed orgiastic rites. DELPHIC: Delphi, in the center of Greece, was the seat of a famous oracle.

Character of Demons

Scripture rightly prohibits the use of magic, but the associates of magicians are apostate and evil spirits and foul demons. For no good spirit obeys a magician.

Origen (185-255 A.D.), *Homilies*.

Eleazar Exorcises a Demon

Eleazar put a ring that had a root of one of those sorts mentioned by Solomon to the nostrils of the demoniac, after which he drew out the demon through his nostrils: and when the man fell down, immediately he abjured him to return into him no more, still making mention of Solomon, and reciting the incantation which he composed. And when Eleazar would persuade and demonstrate to the spectators that he had such a power, he set a little way off a cup or basin full of water, and commanded the demon as he went out of the man to overturn it, and thereby to let the spectators know that he had left the man. And when this was done, the skill and wisdom of Solomon was shown very manifestly.

Josephus, *Antiquities of the Jews.*

Josephus, of the first century A.D., was a historian who was associated largely with Rome.
The incident here narrated occurred in the presence of the Roman Emperor Vespasian.

Types of Demons

There are several other types of beings, that have no name, and that are worshipped by some dark cult. . . . Some have received the name of Daemons. Everyone knows, according to popular opinion, that they are provoked and angered when neglected and receive no permanent veneration, and that they are favorable when they are appeased by prayer.

Porphyry (3rd century A.D.), Greek philosopher.

Character of Demons

The entire art and the power of magicians rest on the aspirations of these demons. As I say, these spirits, defiled and abandoned, wander over the face of the earth and seek solace in their own downfall by destroying men. Thus they fill everything with their stratagems and wiles, their deceits and errors; for they attach themselves to individuals and through the door enter every house. Since they are intangible and impalpable spirits, they insinuate themselves into the bodies of men, and secretly working in their vitals, destroy their health, create disease, and terrify by dreams, and disturb the mind into frenzy.

Lactantius (4th century A.D.) *Divinae Institutiones.*

Demons Fear Cock-Crow

They say that wandering demons, joyful in the darkness of the night, are terrified by cock-crowing, and in their fear fade away.

Prudentius (4th century A.D.), Christian Latin poet. *Hymns.*

Functions of Demons

Some arouse wrath and madness in men; others rule over enmities and provoke hatred among men. The demons, from personal choice, select by lot the spheres of treachery and deceits, crimes and perjury and other vices, in order to be the lords of darkness.

St. Jerome (340-420 A.D.), *Commentarii in Ephesios.*

Characteristics of Demons

Like the gods, they have corporeal immortality, and passions like human beings.

St. Augustine (354-430 A.D.), one of the Church Fathers. Author of *The City of God.*

[93]

Satanic Pact

St. Augustine condemns:
consultations and certain pacts arranged with demons—operations of the magic arts.

St. Augustine (354-430 A.D.), *De Doctrina Christiana*.

Satanic Pact

A *pactum expressum* is entered into by the witch and the demon in writing, or signs, or words.

A *pactum tacitum* assumes, on the part of the witch, the use of Satanic help.

Incubi

It is a widespread belief that Sylvans and Fauns, commonly called incubi, have frequently molested women, sought and obtained coitus from them.

St. Augustine, *De Civitate Dei*.

Mystic Name

The god Demogorgon whose name it is not permissible to know . . . by name cannot be known to any mortal.

Lactantius Placidus (6th century A.D.), Greek commentator.

Solomon and the Devils

And they followed the device which the devils devised against the kingdom of Solomon; and Solomon was not an unbeliever; but the devils believed not, they taught men sorcery.

Al Koran.

The legend runs that the devils composed several magic manuals, and then hid them under King Solomon's throne. After his death they told his courtiers that if they wanted to know how Solomon had secured domination over men, spirits, and wind, they should dig under his throne. Their digging exposed the hidden magic books, filled with unhallowed matter. But ultimately Solomon was cleared of the Devil's imputations.

Solomon Aided by Devils

And we also put the devils in subjection under him: and among them such as were every way skilled in building, and in diving for pearls: and others we delivered to him bound in chains.

Al Koran.

SEE: chapter on Who's Who in Witchcraft: under Solomon.

Renouncing Satan

Those whom St. Boniface converted renounced:
incantations and divination and belief in witches and werewolves.

St. Boniface (680-754 A.D.), *Sermons*.

Number of Demons

According to Talmudic computation, there are 7,405,926 demons.

Appearance of Demons

So horrible and venomous is the appearance of demons that not only does it drive men mad but even kills them.

Caesar of Heisterbach (13th century monk), *Dialogus de Miraculis.*

Pact with Devil

The magician cut a bough of wild hazel, that had not yet produced fruit, with a new knife, at sunrise. Then he brought a bloodstone and two wax candles to some secluded spot: a deserted house, a ruined castle. With the bloodstone he traced a triangle on the floor, and placed the candles by the triangle. A circle was now made around the triangle. Within the triangle, holding a hazel wand, the magician uttered the following conjuration:

Aglon Tetragram Vaycheon Stimulama-
thon

Erohares Retragsammathon Clyoran
Icion

Esition Existien Eryona Onera Erasyn
Moyn

Meffias Soter Emmanuel Saboth Adonai,
I call you. Amen.

Medieval Grimoire.

Demons Who Rule the Earth

Oriens, ruler of the spirits of the East.
Amemon, ruler of the spirits of the
South.
Eltzen, ruler of the spirits of the North.
Boul, ruler of the spirits of the West.

Medieval Grimoire.

A grimoire is a manual of magic. Such handbooks, pseudepigraphically ascribed to King Solomon, certain Popes, Albertus Magnus, and other karcists or putative wizards, were highly popular during the Middle Ages. Among the most notable of such Black Books were: *Liber Spirituum*, the Book of Spirits; *Shemhamphoras*, Hebrew manual of magic; *Oupnekhat*, Sanskrit magic manual translated into Persian and, in 1802, into Latin; *Grimoirium Verum*, published by Alibeck the Egyptian in 1517; *The Constitution of Honorius*, attributed to Pope Honorius III, whose floruit was the thirteenth century. This book, first published in Rome in 1629, describes the ritual of conjuration and other occult ceremonials; *Little Albert; Red Dragon; Arbatel; Tonalamatl*, ancient Mexican Book of Fate, containing magic rituals and formulas; *Y-Kim*, ancient and obscure Chinese text on mysticism, attributed to fourth millennium B.C.; *Red Book of Appin; Hell's Coercion*, attributed to Dr. Faust; *The Great Grimoire; Sanctum Regum; The Black Hen* or *Pullet; The Great and Powerful Sea Ghost*, by Dr. Johann Faustus; *Lemegeton*, also known as the *Lesser Key of Solomon*. This is a manuscript, now in the British Museum, describing the demoniac hierarchy. *The Book of Death* is a volume in which the Devil, during the Sabbat, listed the names of the participants. *The Book of the Sacred Magic* of Abramelin the Mage as delivered by Abraham the Jew unto his son Lamech was a sixteenth century text dealing with magic adventures in a picaresque, novel form. *The Key of Solomon*, ascribed to King Solomon, was one of the most popular grimoires in the Middle Ages, dealing with rituals, the operations of magic, and the requisite preparations for effective consummation. *The Sword of Moses* is a tenth century guide to magic formulas and prescriptions. *The Testament of Solomon* is based on the Old Testament and describes the building of the Temple by King Solomon with demoniac aid and the names and functions of the demoniac powers. *Zekerboni*, a seventeenth century grimoire, gives directions for incantations, spells, and conjurations. Other popular manuals were *Liber*

Pentaculorum; The Sage of the Pyramids; The Almadel. The Book of Raziel, still extant, is a grimoire reputedly derived from the *Book of Signs*, a magic manual attributed to Adam.

The Hierarchy of the Infernal Regions

Here are the names of the principal infernal spirits: Lucifer, Emperor: Beelzebub, Prime Minister: Astorath, Grand Duke. Then come the superior spirits that are subject to the above-mentioned demons:

Lucifuge, Prime Minister
Satanachia, Grand General
Agaliarept, Grand General
Fleuretty, Lieutenant General
Sargatanas, Brigadier
Nebiros, Field Marshal

These six demons just mentioned direct, by their power, the entire infernal might granted to the other demons.

They have at their service eighteen other spirits subordinate to them, as follows:

Baël	Bathim
Agares	Pursan
Marbas	Abigar
Pruslas	Loray
Aamon	Valefar
Barbatos	Foraü
Buer	Ayperos
Gusoyn	Nuberus
Botis	Glasyabolas

After listing these eighteen demons that are inferior to the six previously mentioned, it is advisable to inform you of what follows:

That Lucifuge is in command of the first three demons, Baël, Agares, and Marbas.

Satanachia controls Pruslas, Aamon, and Barbatos.

Agaliarept controls Buer, Gusoyn, and Botis.

Fleuretty controls Bathim, Pursan, and Abigar.

Sargatanas controls Loray, Valefar, and Foraü.

Nebiros controls Ayperos, Nuberus, and Glasyabolas.

And, although there are still millions of demons subject to the above-mentioned one, it is quite useless to name them, since they are employed only at the discretion of the superior demons who may compel them to operate in their stead, because they use all these lower spirits as their workers or slaves.

Thus, in making the pact with one of the six chiefs whom you invoke, it is of no consequence who serves you. However, always ask the spirit with whom you make your pact that one of the three chiefs subordinate to him should serve you.

Here are the exact powers, knowledge, arts, and skills of the above-mentioned demons, so that the initiate who wants to make a pact may find what he requires in each of the talents of the six superior demons. The first is the great Lucifuge Rofocale, infernal Prime Minister. He has the power assigned to him by Lucifer over all the wealth and treasures of the world.

Under him he has Baël, Agares, and Marbas, and several other thousands of demons or spirits who are subject to him. The second is the great Satanachia,

Grand General. He has the power to make women and girls submissive to him and to do his will with them. He commands the great legion of demons. Under him he has Pruslas, Aamon, Barbatos, and others.

Agaliarept, also a general, has the power to discover the most hidden secrets in every royal court, in every cabinet in the world. He also unveils the greatest mysteries. He commands the second legion of spirits. Under him he has Buer, Gusoyn, Botis, and others.

Fleuretty, lieutenant general, has the power to perform any task required during the night. He also brings hail in whatever area he wishes. He commands a very considerable corps of demons. Under him he has Bathim, Pursan, and Abigar.

Sargatanas, brigadier, has the power of conferring invisibility, transporting you anywhere, opening every lock for you, making you see what happens in every home, teaching you every shepherd's trick and wile. He commands many demoniac brigades. Under him he has Loray, Valefar, and Foraü.

Nebiros, field marshal and inspector general, has the power to inflict harm on whomever he wishes. He will find the hand of glory for you, he teaches all the properties of metals, minerals, and vegetables, and animals both clean and unclean. He can also predict the future, being one of the greatest necromancers of all the infernal demons. He goes everywhere, and supervises all the demoniac wiles. Under him he has Ayperos, Nuberus, and Glasyabolas, and others.

The Key of Solomon.

HAND OF GLORY: a hand cut off from a criminal, who had been hanged on a gibbet. In the Middle Ages, such a hand, dried and steeped in various salts, was used in spells.

How to Make a Demoniac Pact

When you want to make your pact with one of the principal demons that I have just named, you will begin, on the evening before the pact, by cutting, with a new knife that has never been used, a wild nut-tree twig that has never borne fruit and that is like the thundering rod already described, at the exact moment that the sun appears on our horizon.

This being done, you will fortify yourself with a blood stone and consecrated candles, and you will then choose a spot for the operation where nobody can disturb you. You may even make the pact in a secluded chamber or in a hut of some old ruined castle, because the demon has the power of transporting whatever treasure he pleases to that spot.

After which, you will trace a triangle with your blood stone, and that only the first time that you make your pact. Then you will set the two candles on the side, placing the sacred name of Jesus behind, to prevent the spirits from inflicting any harm on you.

Then, you will stand in the middle of the triangle, with the mystic wand in your hand, with the great invocation to the demon, the clavicule, the request that you want to make, with the pact and the dismissal of the demon, as indicated in the model of the cabalistic triangle of pacts.

Having performed scrupulously all that

[97]

is indicated, you will begin to recite the following invocation with confidence and assurance:

Great Invocation of the Spirits with whom you wish to make a Pact: Taken from the Great Key of Solomon

Emperor Lucifer, Master of all the rebellious spirits, I beg you to be favorable in the invocation that I make to your great Minister Lucifuge Rofocale, as I wish to make a pact with him. I beg you also, Prince Beelzebub, to protect me in my enterprise.

O Count Astorath! Be propitious, and bring it to pass that, this very night, the great Lucifuge appear to me in human form and without any evil odor, and that he grant me, by means of the pact that I shall offer him, all the wealth that I need.

O great Lucifuge! I beg you to leave your abode, in whatever region of the earth it may be, to come and speak to me. Otherwise I shall constrain you by the power of the great living God, his dear Son, and the Holy Spirit.

Obey promptly, or you will be tortured eternally by the force of the potent words of the Great Key of Solomon that he himself used to bind the rebellious spirits to accept his pact.

So, come forth instanter! Or I shall torture you endlessly by the force of these powerful words of the Key: Agion, Telagram, vaycheon stimulamaton y ezpares retragrammaton oryoram irion esytion existion eryona onera brasim moym messias soter Emanuel Saboot Adonai, te adoro et invoco.

The Key of Solomon.

NEW KNIFE: newness is an efficacious concept in magic ceremonies. Hence fresh, uncontaminated objects were used by magicians. Newly forged weapons, virgin soil, bowls straight from the potter's wheel, had their specific potency. Spells were engraved with a new knife. Periapts were inscribed on fresh parchment. Circles and triangles were drawn with a new blade.

THUNDERING ROD: the magician's wand.

BLOOD STONE: a magic stone that gave its owner the power of fulfilling his wishes.

Magician's Pact with Lucifuge Rofocale

O Emperor Lucifer, Chief of all the spirits which rebelled, I beg thee to favour me in this conjuration, which I am about to perform to Lucifuge Rofocale, thy Minister. O Prince Beelzebub, I adjure thee to protect me in this work. O Earl Astorath, favour me, and permit me tonight to obtain the appearance of the Great Lucifuge, in human shape, and without any evil effluvium. And that he may allow me, in return for the pact which I will sign, the wealth which I am in need of.

O great Lucifuge, I beg thee to leave thy home, wherever it may be, and come to this place to speak with me. If thou doest not this, I will constrain thee to appear, by the force of the Great Living God, his Son and his Spirit. Do my bidding at once, or thou shalt be tormented for ever by the force of the words of Power of the Great Clavicle of Solomon, which he used to compel revolted spirits to obey him and accept his contract.

Appear, then, immediately, or I shall torture thee with the force of these

Words of Power from the Key of Solomon!

Aglon. Tetragram. Vaycheon. Stimulamaton. Ezphares. Retragrammaton. Olyaram. Irion. Esytion. Existion. Eryona. Onera. Orasym. Mozm. Messias. Soter. Emanuel. Sabaoth. Adonay. Te adoro. Et te invoco. Amen.

Lucifuge Rofocale appears.

Magician: I promise the Great Lucifuge to reward him after twenty years for treasures given to me. And I sign . . .

True Grimoire, medieval magic manual.

Pacts between magicians and members of the Satanic hierarchy were motivated by desire for honor, love, power of invisibility and of transvection, wealth. On occasion, the pact had destructive implications: to destroy enemies and cause ruin and cataclysms.

Dismissing a Summoned Infernal Power

I am pleased and contented with thee, Prince Lucifer, for the moment. Leave thou in peace now, and go in quiet and without trouble. Do not forget our pact, or I shall blast thee with my Wand. Amen.

True Grimoire, medieval magic manual.

The magician discharges the spirit that has aided him in his magic operation.

To Summon Demons

To summon demons, utterance of the nine divine and mystic names:

Eheieh
Iod
Tetragrammaton Elohim
El
Elohim Gibor
Eloah Va-Daath
El Adonai Tzabaoth
Elohim Tzabaoth
Shaddai

Key of Solomon, medieval grimoire.

Every Demon Has His Province

There are different kinds of spirits, according to the things over which they preside; some of them govern the Empyrean Heaven, others the Primum Mobile, others the First and Second Crystalline, others the Starry Heaven: there are also spirits of the Heaven of Saturn, which I call Saturnites: there are Jovial, Martial, Solar, Venerean, Mercurial, and Lunar Spirits: there are also Spirits in the Elements as well as in the Heavens: there are some in the Fiery Region, others in the Air, others in the Water, and others upon the Earth, which can all render service to that man who shall have the good fortune to understand their nature, and to know how to attract them.

The Key of Solomon, a medieval grimoire.

Satanic Oath

We Lucifer, and all beforementioned and following spirits, swear to you, to almighty God through Jesus Christ of Nazarus, the Crucified One, our conqueror, that we will faithfully perform everything written in this book: also never to do you any harm, either to your body or your soul, and to execute everything immediately and without refusing.

Liber Spirituum, medieval grimoire.

How to Summon Lucifuge Rofocale

I conjure you, O spirit, to appear within a minute by the power of Great Adonai, by Eloim, by Ariel, Johavam, Agla, Tagla, Mathon, Oarios, Almouzin, Arios, Membrot, Varvis, Pithona, Magots, Silphae, Rabost, Salamandrae, Tabost, Gnomus, Terreae, Coelis, Godens, Aqua, Gingua, Janua, Etituamus, Zariatnetmik.

The Great Grimoire.

The Great Grimoire is a mediaeval manual of magic.
The invocation is to be repeated twice, after which the spirit will appear.
LUCIFUGE ROFOCALE: An arch demon, Prime Minister in the infernal hierarchy.

The Devil Enthroned

In the days of the Emperor Maurice there was in Constantinople a magician named Mesita, who surpassed in the magic art all magicians since the beginning of time.

Now this Mesita—which means in Latin mediator—hired a certain devout, God-fearing notary. Wishing to seduce him into the Black Arts, on a certain day toward evening the wicked Mesita

made his preparations. He also made the notary get ready as if for some useful and necessary service. Mounting fine horses, they both rode out of the gates of the city. When they had gone until midnight, they came to a large level plain, without any dwelling or building on it.

Suddenly a city appeared in view. Dismounting and tying up their horses, Mesita knocked at the gate. It opened to them—said the notary—and a crowd of Ethiopians greeted us, salaaming, until we came to a spacious hall, where we found many lights and golden candelabra without number, and a host of golden candles, numerous benches right and left, and in the centre a lofty golden throne, adorned with every kind of precious stone, and sitting thereon a dark Ethiopian. Other Ethiopians sat on the right and the left.

So Mesita greeted the personage seated on the throne, who welcomed Mesita with great honor and joy, saying:
"What now, Master Mesita? Are your wishes fulfilled or not?"

In reply, Mesita said:
"Yes, Mesita. And for this reason I have come to worship and thank you."

He who sat on the throne said:
"Even greater gifts are yours. Please be seated."

Mesita sat down on the bench at the right.

"Seeing that they were all Ethiopians," said the notary, "I did not approach any of them, but stood behind Mesita. When the abominable creature sitting on the throne observed me, he asked Mesita:
" 'Who is this man with you, Master Mesita?' "

LITTLE BRONZE BELL WITH DEMONS
(Babylon, 9th Century B.C.)

MATTHEW HOPKINS

Matthew Hopkins was a seventeenth century English lawyer who launched a campaign for the extermination of witches. It was said that he was responsible for the execution of thousands of victims.

Note in the illustration the various familiars of the witch and their pet names.

EXECUTION OF WITCHES IN ENGLAND

Witch-hunting was particularly prevalent in the sixteenth and seventeenth centuries. In England, Lancashire was the locale of many investigations, trials, and convictions of women accused of witchcraft. Similar campaigns were organized in the United States, and the Salem witch-hunts became notorious for their ruthless prosecutions.

WITCHCRAFT IN NEW ENGLAND

In the seventeenth century Salem was the scene of notorious witch trials and condemnations. Arthur Miller's play, *The Crucible*, treats the subject dramatically.

Mesita said: "He is your servant, Master."

Then the creature that sat on the throne asked the notary:

"Tell me, young man, are you my servant?"

Crossing himself, the notary replied at once:

"I am the servant of the Father, the Son, and the Holy Ghost."

When he heard these names, the creature that sat on the throne immediately collapsed. The throne disappeared. The lamps went out. The Ethiopians fled howling. Everything vanished. The house, the city faded out. No sign of Mesita. Everything was in a confused mist. No sound was heard, no one was left except the young notary.

He did not look for Mesita, nor turn his gaze to right or left, but untying the horses he mounted them and rapidly returned to the city. Coming to the gate that he had recently left, he beat on it and entered. He told the gate-keepers what he had seen and heard and what had happened. Then, at dawn he went home.

Johannes Monachus (11th century), *Liber de Miraculis.*

Demons under Control

For no beautiful woman would remain undefiled, no ruler or prince would be safe if demons were allowed to listen to and fulfill men's evil desires.

William of Paris (12th century), *De Universo.*

Characteristics of Demons

For Demons are said to love blood; hence, whenever a necromantic act is performed, blood is mixed with water so that they may be exorcised more readily by the color of blood.

Gratian (12th century), *Decretum.*

Worship of Satan

So according to the idolatrous practice of this age Satan is believed to appear in the form of a black cat or a toad and to demand kisses from his adherents: one abominable kiss, under the cat's tail: the other, a horrifying one, in the toad's mouth.

William of Paris (12th century), *De Legibus.*

The Cathari

They are called Cathari from the term cat, whose posterior they kiss, in whose form Satan appears to them.

Errores Haereticorum, medieval treatise.

Satanic Pact of Dr. Faust

The Black Universe asserts that I have a pact with them, but may God protect us, you and me, from him.

Doctor Johannes Faust.

THREEFOLD HARROWING OF HELL: mediaeval magic manual ascribed to Faust.
HIM: Satan himself.

[101]

Habitation of Demons

In these days the belief had spread that spirits dwelt in the desert, spoke, and appeared there.

Maimonides, medieval philosopher (1135-1204).

Activity of Incubus

It is truly recorded of incubi and succubi demons and we ourselves have seen persons known by them and the places in which a man can scarcely even sleep at night without a succubus accosting him.

Albertus Magnus (1206-1280).

Power of Demons Limited

Certain learned men have declared that magic did not exist at all except in the belief of men, who imputed to witchcraft the natural effect whose causes are obscure. But this is contrary to the authority of the saints, who say that demons have power over the bodies and imagination of men, when they are so permitted by God.

Thomas Aquinas (13th century), *Sententiae*.

Satanic Pact

Magicians perform miracles through personal contracts made with demons.

Thomas Aquinas (13th century), *Sententiae*.

The Devil Reveals His Weakness

I have heard that a certain demon, in the guise of a man, served a wealthy master, and, since the man's service and hard work pleased his master, he gave him his daughter to wife along with great riches. But she quarreled day and night with her husband and did not give him any rest. At the end of the year he said to his father-in-law: "I want to leave and go back to my country."

The father-in-law answered: "Haven't I given you many things so that you would lack nothing? Why do you want to leave?"

The man said: "I want to return to my country, by whatever means I can."

The father-in-law said: "Where is your country?"

The other said: "I shall tell you, without concealing the truth. My country is Hell, where I never experienced so much strife and trouble as I suffered this last year from my quarrelsome wife. I'd rather be in Hell than stay any longer with her." So saying, he vanished from their sight.

Exempla, by James of Vitry (d. 1240), cardinal bishop of Tusculum.

These exempla, inserted as illustrations in sermons, were intended to divert and instruct the congregations.

The Devil for Sale

Robert de Roderham appeared against John de Ithon, for that he had not kept the agreement made between them, and therefore complains, that on a certain day and year, at Thorne, there was an agreement between the aforesaid Robert and John, whereby the said John sold to the said Robert the devil, bound in a certain bond, for threepence farthing, and thereupon the said Robert delivered to the said John one farthing as earnest-money, by which the property of the said devil rested in the person of the said Robert, to have livery of the said devil on the fourth day next following, at which day the said Robert came to the aforementioned John, and asked livery of the said devil, according to the agreement between them made. But the said John refused to deliver the said devil, nor has he yet done it, to the grievous damage of the said Robert to the amount of sixty shillings; and he has therefore brought his suit.

The said John came, and did not deny the said agreement; and because it appeared to the court that such a suit ought not to subsist among Christians, the aforesaid parties are therefore adjourned to the infernal regions, there to hear their judgment.

William de Scargell, Senescal, *British Court Rolls,* 1329.

Satan's Hosts

Smooth Devils, Horned Devils,
Sullen Devils, Playful Devils,
Shorn Devils, Hairy Devils,
Foolish Devils,
Devils, Devilesses, and Young Devils,
All the offspring of devildom,
Come from your devilish tricks
Quicker than light.
Passion of St. Quentin, 14th century miracle play.

A Fiend Tempts a Saint

When St. Godric paused, weary from his labor, a certain stranger, standing by, observed him for a long while, then spoke thus: "Did the Fathers of old, whom you believe you are imitating, thus labor in the desert, wan and hungry? Look, from morning to night you have scarcely dug five feet of soil, when you ought to show your devotion to the Lord by the amount of your labor!"

Smilingly, the man of God answered him: "You, then, first show me an example of good work." For Godric thought that the man was righteous, sent by the Lord to teach him. And so, handing him the spade, he said: "The hour of my usual spell of prayer compels me to return to the oratory. I shall come back and listen to you and I will willingly hear what you are good enough to explain." The other quickly seized the spade and energetically began to turn the soil. When Godric came back he found that more work had been accomplished than he was wont to finish in eight days. Then the other man spoke thus: "You ought to have emulated the example of the Fathers, with much sweat and labor."

At the sight, the holy man shuddered, for he realized that the man was not a real man. He was quite dark and hairy and very tall of stature: and for all his labor he showed not a single sign of sweat or effort.

Godric returned to his cell and, taking a book with him, he went back and said: "Tell me who you are and for what purpose you have come here."

The other replied: "Don't you see that

[103]

I am a man like yourself?"

"If you are a man," said Godric, "tell me whether you believe in the Father, the Son, and the Holy Ghost, and adore along with me the Mother of my Lord."

The other one said: "Don't worry about my belief, nor does your question concern me."

And Godric, going up to him, took out the book, containing pictures of the Savior and Holy Mary and St. John, and quickly thrusting it in the man's face, said: "Behold, if you believe in God, kiss these pictures devoutly."

Unable to cope with this, the man spat out a kind of spittle on the book and disappeared mockingly.

Sanctilogium, by John of Tynemouth (d. c. 1349).

Power of Incantations Limited

Hence if any effect follows, it is not from God, who did not so ordain it, nor from the virtue of the incantations; it must therefore be from the demon.

Johann Wünschilburg, *Tractatus de Superstitionibus*, 1440.

Types of Demons

Some are called Fates. Some are incubi and succubi. Some eat and drink with men. Some are formed from the odor and sperm of men and women in intercourse, or from the rays of planets. Some are clean, others are unclean.

Alphonso de Spina, *Fortalicium Fidei*, Nuremberg, 1494.

Names of Satan

Satan may be invoked under a variety of names, each having a special etymological significance. As Asmodeus, he is the Creature of Judgment. As Satan, he becomes the Adversary. As Behemoth, he is the Beast. Diabolus, the Devil, signifies Two Morsels: the body and the soul, both of which he kills. Demon connotes Cunning over Blood. Belial, Without a Master. Beelzebub, Lord of Flies.

Malleus Maleficarum—The Hammer of Witches, a Latin treatise on magic by Heinrich Kramer and Jacob Sprenger, fifteenth century Dominicans.

Necromancy in Medieval Rome

It came to pass through a variety of odd accidents, that I made acquaintance with a Sicilian priest, who was a man of genius, and well versed in the Greek and Latin languages. Happening one day to have some conversation with him, where the subject turned upon the art of necromancy, I, who had a great desire to know something of the matter, told him that I had all my life had a curiosity to be acquainted with the mysteries of this art. The priest made answer, that the man must be of a resolute and steady temper, who entered on that study. I replied, that I had fortitude and resolution enough to desire to be initiated in it. The priest subjoined, "If you think you have the heart to venture, I will give you all the satisfaction you can desire." Thus we agreed to enter upon a scheme of necromancy.

The priest one evening prepared to satisfy me, and desired me to look for a companion or two. I invited one Vincenzio Romoli, who was my intimate acquaintance, and he brought with him a native of Pistoia who cultivated the art of necromancy himself. We repaired to the Coliseum; and the priest, according to the custom of conjurors, began to draw circles on the ground, with the most impressive ceremonies imaginable. He likewise brought with him all sorts of precious perfumes and fire, with some compositions which diffused noisome and bad odours. As soon as he was in readiness, he made an opening to the circle, and took us by the hand, and ordered the other necromancer, his partner, to throw perfumes into the fire at a proper time, intrusting the care of the fire and the perfumes to the rest: and then he began his incantations.

This ceremony lasted above an hour and a half, when there appeared several legions of devils, so that the amphitheatre was quite filled with them. I was busy about the perfumes, when the priest, who knew that there was a sufficient number of infernal spirits, turned about to me, and said, "Benvenuto, ask them something." I answered, "Let them bring me into company with my Sicilian mistress, Angelica." That night we obtained no answer of any sort; but I received great satisfaction in having my curiosity so far indulged.

The necromancer told me that it was requisite we should go a second time, assuring me that I should be satisfied in whatever I asked; but that I must bring with me a boy that had never known woman. I took with me my apprentice, who was about 12 years of age; with the same Vincenzio Romoli, who had been my companion the first time, and one Agnolino Gaddi, an intimate acquaintance, whom I likewise prevailed on to assist at the ceremony. When we came to the place appointed, the priest, having made his preparations as before with the same and even more striking ceremonies, placed us within the circle, which he had drawn with a more wonderful art, and in a more solemn manner, than at our former meeting. Thus having committed the care of the perfumes and the fire to my friend Vincenzio, who was assisted by Gaddi, he put into my hands a pintacolo, or magical chart, and bid me turn it towards the place to which he should direct me; and under the pintacolo I beheld my apprentice. The necromancer, having begun to make his most tremendous invocations, called by their name a multitude of demons who were the leaders of the several legions, and questioned them, by the virtue and power of the eternal, uncreated God, who lives for ever, in the Hebrew language, as also in Latin and Greek; in so much as the amphitheatre was filled, almost in an instant, with demons a hundred times more numerous than at the former conjuration. Vincenzio meanwhile was busied in making a fire with the assistance of Gaddi, and burning a great quantity of precious perfumes. I, by the direction of the necromancer, again desired to be in company with my Angelica. He then turning upon me said, "Know, they have declared that in the space of a month you shall be in her company."

He then requested me to stand by him resolutely, because the legions were now above a thousand more in number than he had designed; and besides these were the most dangerous; so that, after they had answered my question, it behooved him to be civil to them, and dismiss them quietly. At the same time the boy under the pintacolo was in a terrible fright, saying, that there were in the place a million of fierce men who threatened to destroy us; and that, besides, there were four armed giants of enormous stature, who endeavoured to break into our circle. During this time, while the necromancer, trembling with fear, endeavoured by mild means to dismiss them in the best way he could, Vincenzio, who quivered like an aspen leaf, took care of the perfumes. Though I was as much afraid as any of them, I did my utmost to conceal it; so that I greatly contributed to inspire the rest with resolution: but the truth is, I gave myself over for a dead man, seeing the horrid fright the necromancer was in.

The boy had placed his head between his knees; and said, "In this attitude will I die; for we shall all surely perish." I told him that those demons were under us, and what we saw was smoke and shadow; so bid him hold up his head and take courage. No sooner did he look up, than he cried out, "The whole amphitheatre is burning, and the fire is just falling on us." So, covering his eyes with his hands, he again exclaimed, that destruction was inevitable, and he desired to see no more. The necromancer intreated me to have a good heart, and

to take care to burn proper perfumes; upon which I turned to Vincenzio, and bade him burn all the most precious perfumes he had. At the same time I cast my eyes upon Gaddi, who was terrified to such a degree, that he could scarcely distinguish objects, and seemed to be half dead. Seeing him in this condition, I said to him, "Gaddi, upon these occasions a man should not yield to fear, but stir about to give some assistance; so come directly, and put on more of these perfumes." Gaddi accordingly attempted to move; but the effect was annoying both to our sense of hearing and smell, and overcame the perfumes.

The boy perceiving this once more ventured to raise his head, and, seeing me laugh, began to take courage, and said, "The devils are flying away with a vengeance." In this condition we staid, till the bell rang for morning prayers. The boy again told us, that there remained but few devils, and those were at a great distance. When the magician had performed the rest of his ceremonies, he stripped off his gown, and took up a wallet full of books, which he had brought with him. We all went out of the circle together, keeping as close to each other as we possibly could, especially the boy, who placed himself in the middle, holding the necromancer by the coat, and me by the cloak.

As we were going to our houses in the quarter of Banchi, the boy told us, that two of the demons whom we had seen at the amphitheatre, went on before us leaping and skipping, sometimes running upon the roofs of the houses, and sometimes on the ground. The priest declared that, as often as he had entered magic circles, nothing so extraordinary had ever happened to him. As we went along, he would fain have persuaded me to assist at the consecrating a book, from which he said we should derive immense riches. We should then ask the demons to discover to us the various treasures with which the earth abounds, which would raise us to opulence and power; but that those love-affairs were mere follies from which no good could be expected. I made answer, that I would readily have accepted his proposal if I had understood Latin. He assured me that the knowledge of Latin was nowise material; but that he could never meet with a partner of resolution and intrepidity equal to mine, and that that would be to him an invaluable acquisition.

> *Autobiography* of Benvenuto Cellini (1500-1571), Italian sculptor and jeweler.

The incident here recorded is assigned to the year 1534.

Existence of Demons

Therefore it is beyond doubt that demons were created.

> Jerome Cardan (16th century). *De Rerum Varietate.*

Satanic Invocation

May the gods of Acheron be propitious to me!
May the triple divine power of Jehovah prevail!

Fire, air, water, spirit of the earth, hail!
Chief of the East, Beelzebub, monarch of fiery hell, and Demogorgon, we propitiate you, that Mephistopheles may rise and appear.

> Christopher Marlowe (1564-1593) dramatist, author of *The Tragical History of Dr. Faustus.*

The incident here recorded is assigned to the year 1534.
ACHERON: river in Underworld.
BEELZEBUB: Satan as Lord of Flies.
DEMOGORGON: awesome deity of Infernal Regions: invoked in magic ritual.
MEPHISTOPHELES: Satan.

Scottish Succuba

In the region of Gareoth, a village some fourteen miles from Aberdeen, a very handsome young man complained to a priest in Aberdeen that some months previously he had been assailed by a so-called succuba demon, remarkably beautiful and that it had induced him, by much blandishment, to have intercourse.

> Hector Boece, Scottish Chronicler (16th century).

Types of Demons

Terrestrial devils are those Lares, Genii, Fauns, Satyrs, Wood-nymphs, Foliots, Fairies, Robin Goodfellows, Trulli, etc. which as they are most conversant with men, so they do them most harm.

> Robert Burton, *Anatomy of Melancholy* (1577-1640).

Necromantic Conjuration

By the mysteries of the deep, by the flames of Banal, by the power of the East, and by the silence of the night, by the holy rites of Hecate, I conjure and exorcize thee thou distressed Spirit, to present thyself here, and reveal unto me the cause of thy calamity, why thou didst offer violence to thy own liege life, where thou art now in being, and where thou wilt hereafter be.

Reginald Scot, *Discoverie of Witchcraft,* 1584.

HECATE: witch-goddess of the Underworld.

Pact with Demons

Witches are a most pestiferous class, who enter on pacts with demons, and, after making a solemn profession of faith, dedicate themselves, in lasting obedience, to some particular demon. No one can describe the evils of which this class of beings is guilty. Hence they must nowhere be tolerated, but utterly and everywhere exterminated.

Abbot Johann Trithemius (16th century), *Liber Octo Quaestionum.*

Habitation of Demons

In many regions there are still dwellings of demons. Prussia is full of demons. Bilappen swarms with witchcraft. In Switzerland near Lucerne on a very high mountain there is a lake where Satan rages. On a lofty mountain, the Procknesberg, there is a lake, which, when a stone is cast in, produced a great storm throughout the entire region. These are the dwellings of imprisoned demons.

Martin Luther (16th century), *Colloquia.*

Denial of Pact Made with Satan

Satan appeared all in blacke, with a white wande in his hande, demanded of him if hee would continue his faithfull service, according to his first oath and promise made to that effect, whome (as hee then said) he utterly renounced to his face, and said unto him in this manner 'Avoide, Satan, avoide—I utterly forsake thee.'

Newes from Scotland, 1591.

The renunciation was made by John Fian, Scottish sorcerer, who was convicted of witchcraft in 1591.

Satan's Motive

From the very beginning the Devil has been a killer of men, nor has he ever ceased to drive men bereft of piety to slaughter and murder.

Nicholas Rémy. *Demonolatria,* 1595.

Composition of Demons

The Platonic School too affirms that Demons are without body, but that for a specific time they assume bodies and use them, made of air or some denser matter.

Nicholas Rémy. *Demonolatria,* 1595.

Can Demons Possess Wealth?

Strange! Though Demons are believed to guard vast treasures, that lie hidden, and to control them in their power, yet they can never secure any for themselves.

Nicholas Rémy. *Demonolatria,* 1595.

Satanic Pact

These pacts with the Devil are not only vain and useless: they are also dangerous and evil.

Francesco Guazzo. *Compendium Maleficarum,* 1608.

Miltonic Satan

The other shape,
If shape it might be called, that shape had none
Distinguishable in member, joint, or limb,
Or substance might be called that shadow seemed,
For each seemed either; black it stood as night,
Fierce as ten furies, terrible as hell.

John Milton (1608-1674), English poet. Author of *Paradise Lost.*

Types of Demons

There are igneous, aery, phlegmatic, earthly, and subterranean demons.

Sinistrari. *De la démonalité et des animaux incubes et succubes.* French translation, 1876.

Exorcism to Drive out a Poltergeist

I adjure you, ancient serpent, by the Judge of the living and the dead, by the Creator of the universe, who has power to send you to Gehenna, that you depart forthwith from this house. He orders you to do so, cursed devil, who ordered the winds and the sea and the tempests. He orders you who ordered you to be plunged from heaven into the Lower Regions. He orders you, who ordered you to go back. Hearken therefore, Satan, and be afraid, and withdraw, subdued and prostrate.

17th century manual.

Corporeal Demons

They often form for themselves bodies from impure air or vapors and exhalations or clouds mixed with air. To the air water is added, earth, mud, sulphur, resin, wood. Sometimes too there are added bones from the corpses of animals or condemned men: at times too from the semen of beasts or men and such like matter.

Adam Tanner. *Tractatus Theologicus,* 1629.

Curse on Satan!

Then you, ye auld sneck-drawin' dog!
Ye came to Paradise incog.,
An' played on man a cursed brogue,
        (Black be your fa'!),
An' gied the infant world a shog,
        Maist ruined a'.

Robert Burns (1759-1796), Scottish poet. Author of *Address to the Deil.*

[109]

Enter: The Devil

On the study-table a book there lay,
Which Agrippa himself had been reading
    that day;
The letters were written with blood
    therein,
And the leaves were made of dead men's
    skin.

The young man, he began to read
He knew not what, but he would
    proceed,
When there was heard a sound at the
    door,
Which as he read grew more and more.

And more and more the knocking grew,
The young man knew not what to do:
But trembling in fear he sat within,
Till the door was broke, and the Devil
    came in.

Two hideous horns on his head he had
    got,
Like iron heated nine times red-hot;
The breath of his nostrils was brimstone
    blue
And his tail like a fiery serpent grew.
    Robert Southey (1774-1843), Eng-
    lish poet. Author of *Cornelius
    Agrippa: A Ballad.*

CORNELIUS AGRIPPA: 16th century occultist.

The Devil's Due

The Raven croak'd as she sate at her
    meal,
    And the Old Woman knew what he
    said,
And she grew pale at the Raven's tale,
    And sicken'd and went to her bed.

"I have 'nointed myself with infant's fat,
    The fiends have been my slaves,
From sleeping babes I have suck'd the
    breath,
And breaking by charms the sleep of
    death
    I have call'd the dead from their
    graves.

"And the Devil will fetch me now in fire,
    My witchcrafts to atone;
And I who have troubled the dead man's
    grave
    Shall never have rest in my own."

They blest the old woman's winding
    sheet
    With rites and prayers due,
With holy water they sprinkled her
    shroud,
    And they sprinkled her coffin too.

And in He came with eyes of flame,
    The Devil to fetch the dead,
And all the church with his presence
    glow'd
    Like a fiery furnace red.

He laid his hand on the iron chains,
    And like flax they moulder'd asunder,
And the coffin lid, which was barr'd so
    firm,
    He burst with his voice of thunder.

And he bade the Old Woman of Berke-
    ley rise,
    And come with her master away;
A cold sweat started on that cold corpse,
    At the voice she was forced to obey.

The Devil he flung her on her horse,
    And he leapt up before.

[110]

WITCHES' SABBAT

The Sabbat was a seasonal assembly of witches to do homage to the Archfiend. The rendezvous was the Brocken in Germany, or the church of Blokula in Sweden, or an isolated ruined castle or secluded valley. The locale in the illustration is the Blacksberg, in Germany. Note the cat, familiar of witches. Elemental spirits hover over the scene. In one corner a Satanic dance is in progress. In another corner witches are enjoying a grim feast.

(Painting by Michael Herr, 16th century German artist)

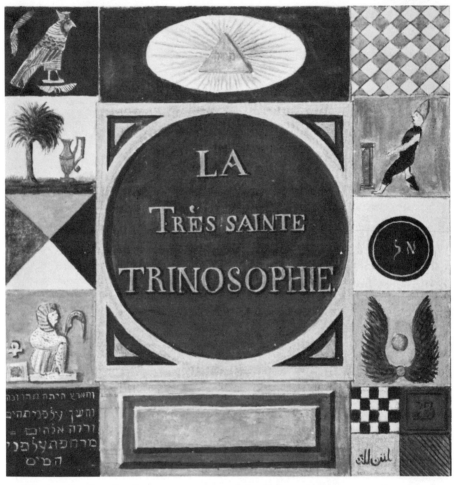

Title page of a French cabalistic manuscript of the eighteenth century: attributed to the Comte de Saint-Germain.

Bibliothèque Municipale, Troyes, France.

WITCHES' SABBAT

A gathering of witches doing homage to his Satanic Majesty. Note the witch arriving on the back of a goat. The cat is the witch's familiar. The Sabbat was a popular subject for artistic expression.

(Painting by Hans Baldung, 16th century German artist)

Courtesy of The Metropolitan Museum of Art, N. Y.

BEASTS OF THE BLACK ARTS

Fantastic creatures, half animal and partly human, characteristic of Goya's interest in
magic subjects. A possible reminiscence of Circe's magic animal transformations.
(Painting by Goya, 18th century Spanish artist)

Courtesy of The Metropolitan Museum of Art, N. Y.

And away like the lightning's speed they
    went,
And she was seen no more.
    Robert Southey (1774-1843), Eng-
    lish poet. Author of *The Old Wom-
    an of Berkeley: A Ballad.*

Poem based on a ninth century tale of a
witch: appears in old chronicles: William
of Malmesbury, Matthew of Westminster,
Olaus Magnus, Nuremberg Chronicle.

Appearance of Satan

Old Nick is a black-looking fellow at
    best,
Ah, e'en when he 's pleased; but never
    before
        Had he looked so black
        As on seeing his sack
Thus cut into slits on the Red Sea Shore.
    Richard H. Barham (1788-1845),
    British humorist. Author of *Ingolds-
    by Legends.*

Devil's Livery

According to mediaeval legend, the
livery of the Devil is Black and Yellow:
Black indicating death, Yellow implying
Quarantine.

St. Dunstan and Satan

St. Dunstan stood in his ivied tower,
    Alembic, crucible, all were there;
When in came Nick to play him a trick,
    In guise of a damsel passing fair.

Everyone knows
        How the story goes:
He took up the tongs and caught hold of
    his nose.
    Richard H. Barham (1788-1845),
    British humorist. Author of *Ingolds-
    by Legends.*

Raising the Devil
A Legend of Cornelius Agrippa

'And hast thou nerve enough?' he cried,
    That grey Old Man, above whose head
    Unnumber'd years had roll'd,—
'And hast thou nerve to view,' he cried,
    'The incarnate Fiend that Heaven
        defied!—
    —Art thou indeed so bold?

'Say, canst Thou, with unshrinking gaze,
Sustain, rash youth, the withering blaze
    Of that unearthly eye,
That blasts where'er it lights,—the breath
That, like the Simoon, scatters death
    On all that yet can die?

—'Darest thou confront that fearful form,
That rides the whirlwind, and the storm,
    In wild unholy revel!—
The terrors of that blasted brow,
Archangel's once,—though ruin'd now—
    —Ay,—dar'st thou face THE DEVIL?'—

'I dare!' the desperate youth replied,
And placed him by that Old Man's side,
    In fierce and frantic glee,
Unblench'd his cheek, and firm his limb
—'No paltry juggling Fiend, but HIM!
    —The Devil!—I fain would see!—

[111]

'In all his Gorgon terrors clad,
His worst, his fellest shape!' the Lad
    Rejoin'd in reckless tone.—
—'Have then thy wish!' Agrippa said,
And sigh'd and shook his hoary head,
    With many a bitter groan.

He drew the mystic circle's bound,
With skull and cross-bones fenc'd around;
He traced full many a sigil there;
He mutter'd many a backward pray'r,
    That sounded like a curse—
'He comes!'—he cried with wild grimace,
'The fellest of Apollyon's race!'—
—Then in his startled pupil's face
    He dash'd—an EMPTY PURSE!

    R. H. Barham (1788-1845), English humorist. Author of *The Ingoldsby Legends.*

CORNELIUS AGRIPPA: 16th century occultist.
GORGON: In classical mythology, a monster the sight of whom turned a person to stone.
CIRCLE: magic circle drawn around sorcerer in performing occult rites.
SIGIL: magic symbol.
BACKWARD: to produce certain magic effects, certain formulae were recited backward, especially mystical names, incantations, the Pater Noster.
APOLLYON: the Archfiend.

Exorcism of Demon

According to the religious beliefs of the Tartars, all illness is owing to the visitation of a Tchutgour or demon; but the expulsion of the demon is first a matter of medicine. The Lama physician next proceeds, as Lama apothecary, to give the specific befitting the case; the Tartar pharmacopoeia rejecting all mineral chemistry, the Lama remedies consist entirely of vegetables pulverized, and either infused in water or made up into pills. If the Lama doctor happens not to have any medicine with him, he is by no means disconcerted; he writes the names of the remedies upon little scraps of paper, moistens the papers with his saliva, and rolls them up into pills, which the patient tosses down with the same perfect confidence as though they were genuine medicaments. To swallow the name of a remedy, or the remedy itself, say the Tartars, comes to precisely the same thing.

    The medical assault of the usurping demon being applied, the Lama next proceeds to spiritual artillery, in the form of prayers, adapted to the quality of the demon who has to be dislodged. If the patient is poor, the Tchutgour visiting him can evidently be only an inferior Tchutgour, requiring merely a brief, off-hand prayer, sometimes merely an interjectional exorcism. If the patient is very poor, the Lama troubles himself with neither prayer nor pill, but goes away, recommending the friends to wait with patience until the sick person gets better or dies. But where the patient is rich, the possessor of large flocks, the proceedings are altogether different. First, it is obvious that a devil who presumes to visit so eminent a personage must be a potent devil, one of the chiefs of the lower world; and it would not be decent for a great Tchutgour to travel like a mere sprite; the family, accordingly, are directed to prepare for him a handsome suit of clothes, a pair of rich boots, a fine horse, ready saddled and bridled, otherwise the devil will never think of going, physic or exorcise him how you may. It is even possible, indeed, that one horse will not suffice, for the demon, in very rich cases, may turn out, upon inquiry, to be so high and mighty a prince, that he has with him a number of courtiers and attendants, all of whom have to be provided with horses.

Everything being arranged, the ceremony commences. The Lama and numerous co-physicians called in from his own and other adjacent monasteries, offer up prayers in the rich man's tents for a week or a fortnight, until they perceive that the devil is gone—that is to say, until they have exhausted all the disposable tea and sheep. If the patient recovers, it is a clear proof that the prayers have been efficaciously recited; if he dies, it is a still greater proof of the efficaciousness of the prayers, for not only is the devil gone, but the patient has transmigrated to a state far better than he has quitted.

The prayers recited by the Lamas for the recovery of the sick are sometimes accompanied with very dismal and alarming rites. The aunt of Tokoura, chief of an encampment in the Valley of Dark Waters, visited by M. Huc, was seized one evening with an intermittent fever. "I would invite the attendance of the doctor Lama," said Tokoura, "but if he finds that there is a very big Tchutgour present, the expenses will ruin me." He waited for some days; but as his aunt grew worse and worse, he at last sent for a Lama; his anticipations were confirmed. The Lama pronounced that a demon of considerable rank was present, and that no time must be lost in expelling him. Eight other Lamas were forthwith called in,

who at once set about the construction, in dried herbs, of a great puppet which they entitled the *Demon of Intermittent Fevers,* and which, when completed, they placed on its legs by means of a stick, in the patient's tent.

The ceremony began at eleven o'clock at night; the Lamas ranged themselves in a semi-circle around the upper portion of the tent, with cymbals, sea-shells, bells, tambourines, and other instruments of the noisy Tartar music. The remainder of the circle was completed by the members of the family, squatting on the ground close to one another, the patient kneeling, or rather crouched on her heels, opposite the *Demon of Intermittent Fevers.* The Lama doctor-in-chief had before him a large copper basin filled with millet, and some little images made of paste. The dung-fuel threw, amid much smoke, a fantastic and quivering light over the strange scene.

Upon a given signal, the clerical orchestra executed an overture harsh enough to frighten Satan himself, the lay congregation beating time with their hands to the charivari of clanging instruments and ear-splitting voices. The diabolical concert over, the Grand Lama opened the Book of Exorcisms, which he rested on his knees. As he chanted one of the forms, he took from the basin, from time to time, a handful of millet, which he threw east, west, north, and south, according to the Rubric. The tones of his voice, as he prayed, were sometimes mournful and suppressed, sometimes vehemently loud and energetic. All of a sudden, he would quit the regular cadence of prayer, and have an outburst of apparently indomitable rage, abusing the herb puppet with fierce invectives and furious gestures. The exorcism terminated, he gave a signal by stretching out his arms, right and left, and the other Lamas struck up a tremendously noisy chorus, in hurried, dashing tones; all the instruments were set to work, and meantime the lay congregation, having started up with one accord, ran out of the tent, one after the other, and tearing round it like mad people, beat it at their hardest with sticks, yelling all the while at the pitch of their voices in a manner to make ordinary hair stand on end. Having thrice performed this demoniac round, they re-entered the tent as precipitately as they had quitted it, and resumed their seats. Then all the others covering their faces with their hands, the Grand Lama rose and set fire to the herb figure. As soon as the flames rose, he uttered a loud cry, which was repeated with interest by the rest of the company. The laity immediately rose, seized the burning figure, carried it into the plain, away from the tents, and there, as it consumed, anathematized it with all sorts of imprecations; the Lamas meantime squatted in the tent, tranquilly chanting their prayers in a grave, solemn tone.

Upon the return of the family from their valorous expedition, the praying was exchanged for joyous felicitations. By and by, each person provided with a lighted torch, the whole party rushed simultaneously from the tent, and formed into a procession, the laymen first, then the patient, supported on either side by a member of the family, and lastly, the nine Lamas, making night hideous with their music. In this style the patient was conducted to another tent, pursuant to the orders of the Lama, who had declared that she must absent herself from her own habitation for an entire month.

After this strange treatment, the malady did not return.

M. Huc. *Travels in Tartary, Thibet and China during the years 1844-5-6.*

The Apparition

I was exhausted. I fell into a profound sleep early that night; it might be a little after twelve when I woke, and woke as fully, as completely, as much restored to life and consciousness, as it was then my habit to be at the break of day. And, so waking, I saw, on the wall opposite my bed, the same luminous phantom I had seen in the wizard's study at Derval Court. I have read in Scandinavian legends of an apparition called the Scin-Laeca, or shining corpse. It is supposed, in the northern superstition, sometimes to haunt sepulchres, sometimes to foretell doom. It is the spectre of a human body seen in a phosphoric light, and so exactly did this phantom correspond to the description of such an apparition in Scandinavian fable that I know not how to give it a better name than that of Scin-Laeca—the shining corpse.

There it was before me, corpse-like, yet not dead; there, as in the haunted study of the wizard Forman—the form and the face of Margrave. Constitutionally, my nerves are strong, and my temper hardy, and now I was resolved to battle against any impression which my senses might receive from my own deluding fancies. Things that witnessed for the first time daunt us, witnessed for the second time lose their terror. I rose from my bed with a bold aspect, I approached the phantom with a firm step; but when within two paces of it, and my hand outstretched to touch it, my arm became fixed in air, my feet locked to the ground. I did not experience fear; I felt that my heart beat regularly, but an invincible something opposed itself to me. I stood as if turned to stone, and then from the lips of this phantom there came a voice, but a voice which seemed borne from a great distance—very low, muffled, and yet distinct: I could not even be sure that my ear heard it, or whether the sound was not conveyed to me by an inner sense.

"I, and I alone, can save and deliver you," said the voice. "I will do so; and the conditions I ask, in return, are simple and easy." "Fiend or spectre, or mere delusion of my own brain," cried I, "there can be no compact between thee and me. I despise thy malice, I reject thy services; I accept no conditions to escape from the one to obtain the other."

"You may give a different answer when I ask again."

The Scin-Laeca slowly waned, and, fading first into a paler shadow, then vanished.

A Strange Story, by Bulwer Lytton (1803-1873), English novelist and occultist. Another of his novels dealing with occultism is *The Coming Race.*

The narrator is Dr. Allen Fenwick, a physician who is interested and involved in occult practices.

Conversation with a Spirit

I slowly moved the sand as if describing a circle. Before I had performed half the circle, the wand of itself stopped, resisting palpably the movement of my hand to impel it onward. I had not held it thus fixed for many seconds, before a cold air passed by me, stirring the roots of my hair; and, reflected against the opposite wall, stood the hateful Scin-Laeca. The Shadow was dimmer in its light than when before beheld, and the outline of the features was less distinct —still it was the unmistakable lemur, or image, of Margrave.

And a voice was conveyed to my senses saying, as from a great distance, and in weary yet angry accents—"You have summoned me? Wherefore?"

I overcame the startled shudder with which, at first, I beheld the Shadow and heard the Voice.

"I summoned you not," said I; "I sought but to impose upon you my will, that you should persecute, with your ghastly influences, me and mine no more. And now, by whatever authority this wand bestows on me, I so abjure and command you!"

I thought there was a sneer of disdain on the lip through which the answer seemed to come: "Vain and ignorant; it is but a shadow you command. My body you have cast into a sleep, and it knows not that the shadow is here; nor, when it wakes, will the brain be aware of one reminiscence of the words that you utter or the words that you hear."

"What, then, is this shadow that stimulates the body? Is it that which in popular language is called the soul?"

"It is not: soul is no shadow."

"What then?"

"Ask not me. Use the wand to invoke Intelligences higher than mine."

"And how?"

"I will tell you not. Of yourself you may learn, if you guide the wand by your own pride of will and desire; but in the hands of him who has learned not the art, the wand has its dangers. Again, I say you have summoned me! Wherefore?"

"Lying shade, I summoned thee not."

"So wouldst thou say to the demons, did they come in their terrible wrath, when the bungler, who knows not the springs that he moves, calls them up unawares, and can neither control nor dispel. Less revengeful than they, I leave thee unharmed, and depart."

"Stay. If, as thou sayest, no command I address to thee—to thee, who art only the image or shadow—can have effect on the body and mind of the being whose likeness thou art, still thou canst tell me what passes now in his brain. Does it now harbour schemes against me through the woman I love? Answer truly."

"I reply for the sleeper, of whom I am more than a likeness, though only the shadow. His thought speaks thus: 'I know, Allen Fenwick, that in thee is the agent I need for achieving the end that I seek. Through the woman thou lovest I hope to subject thee. A grief that harrows thy heart is at hand; when that grief shall befall, thou wilt welcome my coming. In me alone thy hope will be placed —through me alone wilt thou seek a path out of thy sorrow. I shall ask my conditions: they will make thee my tool and my slave!'"

The shadow waned—it was gone.

A Strange Story, by Bulwer Lytton (1803-1873), English novelist and occultist.

The Devil in the Twentieth Century

The road wound hither and thither for no conceivable reason, it climbed the shoulder of a hill when its obvious course was comparatively level. . . . The men declared Auld Hornie himself took an interest in the Boscath road and that their labours were in vain.

D. E. Stevenson. *Winter and Rough Weather*, 1951.

AULD HORNIE: the Old Horned One; i.e., the Devil. A traditional Scottish designation.

Chapter V

Black Mass, Sabbat

Chapter 5

BLACK MASS

SABBAT

Introduction

The mysteries of witchcraft, throughout the dim, perplexed centuries down to the present day, are uncannily interwoven with antique pagan cults. The introduction of Christianity swept many of the occult traditions and rites into dark hiding, across the entire extent of Europe. But they did not banish them completely. Wizardry and arcane rituals and beliefs still flourished, persisting in their grim mystery.

In furtive Hungarian hamlets, in remote hillsides of Central France, among the forbidding glens of the Scottish Highlands, and elsewhere, the vestiges of the pagan primal ways survived the sweep and impact of Christianity. Reluctantly, slowly, the ancient worships, at the cost of much blood, torture, and massacre—as we learn from the mediaeval demonographer Martin Delrio, from the horrendous Witches' Hammer, and the Compendium of Witches of Father Guaccius—faded away; never however, into complete oblivion or negation.

The essence of the occult performances always dwelt on the distinction between Christian dogmas and the mores of the "old religion," as it was called, which was the religion of witchcraft. One of the most tenebrous and malefic performances among such practices was the Black Mass. The Black Mass, that grew in geographical extent and in rampant prevalence, reached its demoniac apogee in the Middle Ages, continuing potently though secretly into the eighteenth century, and making its deepest impression on French society.

The Black Mass is a subtle, corrupt, obscene travesty of Christian rites. It denies or distorts Christian doctrine by means of inverted rituals, mysterious and lascivious formulae, secretive assemblies, weird pronouncements. Essentially, it dethrones Christianity and in its stead raises and exalts the Arch Fiend, the Satanic Power, the Prime Archon of the Infernal Regions, as the dominant ruler and emperor of the actively evil forces in the universe.

The Black Mass was regularly associated with the Witches' Sabbat, that strange periodic gathering of the covens of warlocks and wonder-workers, witches and necromancers, in secluded regions of Auvergne, on the mountain heights of the Blocksberg in Germany, in abandoned ruins sunk in forlorn countrysides in Brittany, among isolated menhirs, in wooded terrain such as the Schwarzwald in Germany, or even, in some notorious instances, in chapels and other sanctified places, as in the church of Blokula in Sweden, the frequent scene of Satanic rites. At these macabre reunions the adepts in the occult arts celebrated their degenerate and phallic devotion to the demons of the Satanic realms, and notably to the Arch Demon himself, the Devil Incarnate, by frenzied orgies, perverted back-to-back dancing in the dark of the night, demoniac conjurations, sacrificial oblations of animals—and, it was commonly credited, of young children as well, and obscene obeisance to the Devil himself.

There is still discussion about the relationship of the Sabbat to the Black Mass, and the view is generally proposed, by a number of demonographers, that the Sabbat was essentially of pagan design, while the Black Mass deliberately distorted and borrowed Christian ceremonials. It is an unsettled question, and can scarcely be resolved. The greater probability is that the Sabbat overlapped into the Black Mass ceremonials, and that this merging of practices became symbolically one unit, whose one aim was contact with the dark forces in the cosmos and a rejection of all Christian doctrine that opposed and conflicted with the "old religion."

With the succession of the ages, however, the Black Mass gathered a certain sinister and individual importance of its own, and became an independent ritual quite often divorced from the Sabbat. It maintained its own cryptic locale, its own devotees who were not necessarily witches, seers, diviners, and professional warlocks but who had intense, unhallowed interest in the obscene and fiend-ridden manifestations that were features of the Black Mass. They were inspired, these awestruck peasants or high-born ladies, these sinister priests and prelates, these adventurous dukes and speculative savants, members of royal families and amateurs of the esoteric, apart from this personal curiosity, by the impulse of possible profitable benefits to themselves in enlisting demoniac favors for their baleful, illicit occasions.

The Devil, in actual palpable manifestation, is the object of the Black Mass

[120]

R.Holata Outina.

CONSULTING A SORCERER

Outina, an Indian chief, consults a sorcerer. The sorcerer laid a shield on the ground, drew a magic circle around it and inscribed it with magic signs. Then, kneeling, he whispered as if in conversation. He was then seized with convulsions but finally became calm, stepped out of the circle, and revealed the number of the enemy and the location of the combat.

(Sixteenth century illustration)

PREPARATION OF A CHARM
The young witch is preparing a magic brew. Note the cat, her familiar, at the fireside.
(Nineteenth century Engraving)

WITCH BURNING

A German woodcut depicting the burning of witches at Dernburg, in the sixteenth
century.

WITCHES PRODUCING RAIN

Rain making was a function of medieval witches, who were reputed to control all natural phenomena. Ulrich Molitor was a 15th century German demonographer.

worship. He is the ultimate master. His satellites, the lords of Hell, who are ranged in a hierarchy of nobility, and actually include—according to the mediaeval chroniclers—counts and dukes, princelings and chiefs, sweep through the interstices of the cosmos on their unnamable missions.

The Devil—Diabolus—is protean in form, and in various places, on different occasions, he assumes a diversity of names among his neophytes and adherents. But in inherent characteristics, in the malefic power he exerts, in the febrile devotion he attracts, he remains essentially identical in function. He is Satan the adversary, the obstructor, regularly represented pictorially as goat-headed. Or he is Beelzebub—Lord of the Flies. He is Asmodeus and Mephistopheles. He is Mulciber, and he is everlastingly the opponent of the principles of goodness, eternally battling, with the support of his numberless legions of demons, against the lucent powers. Mediaevally, he stands in his black baleful skin, with horned head, his cloven feet rooted in the earthy soil, his toothed shapeless mouth belching fire. The old Neo-Platonic philosophers had a mystic name for him: Pentamorph—He of the Five Shapes, although that name was so obscure and traditional that the five shapes were not all identifiable.

Satan has capacities and functions that include ubiquity and levitation. He is everywhere, scouring the heavens and the seas with unmeasured speed. But his headquarters are quintuple. He dwells amid smoke and wind, fire, water, and darkness, and these elements constitute his realms. But being endowed with self-movement throughout all points of the cosmos, he never fails to appear at disparate gatherings of his adherents. At the Black Mass he is invariably present, virtually at least, in the symbolism of the ritual, in the significance of the invocations.

The locale of the Black Mass was frequently some dank deep spacious cellar, hidden from profane eyes where the foul parody of Christian ritual might be performed without hindrance or interruption from constituted authorities. Sometimes the milieu would be cloisters. On occasion the rendezvous chosen was some old deserted chapel. During the seventeenth century, in the supersophisticated society of the French court, the Black Mass was a feature of many court intrigues and subterranean cabals. In one of the episodes the beautiful and notorious Madame de Montespan was actively, personally involved. There was a certain witch woman, a fortune-teller and a concoctor of love-philtres, one Catherine La Voisin, who, with an accomplice, the unscrupulous Abbé Guibourg, inveigled de Montespan into wild, obscene performances at these Black Masses. The officiating priests were clothed in lavish raiment, gold trimmed, lace lined, scarlet shoes on their feet. Their robes were interwoven with strange cabalistic symbols, with esoteric designs. Wine was drunk, spiced with aphrodisiacs. Unhallowed invocations were chanted to the Arch Fiend. Madame de Montespan herself, naked, was the central performer. And, darkly, children were sacrificed at the foul Black Mass, while powerful wreaths of incense rose throughout the chambers, inviting the presence of the evil spirits. Later, the victims were disposed of, as was discovered, in a furnace attached to La Voisin's house.

Then, at the height of the ceremonial, in the frantic excitement of the obscenities, an unbridled sexual orgy took place, in which the chief performer was the priestly officiant himself. Not all these features were always present at every Black Mass, but, in their totality, the picture is valid for the generality of the Black Mass rites.

At another Black Mass the officiants, black robed, administered the ritual over the body of a girl lying nude on the altar, arms and limbs outstretched to form the design of a cross. In her hands she upheld candlesticks in which flared black tapers. The blood of a sacrificed child, mixed with the chalice contents, was offered to Asmodeus, and also to Astorath, who is Astarte, goddess of lust and sexuality.

Many strange figures have, in a historical sense, been associated with the Black Mass. In the fifteenth century there was the notorious Gilles de Rais, a wealthy spendthrift who, after squandering a fortune, sought to recoup himself through demoniac contacts. He enlisted the services of a Florentine, the sorcerer-priest Francesco Prelati, who abetted de Rais in his Satanic researches.

During the latter decades of the seventeenth century, and spreading into the eighteenth, in the wanton society of London, there were coteries and sodalities, clubs and fraternities of men about town who stopped at nothing and often, in their passionate search for diversion, celebrated the Black Mass in secret halls and country houses. These men were known as Mohawks and Sons of Midnight, appropriately enough, and their activities were, apart from exuberance, sinister and demoniac.

In this connection arises the story of the Friars of Medmenham, a foul episode in the sequence of English social life. Sir Francis Dashwood, a wealthy, leisurely profligate, endowed with fine esthetic tastes that, however, had merged into vice and wantonness, had, in his earlier days, gone on the grand tour of Europe. He had absorbed in his travels the more recondite skills, dabbling in Satanic and occult mysteries. On his return he established himself in a fantastic set-up in the ancient ruins of Medmenham Abbey. The Abbey was renovated and refurbished. A library of rare books—mostly pornographic —was installed. A refectory, serving exotic dishes and unique gastronomic delights, was outfitted. The walls of the corridors and cells were adorned afresh with friezes and engravings, all depicting the most debauched lubricities. Here, Dashwood summoned his cronies, members of the Hell Fire Club. These members had similar tastes and in their combined efforts they produced a sensational phenomenon. It was, virtually, an Abbey in reverse. Dashwood set himself up as the Superior of these Franciscan Friars, and together with his fraternal monkish crew he pursued a course of the utmost unprincipled lewdness. The Abbey seethed in putrescence. Actually, it was a cryptic brothel, lavish, lust-ridden, secretive. In their private "cells," in the refectory, in the secluded gardens and along the porticoes the Friars practiced their blasphemous devilry. But the height of their abominations was the ritualistic celebration of the Black Mass by the Satanist himself, Sir Francis Dashwood, epicure and Satanist in excelsis.

The Black Mass has not disappeared entirely. To this very day it is reputed to be administered among Satanic circles, in the highly cosmopolitan locales of two continents: in New York and London, in Paris and in lesser provincial cities. In the metropolitan areas the cult has its own adherents, its own carefully guarded chambers, its own secret communications. At such rituals the atmospheric aura of purposeful maleficence is heightened, among the celebrants, by the subtle use of black: black wine and black candles, while the sense of impalpable yet potent evil is intensified by the clamorous demoniac falsifications, by the acknowledgment of alien allegiance, Satanic loyalties. In the thirties of this century the most perplexing personality who dominated such practices was Alesteir Crowley, the occultist, a professed Satanist, at whose death a Black Mass was administered at his grave, by his passionate disciples.

Notes on the Black Mass

The Black Mass is virtually a reversal of the Mass of the Christian liturgy.

According to the demonographer Cotton Mather, the Black Mass related to the witches' "Diabolical Sacraments, imitating the Baptism and the Supper of our Lord."

In the Black Mass the host was called White John.

Black Mass Prayer

Lamb, which the priests of Adonai have made a symbol of sterility raised to the rank of a virtue, I sacrifice you to Lucifer. May the Peace of Satan always be with you.

Intoned after sacrifice of lamb.

Black Mass Sequel

On the eighth of April, 1554, then being Sunday, a cat with her head shorn, and the likeness of a vestment cast over her with her fore feet tied together, and a round piece of paper like a singing cake betwixt them, was hanged in the parish of St. Matthew: which cat being taken down, was carried to the Bishop of London.

Holinshed, 16th century chronicler.

SINGING CAKE: the Host.

Celebration of Black Mass

I cannot write without horror of the way in which it is celebrated: for the person who is to say the office is robed in a black cape without a cross on it: after putting the water in the chalice he turns his back to the altar, and then, instead of the Host, elevates a black colored turnip. Then all the witches exclaim: "Master, help us."

Henri Boguet, *Discours des Sorciers,* 1608.

Black Mass Consecration

Astaroth, Asmodeus, I beg you to accept the sacrifice of this child which we now offer to you, so that we may receive the things that we ask.

Report on Black Mass (France, 18th century).

The offering was made to Satan, after the sacrifice of a child, whose blood was mixed with the chalice contents.

ASTORATH: also Astarte; equated with Aphrodite.

ASMODEUS: king of the Demons, according to Hebraic legend. Represented pictorially with three heads, goose feet, a snake's tail.

Black Mass Invocation

The priest mounted the steps backward, made a genuflexion on the last step, and exclaimed, in a shrill, tremulous voice:

"Master of Slanders! Dispenser of the Blessings of love, Steward of Voluptuous sins and monstrous vices, Satan, it is you that we worship."

J-K Huysmans (1848-1907), French novelist. Author of *Là-Bas,* novel on Satanism.

BACKWARD: to counteract or produce magic effects, and particularly in Satanic rites, recitations of formulas, prayers, and supplications were delivered backward. In Satanism, the Pater Noster was said backward. Likewise, incantations were so chanted in reverse, words were written backward, and mystical names and invocations were subjected to this retroversive technique.

Notes on the Sabbat

According to H. C. Lea, in his *Materials Towards a History of Witchcraft,* the Witches' Sabbat is first mentioned in relation to the Inquisition.

The Sabbat always took place at night, usually on a Good Friday: or, according to the demonographer Boguet, on any night ordained by Satan.

In the fifteenth century Sabbat assemblies reached their height on the European continent: with additional widespread belief in acts of cannibalism at these conventions.

The officiating priestess, though usually young, was commonly known as The Ancient One.

The opening words of the officiating priestess were: "I will come to the altar. Save me Lord Satan from the treacherous and the violent."

The Sabbat

The derivation of the term Sabbat is in doubt. Dr. Margaret Murray considers the word stems from French s'ébattre, to revel or frolic. The Oxford English Dictionary, on the other hand, derives the term from Hebrew Sabbath.

In any case, the reality of the Sabbath, in relation to the reality of witchcraft, is unquestionable.

In a demonological sense, the Sabbat, during the Middle Ages, was the occasion of the Satanic convention of witches: particularly on May Eve—Roodmas: in Midsummer—Beltane: on November Eve —Hallowmass.

Each local or regional group—called a coven—consisted of twelve members and a president called the Devil: the thirteen members being associated with the thirteen lunar months. From various countries covens sent representatives to the Sabbat gathering. The locale was usually some remote wooded spot, or a mountain crag, or a cave, or any rendezvous far from human habitation. In early times Mount Atlas, in North Africa, was a favorite meeting place. The Mountain of the Bructeri, by some called Meliboeus, in the Duchy of Brunswick, was notorious as a witches' haunt, to which they ride through the air on broomsticks, goats, or cats.

Gulfora, Queen of the Sabbat

Not only do old hags bestride cats and goats and pigs, but many dignitaries too, and civic officials and those who administer justice to the people in the august senate range themselves to be governed under Gulfora's sway. They observe the days of Jupiter; they anoint their limbs, hurrying to pay court to the Mistress, who is called Gulfora.

Girolamo Folengo. *Maccaronea,* 1519.

DAYS OF JUPITER: when witches rode through the air on their malefic missions.

Irish Witchery

They found a pipe of ointment, where-with she greased a staffe, upon which she ambled and gallopped thorough thicke and thin.

R. Holinshed (16th century), English chronicler.

The reference is to an Irish witch, Alice Kettle, who flourished in the fourteenth century.

Sabbat Preparation

Some set out on foot with their children, whom they intended to sacrifice in solemn assembly: then they were carried home by the Demon through the air.

Nicholas Rémy. *Daemonolatria*, 1595.

Flight to the Sabbat

As I was writing thus, there came into my hands the reports of certain matters, from which I learned, as I had not hitherto done, that witches were wont to fly off from their marriage bed to their assemblies.

Nicholas Rémy. *Daemonolatria*, 1595.

The reference is to the witches of Lotharingia, Germany.

Sabbat Orgy

It more frequently happens that witches are corporeally present at Sab-bats and have actual carnal and physical intercourse with the Demon.

Ludovico Maria d'Ameno Sinistrari (1622-1701). Author of *De La Démonalité et des animaux incubes et succubes.*

Sabbat Riding Questioned

Certain women, converted to Satan, believe and confess that in the night hours they ride with Diana the goddess of the pagans or with Herodias and Minerva and a numberless train of women, and obey their commands. But you are crassly stupid to believe that these acts, which are imaginative, actually occur.

12th century tract, authorship uncertain.

DIANA: the Moon goddess, synonymous with Herodias.
MINERVA: Pallas Athene, Greek goddess of wisdom.

Transvection of Witches

Certainly I do not deny that women of this kind can be transported on an ass, a horse, an ox or a camel like everybody and by natural means. But we are speaking of cases where it is a question of transportation beyond usual means.

Ulrich Molitor, *De lamiis et phitonicis muliebribus*, 1489.

WOMEN OF THIS KIND: i.e., witches.

Food at the Sabbat

The meal, whether perceived by the eyes or by the sense of smell, produces nausea. The taste of the food itself is so unpleasant and tart and bitter that it has to be vomited out as soon as tasted.

Nicholas Rémy, *Daemonolatria* (16th century).

Sabbat Gathering

For as we learn from the confession of witches, before they anoint themselves they hear a thunderous noise at night of their mistress as she passes with her retinue of dancing spirits; and only then are they wont to anoint themselves so that they may be borne through the air and follow until they all come to the assigned spot.

Bartolomeus Spina, *Quaestio de strigibus,* 1576.

MISTRESS: i.e., Diana, the Moon goddess, also called Herodias.

Peculiarity of the Sabbat

But it is always a condition of these Satanic nocturnal assemblies that upon the crowing of the cock everything vanishes.

Boguet, *An Examen of Witches,* 1590.

The Sabbat in France

They still say that Satan presides at the assemblies of this wretched rabble that sacrifices to him in the form of the most hideous goat imaginable.

Gabriel Naudé. *Apologie pour les Grands Hommes Soupçonnez de Magie* Paris, 1625.

Witches Flying Merrily

'Hey Cockalorum! my Broomstick gay!
We must rush back ere the dawn of the
   day;
Hey up the chimney! away! away!'-
   Old Goody Price Mounts in a trice,
In showing her legs she is not over nice:
   Old Goody Jones, all skin and
   bones,
Follows 'like winking'—Away go the
   crones.

R. H. Barham (1788-1845), English humorist. Author of *The Ingoldsby Legends.*

Confession of a Sabbat Participant

Ann Armstrong saith, that since she gave information against severall persons who ridd her to severall places where they had conversation with the divell, she hath been severall times lately ridden. On Monday last at night, she, being in her father's house, see one Jane Baites, of Corbridge, come in the forme of a gray cat with a bridle hanging on her foote, and breath'd upon her and struck her dead, and bridled her, and rid upon her in the name of the devill southward, but the name of the place she does not now remember. And the said Jane allighted and pulled the bridle of her head.

Sir Walter Scott (1771-1832) *Letters on Daemonology and Witchcraft.*

Ann Armstrong was a seventeenth century Northumbrian witch.

Sabbat in Italy

In Benevento a nut-tree stands
And thither by night from many lands,
Over the waters and on the wind,
Came witches flying of every kind,
On goats, and boars, and bears, and cats,
Some upon broomsticks, some like bats,
Howling, hurtling, hurrying, all,
Come to the tree at the master's call.

C. G. Leland (19th century). Translation of Dom Piccini's *Ottava della Notte*.

CHINESE MAGICIANS
The magicians of China were as skilled as those of the West. Note the toad, the magicians' familiar.
(An eighteenth century illustration)

CHINESE SORCERERS

Note the usual magic paraphernalia and circumstances: magic wand, creatures who are
familiars, and occult scroll.

(An eighteenth century illustration)

THE WOLF CHARMER

An evident reminiscence of the legends about werewolves, men who had the reputed power of transforming themselves into wolves and back into human form. Belief in the werewolf is as old as Petronius, the Roman novelist of the first century A.D. who described a werewolf scene in his *Satyricon*.

(Painting by John La Farge, 1836-1910)

APPARITIONS
A scene from Coleridge's *The Rime of the Ancient Mariner,* alluding to the mysterious
zones of beings beyond human familiarity.
(Gustave Doré, 19th century French artist)

Chapter VI

Witches and Warlocks
Appearance, Characteristics, Habits

Chapter 6

WITCHES AND WARLOCKS

APPEARANCE — CHARACTERISTICS — HABITS

Introduction

In the scheme of magic, the witch and the warlock, the necromancer and the occultist have their personal insignia, traits that distinguish them, habits and powers that detach them from the normal world. Their appearance and ways have been described by adepts and poets, by demoniacs and demonographers. A Greek poet hints at the tenebrous doings of a witch, gathering mephitic herbs for her philtres in the remote fastnesses of Thessaly, the breeding ground of ancient Greek witchcraft. The Roman poets, again, know the witch as always bare of foot, dishevelled, performing her obscene rites, her awesome ceremonials, under the glimmering moon. She shrieks her darksome invocations, her mystic runes, her mantic spells at dead of night, by the crossroads, or in horrendous graveyards. And, both to the Greeks and the Romans, to the Assyrians and the Akkadians, the witch is a member of society, an integral element in the communal fabric, although, of course, a malefic one. So, in Babylonia and Malaya, in the West Indies and in the sundered islands of the Pacific, the witch dwells among people, but is not of them.

Sometimes, for their sinister conclaves, the witches throng to forsaken ruins, to mountain tops, or forest groves. They haunt tombs and charnel houses. For their operations must be secretive and their rituals, their sacrifices, of humans and of animals, must be hidden from the common glance.

One of their organizations is the coven, consisting as a rule of thirteen

[133]

members, the thirteenth, by occult symbolism, typifying Satan himself, the Grand Master. Yet the term coven is not only, etymologically, innocuous, but associated with religious devotion. For the coven was originally the convent, the religious assembly. But the religious assembly, in certain European countries and under political and social stresses, developed into a specialized sodality, confined to adepts who sought the ancient forms of pagan cults, who hungered after the dark mysteries of Satanic worship.

The term witch, now applied to a female magician, stems from Old English wicca, a man who practices magic. In the Middle Ages the term was of common gender. In appearance, a witch may seem young and attractive, seductive enough to lure hapless victims, as she is depicted in mediaeval prints, in ancient woodcuts, in the Latin chronicles, even in the paintings of Goya. But that is merely a superficial carapace. In actuality, she is old, wizened, repulsive, branded on the body with the Devil's Mark, wearing the Devil's Girdle. On occasion, she eats human flesh, drinks human blood. She produces mannikins to represent humans. She is responsible for changelings. Copulation with humans is one of her traits, while she constantly disrupts the forces of nature, the course of the seasons, the flow of rivers. The witch ranges over every goetic operation, from the concoction of love philtres to the fashioning of images representing prospective victims. And all her ways and all her spells and bindings, her divinations and conjurations, are uniformly evil in intent, malefic and disastrous.

The witch may act alone, in intimate communion with spectral or infernal agencies. But she has her satellites as well, her families that attend her. They may have the form of cats, dogs, ferrets, apes, hares: devoted to their furtive doings, they are tainted with the same evil powers.

An outcast in her community, living in some obscure burrow secluded from other human habitation, in dark cave or wooded retreat, the witch wreaks vengeance on those who scorn her. She shatters an obdurate neighbor by fascinatio, the Evil Eye. She can conjure the dead, and extract from the sepulchral spirits the scheme of the future, the design of the past. By periapts and mystic formulas she summons the infernal hosts, the demons of the Satanic hierarchy, to assault and confound her enemies; or she enlists their aid for her own advantage. The ability to change form is also hers, to turn man into beast or winged creature, to ride the skies and levitate. The language of animals is no secret to her omniscience. She can produce visual illusions, or appear in several places synchronously, or endow statues with animation.

What are the tools and weapons of the magician? What is his professional apparatus? What are the elements of his occult pharmacopoeia, his thaumaturgic laboratory? Candles and smoke, scarabs and colored threads, complicated knots, bells and rings and numbers—particularly the Pythagorean and cabbalistic numbers 3, 7, 9—these have their magic significance, their arcane potency. Pots and wands, twigs, ashes and animal bones, mirrors, nails, lamps, coral and human excrement, drums and cups and cauldrons, squill and hellebore, laurel, skulls, and blood, wolf's entrails, saliva, owl's wings and marrow are among the common stock in trade of every recognized, authentic karcist. Herbs too are utilized in abundance to create invisibility, for apotropaic purposes, for exorcisms: among them, alsine pubescens, sium, solanum somniferum, pentaphyllon and teriac, suntull, enzian, veronica, centifolium, symplocarpus, acorum vulgare, and lungwort. Figurines and metallic objects serve the magician. The Golden Disc of the Four Castles, now in the British Museum, was used by the occultist Dr. John Dee. Swords in particular belong in the dark rites: Angurvadel, the magic blade of Icelandic wizardry; Fragarach, the sword endowed with magic virtues, in Irish lore; Gram, a sword equally effective in Nordic witchcraft. The bloodstone is the magician's standby, although other stones, found obscurely, and shaped fantastically, have their purposes: as the anachitis, used for conjuring water spirits; the anancithidus, used for invoking demons; Glosopetra, that reputedly fell from heaven during a waning moon and was shaped like a human tongue. Similarly, the Hekakontalithos was a stone used as a demoniac offering, in occult rites. The Lapis Iudaicus, the Jewish Stone, likewise had efficacious properties. To compel demons to answer questions, the pontica, a stone displaying blood-like stains, was employed.

No object was too trifling, or too sacred, or too rare, to be brought under contribution, converted to mystic purposefulness. A witch's hair, for instance, possessed potency; hence, in the Middle Ages, witches on trial were shorn clean. Haman, a stone shaped like a ram's horn, was an aid in revealing cosmic mysteries. The Hand of Glory was a hand cut off from a hanged felon. Dried and preserved in salts, it was used in spells. The hexagram, a six-pointed figure, also known as The Shield of David, controlled demons. The Stone of Knellar, in Aberdeenshire, Scotland, has Druidic symbols inscribed on it. Among Moslems a stone called the Seal of the Snake is efficacious as a love charm. The Quirin, or Traitors' Stone, found in lapwings' nests, when placed on the head of a sleeping person, induces the utterance of the innermost thoughts. The pentacle, a five-pointed figure, had a protective purpose.

All instruments, all objects to be handled by the karcist must be new, or cleansed, or specially and freshly acquired or made, by the light of the moon, in desolate spots, in the dead of night. Swords and poniards, inks and incenses, beeswax tapers, knives of tempered steel: hazel wands, box-wood sacrificial

[135]

knive handles formed the normal collection of the warlock's mystic laboratory. For parchment a lamb or kid was killed ritually. All operations were accompanied by fumigations and incantations, the tracing of magic circles, infernal invocations. Rigid, scrupulous measures were essential for success. Every step in the ritual performance must conform to thaumaturgic prescriptions. The slightest deviation meant not only failure, but, on occasion, black disaster and eternal damnation.

So the wizard searches, from the sea depths and the grasslands, from cave and heath, objects that, harmless possibly in themselves, become instruments of baleful implication, directed toward the consummation of monstrous phenomena not merely conceptual, but material and palpable, equally inexplicable to the victim, equally malignant.

Beware Witches

Since the ancient Witch of Endor, plying her necromantic faculty, exorcised King Saul, women have been intimately and potently associated with the Black Art. Legends and sagas, ballads and folk songs are a-tremble with their ways—from the Finnish Kalevala through the fairy tales of Central Europe, from the Hindu epic Ramayana to the mediaeval grimoires, from the Tonkinese Bacoti to the mamaloi, the priestess-witch of West Indian voodoo. Universally, the cryptic thaumaturgy of the witch's potency has cast its grim spell.

The witch can bring down the moon, like the Roman poet Horace's Sagana, or her associate Canidia. Canidia in particular receives more extended treatment. She tortures children to death and extracts their marrow and spleen as ingredients for her malefic love-philtres. The witch can enchant and exorcise the spirits of the dead. She can cast the evil eye and thus wither man or beast. Her obscene potions are sought after by passionate or forlorn maidens, by incestuous poisoners and perverted wives. The witch peers into the future, unraveling the woof and warp of destiny. Her invocations to the infernal demons, her dread utterances of the tetragrammaton and the secret names of the hierarchy of Hell produce at her will earthquakes and cosmic cataclysms, freak tempests and devastation. Her pastime is to converse with strange creatures, neither animal nor human. She has her dark attendants, too, snarling hounds that appear as her familiars at the tenebrous cross-roads. She can disembody herself, or sweep through the night astride her coursing broomstick, bound for a Sabbat assembly on some mountain top, or making for a Black Mass to be celebrated in shadowy valleys. She can shed her withered repulsiveness, her aged carapace, and stand forth fresh and fair in all the seductiveness of an alluring maiden.

The Greek minstrel Homer describes Circe the Sorceress, who lured the hapless Ulysses and held him bound. She dwells in a palace of hewn stones, within a spacious valley. Around her prowl mountain lions and wolves, once men, now transformed into brutes by her powerful drugs. Circe is the prototype of them all, the subtle and sinister, the voluptuous yet fatal witch who is the bane of men, the doom of wandering mortals. But there were others, almost equally grim, equally efficient in their evil. The Greek orator, Demosthenes, who flourished in the fourth century B.C., has given factual historical validity to another of the black sisterhood—a certain Theodoris of Lemnos, who was condemned to death for practicing her baleful enchantments. Greece, in fact, was always rife with the demoniac arts, that seeped into the very life of Hellas, into the social and domestic pattern of the ancient mores, affecting priest and chieftain, princeling and herdsman, cobbler and artist, orator and helot. In a pastoral sketch, the bucolic poet Theocritus sings of Simaetha, a Greek maid who by means of a magic wheel and esoteric rites tries to win back her neglectful lover Delphis.

Murmurously, tense and expectant, she chants:

[137]

My magic wheel, draw home to me the man I love!

It is a modern theme, a crooning plea, with only an ancient twist, a mystic Hellenic tone pervading the enticement. It suits any time, any age, and it is always entirely potent, completely magical.

Simaetha takes stronger measures too. She moulds her lover's image, and by sympathetic magic bends him to her desire, destroys him in her inflamed love turned to hate:

Even as I melt this wax—she shrieks —with the god as aid, so speedily may my love be molten!

Then, in a final outburst of rancor and embittered contempt, she clamors:

Now with magic rites I will strive to bind him, but if he still vexes me, he shall beat at the gate of Hell, by the Fates I vow it!

In Imperial Rome, the epic poet Lucan describes, in startling detail, the enchantments and spells, the conjurations and philtres, the metamorphoses and phantasmic horrors associated with the ancient witches of Thessaly: particularly Erichtho, noted for her necromantic machinations. And throughout the stream of Roman life and literature, through Roman drama and lyric poetry, legend and history, strides Medea, 'the cunning one.' Appropriately, she belongs, as a niece, to the family of Circe. Girt with similar wiles, with commensurate potency, Medea is the arch-mistress of the antique coven. Skilled in herb lore and in necromancy, in divination and the use of periapts, she performs awesome feats, changing the course of nature itself, bending the Fates to her wild domination, forcing

drifting mortals to her compulsive bidding. Above all, she can rejuvenate, she can bring back virility: as she did in the case of old Aeson, Jason's father, whose manhood was restored when he was boiled in a cauldron by the wonder-working Medea.

In the actual annals of Roman history, the historian Tacitus, that dour and sullen chronicler of court intrigues and witchcraft, of astrology and royalty, tells of Vellada, the priestess-diviner. She roamed the forests of Gaul and Germany, and performed her goetic amazements among the groves of the Druids, in remote altar-strewn recesses.

Periodically, witchcraft went underground. Periodically, hordes of diviners and thaumaturgists, warlocks and astrologers, alchemists and occultists were banished from the Imperial City, from court and port. And just as periodically, they returned, insinuating their secretive ways into the vitals of the Empire. Thus specific names of practitioners, of witches and sorceresses, become, fitfully, rare: and, correspondingly, emerge into later recognition. A strange, sudden figure of this type was Mary the Jewess, who appeared in the fourth century A.D. Adept in occult practices, she is traditionally known as the earliest woman alchemist.

The witch, then, is all-powerful, drawing her strength, in all its wanton and evil implications, from Selene, the moon-goddess: from the nameless deities of the Underworld, and dominantly from Hecate, the triple goddess, the presiding patron of the witch brood, herself a supreme adept. According to the Greek poet Hesiod, her presence is marked by the weird, prolonged howling of dogs, while her escort consists of tenuous ghastly souls of the dead.

Throughout the ages, the roster of witches rolls on endlessly, impinging on the lives of close neighbors, of small farmers and love-sick girls, petty burghers and ambitious prelates, royal mistresses and secretive scholars. Some names rise and pass into oblivion, leaving a furtive hint, a dark warning, in folk talk and peasants' chants, in obscure archives or family reminiscences. Wrapped in Latin, there is the tale of the priestess-witch Oenothea, told by the magician—novelist Apuleius himself. In the fourth century, Fredegonde, a Frankish queen, was endowed with the Evil Eye, and also practiced witchcraft. Centuries later appeared Lady Alice Kyteler, an Irish witch, tried for sorcery that involved the death of her four husbands. Craca was another mediaeval witch, whose specialty was changing food into stone. Isobel Gowdie, a notorious Scottish witch, bore on her shoulder, according to hushed talk, the Devil's Mark. Jeannette Biscar was brought by the Devil himself to a Sabbat assembly, under the guise of a goat. Alison Gross was an ugly witch who cast her spells, in the remote Scottish Highlands, on her personal enemies. One of the most remarkable practitioners was Catherine La Voisin, who was implicated in the occult ceremonials of Madame de Montespan, one of the mistresses of Louis the Fourteenth. Madame de Montespan herself, to retain the affection of the king, participated in magic operations, concocted love-potions, and even practiced, with the cooperation of Catherine La Voisin, child sacrifice. France, in short, was

seeped in wizardry, from king to serf. There was Madeleine Amalaric, who was convicted of causing the death of a dozen persons by witchcraft. Madeleine Bavan was known for her obscene practices at the Sabbat. Stevenote de Audebert made a pact with the Devil in 1616. Perron Megain's black craft gave her widespread notoriety. Over the face of Europe they appeared, manipulating their magic puppets, destroying or transforming with muttered incantations. In Italy arose Catherine di Medici, patron of astrologers and warlocks, herself no mean adept. In England, Elizabeth Style signed away her soul in a demoniac pact. In the Northern regions, the infamy of the Nordic witch, Thöck, brooded timelessly.

During those middle centuries witches became so numerous, affecting social, religious and political conditions to such an extent that in England, in the reign of Queen Elizabeth, a Bill, passed in 1563, was responsible for putting to death some 70,000 witches, according to one estimate. Germany was notably riddled with sorceresses. The Tower of the Witches, in Lindheim, was reputedly a meeting place for witches during the Middle Ages. In Bamberg, in the seventeenth century, the Hexenhaus—the House of the Witches—was used as an assembly chamber for the trial of sorceresses.

Certain locations in Europe were particularly associated with gatherings of witches, rituals and ceremonies. In the Carpathian Mountains there was the Old Women's Mountain. In Germany, witches met at the Huiberg Mountain, the Köterberg, and the Horselberg. In Italy, at the Paterno di Bologna, the Tossale di Bergamo. In France, at the Puy de Dôme. And now, with the advance of civilization, they congregate in tea-rooms and in salons, in night clubs and bars.

Terms Used for Witches

Witchcraft was widespread over Europe since proto-historic times: but it reached a climax during the Middle Ages, when Latin was the common literary medium. Hence various names for witches have, apart from vernacular and local terminology, Latin designations, especially among the demonographers:

Incantatrix: female enchanter.

Lamia: general name for witch: looks like a woman but has horse's hoofs.

Maga: generic name for witch: usually acts for own pleasure.

Malefica: witch taught by demon: her object is to inflict injury.

Saga: usually a fortune-teller.

Sortilega: diviner.

Strix: plural, striges. Sorceress. The term is associated etymologically with 'screech-owl'. Believed to suck blood of children.

Venefica: witch who uses poisons and philtres.

Versatility of Sorcerers

The wizard has charmed me with the charm, has charmed me with his charm:

The witch has charmed me with the charm, has charmed me with her charm:

The sorcerer has bewitched me with the spell, has bewitched me with his spell:

The sorceress has bewitched me with the spell, has bewitched me with her spell:

He who enchants images has charmed away my life by image.

He has taken the enchanted philtre, and has soiled my garments with it.

He has torn my garment and dragged it in the dust of my feet.

May the God fire, the hero, dispel their enchantments.

> Assyrian magic tablet.

Reference is here made to image magic, spellbinding, and potions.

Power of Witchcraft

If I command the moon, it will come down; and if I wish to withhold the day, night will linger over my head; and again, if I wish to embark on the sea, I need no ship; and if I wish to fly through the air, I am freed from my weight.

> Ancient Greek magical papyrus.

Familiar Spirits

And the spirit of Egypt shall fail in the midst thereof; and I will destroy the counsel thereof: and they shall seek to the idols, and to the charmers, and to them that have familiar spirits, and to the wizards.

> *Isaiah*, 19.3.

Familiars, demons who attended on witches and wizards, could assume the form of insects and animals: toads, rats, spiders, but

[140]

JAPANESE WITCH

The Japanese witch Omibaba is performing an operation on a victim. Note the skulls, also the flaming apparition in the background. Japanese literature teems with magic tales. Lafcadio Hearn translated many of them into English.

(Kasuo Kuniyoshi, modern Japanese artist)

AFRICAN 'WITCH DOCTOR'

A Matabeli witch doctor. Note the charms, consisting of animal teeth, claws and similar objects, around his neck. The term witch doctor is anthropologically erroneous. Ritual specialist is near the significance of the African expression.

Courtesy of The American Museum of Natural History, N. Y.

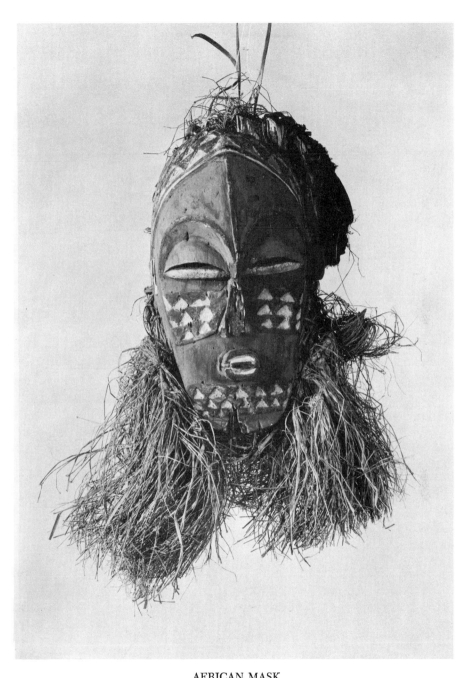

AFRICAN MASK
This fringed mask, from Lumbajoso, Africa, represents a tribal spirit. It was used to
conceal the identity of the performer during ritual ceremonies.
Courtesy of The American Museum of Natural History, N. Y.

MEDICINE MEN

A Kaffir, South African doctor, and his assistant, with their medicines hanging on them.
Some of the medicines are in the form of charms and periapts.

usually that of a dog. The mediaeval occultist Agrippa von Nettesheim had a black dog as a familiar, while Oliver Cromwell, who was reputed to be an adept in the Black Arts, had one called Grimoald.

The Bible and Familiar Spirits

When they say unto you, Seek unto them that have familiar spirits and unto wizards, that chirp and mutter: should not a people seek unto their God?

Isaiah.

Prevalence of Witchcraft in Bible Times

Stand now with thine enchantments, and with the multitude of thy sorceries, wherein thou hast laboured from thy youth; if so be thou shalt be able to profit, if so be thou mayest prevail.

Thou art wearied in the multitude of thy counsels. Let now the astrologers, the stargazers, the monthly prognosticators stand up, and save thee from these things that shall come upon thee.

Isaiah, 47.12-13.

Biblical Enchantment

And he caused his children to pass through the fire in the valley of the son of Hinnom: also he observed times, and used enchantments, and used witchcraft, and dealt with a familiar spirit, and with wizards: he wrought much evil in the sight of the Lord, to provoke him to anger.

II Chronicles, 33.6.

The reference is to King Manasseh.

The Witch of Endor

Then said Saul unto his servants, Seek me a woman that hath a familiar spirit, that I may go to her, and enquire of her. And his servants said to him, Behold, there is a woman that hath a familiar spirit at Endor.

And Saul disguised himself, and put on other raiment, and he went, and two men with him, and they came to the woman by night: and he said, I pray thee, divine unto me by the familiar spirit, and bring me him up, whom I shall name unto thee.

And the woman said unto him, Behold, thou knowest what Saul hath done, how he hath cut off those that have familiar spirits, and the wizards, out of the land: wherefore then layest thou a snare for my life, to cause me to die?

And Saul sware to her by the Lord, saying, As the Lord liveth, there shall no punishment happen to thee for this thing.

Then said the woman, Whom shall I bring up unto thee? And he said, Bring me up Samuel.

And when the woman saw Samuel, she cried with a loud voice: and the woman spake to Saul, saying, Why hast thou deceived me? for thou art Saul.

And the king said unto her, Be not afraid: for what sawest thou? And the woman said unto Saul, I saw gods ascending out of the earth.

[141]

And he said unto her, What form is he of? And she said, An old man cometh up; and he is covered with a mantle. And Saul perceived that it was Samuel, and he stooped with his face to the ground, and he bowed himself.

And Samuel said to Saul, Why hast thou disquieted me, to bring me up? And Saul answered, I am sore distressed; for the Philistines make war against me, and God is departed from me, and answereth me no more, neither by prophets, nor by dreams: therefore I have called, thee, that thou mayest make known unto me what I shall do.

Then said Samuel, Wherefore then dost thou ask of me, seeing the Lord is departed from thee, and is become thine enemy?

And the Lord hath done to him, as he spake by me: for the Lord hath rent the kingdom out of thine hand, and given it to thy neighbor, even to David:

Because thou obeyedst not the voice of the Lord, nor executedst his fierce wrath upon Amalek, therefore hath the Lord done this thing unto thee this day.

Moreover the Lord will also deliver Israel with thee into the hand of the Philistines: and tomorrow shalt thou and thy sons be with me: the Lord also shall deliver the host of Israel into the hand of the Philistines.

Then Saul fell straightway all along on the earth, and was sore afraid, because of the words of Samuel: and there was no strength in him; for he had eaten no bread all the day, nor all the night.

And the woman came unto Saul, and saw that he was sore troubled, and said unto him, Behold, thine handmaid hath obeyed thy voice, and I have put my life in my hand, and have hearkened unto thy words which thou spakest unto me.

Now therefore, I pray thee, hearken thou also unto the voice of thine handmaid, and let me set a morsel of bread before thee; and eat, that thou mayest have strength, when thou goest on thy way.

But he refused, and said, I will not eat. But his servants, together with the woman, compelled him; and he hearkened unto their voice. So he arose from the earth, and sat upon the bed.

And the woman had a fat calf in the house; and she hastened, and killed it, and took flour, and kneaded it, and did bake unleavened bread thereof:

And she brought it before Saul, and before his servants; and they did eat. Then they rose up, and went away that night.

I Samuel, 28.7-25

Simon Magus the Sorcerer

But there was a certain man, called Simon, which beforetime in the same city used sorcery, and bewitched the people of Samaria, giving out that himself was some great one:

To whom they all gave heed, from the least to the greatest, saying, This man is the great power of God.

And to him they had regard, because that of long time he had bewitched them with sorceries.

Acts of the Apostles, Chapter 8.

The reference is to Simon Magus, a pupil of Dositheus, a thaumaturgist. Magus reappears in Irish legend as Simon the Druid.

Biblical Sorcerer

And there they came across a Jewish magician and false prophet named Bar-Jesus.

Acts, 13.6.

The place was Paphos. Bar-Jesus is also known as Elymas.

The Sirens

They bewitch all men, whoso shall come to them, whoso draws nigh them unwittingly and hears the sound of the Sirens' voice never doth he see wife or babes on his return; but the Sirens enchant him with their clear song.

Homer (9th century B.C.), Greek poet. Author of *Odyssey*.

Circe the Sorceress

They found the fair abode where Circe
    dwelt,
A palace of hewn stone within the vale,
Yet nobly seated. There were mountain
    wolves
And lions round it, which herself had
    tamed
With powerful drugs.

Homer, Greek poet of possibly ninth century B.C., *Odyssey*, Book 10.

Human Sacrifice

Amestris, wife of Xerxes, sacrificed seven children to the god of darkness and the infernal regions.

Herodotus (c. 484-425 B.C.), Greek historian, author of *History of the Persian Wars.*

XERXES (519 B.C.-465 B.C.): Persian king.

Calming Storms by Magic

But at length the Magi, having sacrificed victims and endeavored to charm the winds by incantations, and moreover, having offered sacrifices to Thetis and the Nereids, laid the storm on the fourth day.

Herodotus (5th century, B.C.), Greek historian. Author of *History of the Persian Wars*. Translated by H. F. Cary.

THETIS: sea goddess.
NEREIDS: sea divinities.

Comedy in Witchcraft

Strepsiades: I have a scheme for not paying my debts.
Socrates: Let us hear it.
Strepsiades: Tell me, if I purchased a Thessalian witch, I could make the moon descend during the night and shut it, like a mirror, into a round box and there keep it carefully.
Socrates: How would you gain by that?
Strepsiades: How? Why, if the moon did not rise, I would have no interest to pay.
Socrates: Why so?
Strepsiades: Because money is lent by the month.

Aristophanes (c. 450-c. 385 B.C.), Greek comic poet. Author of *The Clouds.*

Strepsiades (heavily in debt) and Socrates (the philosopher) are two of the characters in the comedy.
THESSALIAN WITCH: Thessaly, a region in

Northern Greece, notorious for witchcraft. Sophocles, the Greek dramatist, and the comic writer Menander refer to Thessalian magicians, while the Roman poets Vergil, Ovid, and Lucan describe Thessaly as the home of magic.

Witches' Food

Witches that feed on human entrails.
Plautus (251 B.C.-184 B.C.), Roman comedy writer. *Pseudolus,* 3.2.31.

Witch Howl

Now she holds the crowd of infernal spirits by her magic howl.
Tibullus (c. 48-19 B.C.), Roman poet.

Circe's Home

They run
Fair Circe's magic coast along,
Where she, bright daughter of the sun,
Her forest fastness thrills with song,
And for a nightly blaze consumes
Rich cedar in her stately rooms,
While, sounding shrill, the comb is sped
From end to end adown the thread.
Thence hear they many a midnight roar:
The lion strives to burst his cell:
The raging bear, the foaming boar
Alternate with the gaunt wolf's yell:
Whom from the human form divine
For malice' sake the ruthless queen
Had changed by pharmacy malign
To bristly hide and bestial mien.
Vergil (70-19 B.C.), Roman poet. *Aeneid,* Book 7.

Thessalian Witchcraft

What witch, what magician will be able to free you from Thessalian sorceries?
Horace (65-8 B.C.), Roman poet.

THESSALIAN: Thessaly, a district of Greece, was traditionally notorious for witchcraft.

Power of Temple Priestess

She undertakes by her incantations to give peace to minds at will, or to fill them with heavy cares; to arrest the flow of rivers and turn back the stars in their course: she summons the nocturnal spirits: you will see the ground rumble beneath her feet; and the ash trees descend from the mountains.
Vergil (70-19 B.C.), Roman poet. *Aeneid,* 4.

Appearance of Witch

She goes forth from her hut, clad in a coarse garment, bare of foot, hair unbound and flowing on to her shoulders.
Ovid (43 B.C.-c. 17 A.D.), Roman poet. Author of *Metamorphoses.*

Powers of the Witch

There is a certain old hag—whoever wants to find a procuress, let him listen! —her name is Dipsas. She knows the Black Arts and the spells of Aeaea and by her skill turns back the waters to their source.
She knows what the herbs, what the threads twisted by the magic circle, what

the poison of the loving mare can do. At her will, the clouds mass in the entire heavens. At her will, the day shines in the clear sky. I have seen the stars dripping with blood—if you may believe me—and the face of the moon glowing red with blood. I suspect that she flits through the shades of night, and that her aged body is covered with feathers. She summons from the ancient tombs her antique ancestors, and makes the ground yawn open by her incantation.

Ovid (43 B.C.-17 A.D.), Roman poet. Author of *Amores*.

AEAEA: another name for Circe, celebrated, in Homer's Odyssey, for her skill in magic arts.
POISON OF THE LIVING MARE: this is the notorious hippomanes, a protuberance that was said to appear on the forehead of newborn foals: used as a love philtre.

Erichtho the Witch

These rites of criminality, these spells of the direful race, the wild Erichtho has condemned as being of piety too extreme, and has applied the polluted art to new ceremonies. For to her it is not permitted to place her deadly head within a roof or a home in the city; and she haunts the deserted piles, and, the ghosts expelled, takes possession of the tombs, pleasing to the Gods of Erebus. To hear the counsels of the dead, to know the Stygian abodes and the secrets of the concealed Pluto, not the Gods above, not a life on earth, forbids.

Leanness has possession of the features of the hag, foul with filthiness, and, unknown to a clear sky, her dreadful visage, laden with uncombed locks, is beset with Stygian paleness. If showers and black clouds obscure the stars, then does the Thessalian witch stalk forth from the spoiled piles, and try to arrest the lightnings of the night. The seeds she treads on of the fruitful corn she burns up and by her breathing makes air noxious that was not deadly before. She neither prays to the Gods of heaven, nor with suppliant prayer calls the Deity to her aid, nor does she know of the propitiating entrails; upon the altars she delights to place funereal flames, and frankincense which she has carried off from the lighted pile.

Her voice now first heard as she demands, the Gods of heaven accede to all the wickedness, and dread to hear a second address. Souls that live, and still rule their respective limbs, she buries in the tomb and death reluctantly creeps on upon those who owe lengthened years to the Fates; the funeral procession turning back, the dead bodies she rescues from the tomb; corpses fly from death. The smoking ashes of the young and the burning bones she snatches from the midst of the piles, and the very torch which the parents have held; the fragments, too, of the funeral bier that fly about in the black smoke, and the flowing robes does she collect amid the ashes, and the embers that smell of the limbs.

But when corpses are kept within stone, from which the moisture within is taken away, and, the corruption withdrawn, the marrow has grown hard; then does she greedily raven upon all the limbs, and bury her hands in the eyes, and delight to scoop out the dried-up balls, and

[145]

gnaw the pallid nails of the shrunken hand; with her mouth she tears asunder the halter and the murderous knots; the bodies as they hang she gnaws, and scrapes the crosses; the entrails, too, smitten by the showers she rends asunder, and the parched marrow, the sun's heat admitted thereto. Iron fastened into the hands, and the black corruption of the filthy matter that distils upon limbs, and the slime that has collected, she bears off, and hangs to the bodies, as the sinews hold fast her bite.

Whatever carcase, too, is lying upon the bare ground, before the beasts and the birds of air does she sit; nor does she wish to separate the joints with iron and with her hands, and about to tear the limbs from their parched jaws, she awaits the bites of the wolves. Nor do her hands refrain from murder, if she requires the life-blood, which is the first to spring from the divided throat. Nor does she shun slaughter, if her rites demand living gore, and her funereal tables demand the quivering entrails. So, through the wounds of the womb, not the way in which nature invites, is the embryo torn out, about to be placed upon the glowing altars. And as often as she has need of grim and stalwart shades, she herself makes the ghosts; every kind of death among mankind is in her employ.

She from the youthful body tears the down of the cheek, she with her left hand from the dying stripling cuts off the hair. Full often, too, at her kinsman's pile has the dire Thessalian witch brooded over the dear limbs, and imprinting kisses, has both cut off the head, and torn away the cheeks pressed with her teeth, and biting off the end of the tongue as it cleaves to the dried throat, has poured forth murmurs into the cold lips, and has dispatched accursed secrets to the Stygian shades.

When the rumours of the spot brought her to the notice of Pompey, amid the depths of the night of the sky, at the time when Titan is bringing the midday beneath our earth, along the deserted fields he takes his way. The faithful and wonted attendants upon his crimes, wandering amid the ruined tombs and graves, beheld her afar, sitting upon a lofty crag, where Haemus, sloping down, extends the Pharsalian ridges. She was conning over spells unknown to the magicians and the Gods of magic, and was trying charms for unwonted purposes. For, fearing lest the shifting warfare might remove to another region, and the Emathian land be deprived of slaughter so vast, the sorceress has forbidden Philippi, polluted with spells and sprinkled with dreadful potions, to transfer the combats, about to claim so many deaths as her own, and to enjoy the blood of the world; she hopes to maim the corpses of slaughtered monarchs, and to turn to herself the ashes of the Hesperian race, and the bones of nobles, and to obtain ghosts so mighty. This is her pursuit, and her sole study, what she is to tear away from the corpse of Magnus when exposed, what limbs of Caesar she is to brood over. Her does the degenerate offspring of Pompey first address:

"O thou honor to the Haemonian females, who art able to reveal their fates to nations, and who art able to turn them away from their course when about

[146]

to come to pass, I pray thee that it may be permitted to know the assured end which the fortune of war provides. Not the lowest portion am I of the Roman multitude; the most renowned offspring of Magnus, either ruler of the world, or heir to a fall so great. Smitten with doubts, my mind is in alarm, and again is prepared to endure the fears that spring from certainty. This power do thou withdraw from events, that they may not rush on sudden and unseen; either extort it from the Deities, or do thou spare the Gods, and force the truth from the shades below. Unlock the Elysian abodes, and Death herself, called forth, compel to confess to thee whom of us it is that she demands. Not mean is the task; it is worthy for even thee to have a care to seek which way inclines the hazard of destinies so mighty."

The impious Thessalian witch rejoices as the mention of her fame spread abroad, and answers on the other hand: "O youth, if thou wouldst have influenced more humble destinies, it had been easy to force the reluctant Gods to any action thou mightst wish. To my skill it is granted, when with their beams the constellations have urged on death, to interpose delays; and although every star would make a man aged, by drugs do we cut short his years in the midst. But together does the chain of causes work downward from the first origin of the world, and all the fates are struggling, if thou shouldst wish to change anything, and the human race stands subject to a single blow; then do we, the Thessalian throng, confess. Fortune has the greater might. But if thou art content to learn the vents beforehand, paths

easy and manifold will lie open to truth; earth, and sky, and Chaos, and seas, and plains, and the rocks of Rhodope, will converse with us. But it is easy, since there is a supply so vast of recent deaths, to raise a single body from the Emathian plains, that, with a clear voice, the lips of a corpse just dead and warm may utter their sounds, and no dismal ghost, the limbs scorched by the sun, may send forth indistinct screechings."

Thus she says; and, the shades of night redoubled by her art, wrapped as to her direful head in a turbid cloud, she wanders amid the bodies of the slain, exposed, sepulchres being denied. Forthwith the wolves take to flight, their talons loosened, the birds fly unfed, while the Thessalian witch selects her prophet, and, examining the marrow cold in death, finds the fibres of the stiffened lungs standing without a wound, and in the dead body seeks a voice. Now stand in doubt destinies full many of men who have been slain, which one she is to choose to recall to the world above. If she had attempted to raise whole armies from the plains, and to restore them to the war, the laws of Erebus would have yielded, and a people dragged forth by the powerful miscreant from Stygian Avernus, would have mingled in fight.

A body selected at length with pierced throat she takes, and, a hook being inserted with funereal ropes, the wretched carcase is dragged over rocks, over stones, destined to live once again; and beneath the lofty crags of the hollowed mountain, which the dire Erichtho has destined for her rites, it is placed.

Downward sloping, not far from the black caverns of Pluto, the ground pre-

[147]

cipitately descends, which a wood covers, pale with its drooping foliage, and with no lofty tops looking upwards to the heavens, and a yew-tree shades, not pervious to the sun. Within is squalid darkness, and mouldiness pallid within the caves amid the lengthened gloom; never, unless produced by charms, does it receive the light. Not within the jaws of Taenarus, the baleful limit of the hidden world, and of our own, does the air settle thus stagnant; whither the sovereigns of Tartarus would not fear to send forth the shades. For although the Thessalian witch uses violence against destiny, it is matter of doubt whether she beholds the Stygian ghosts because she has dragged them thither, or whether because she has descended to Tartarus.

A dress, of various colours and furylike with varied garb, is put on by her; and her locks removed, her features are revealed, and, bristling, with wreaths of vipers her hair is fastened round. When she perceives the youth's attendants alarmed, and himself trembling, and, casting down his eyes with looks struck with horror, she says:

"Banish the fears conceived in your timid mind; now anew, now in its genuine form shall life be restored, that even tremblers may endure to hear him speak. But if I can show the Stygian lakes, and the shores that resound with flames; if, I being present, the Eumenides can be beheld, and Cerberus shaking his necks shaggy with serpents, and the Giants chained with their hands to their backs, what dread is there, cowards, to behold the frightened ghosts?"

Then in the first place does she fill his breast, opened by fresh wounds, with reeking blood, and she bathes his marrow with gore, and plentifully supplies venom from the moon. Here is mingled whatever, by a monstrous generation, nature has produced. Not the foam of dogs to which water is an object of dread, not the entrails of the lynx, not the excrescence of the direful hyaena is wanting, and the marrow of the stag that has fed upon serpents; not the sucking fish, that holds back the ship in the midst of the waves, while the eastern breeze stretches the rigging; the eyes of dragons, too, and the stones that resound, warmed beneath the brooding bird; not the winged serpent of the Arabians, and the viper produced in the Red Sea, the guardian of the precious shell; or the slough of the horned serpent of Libya that still survives or the ashes of the Phoenix, laid upon an eastern altar.

With this, after she has mingled abominations, vile, and possessing no names, she added leaves steeped in accursed spell, and herbs upon which, when shooting up, her direful mouth had spat, and whatever poisons she herself gave unto the world; then, a voice, more potent than all drugs to charm the Gods of Lethe, first poured forth its murmurs, discordant, and differing much from the human tongue. The bark of the dogs has she, and the howling of wolves; she sends forth the voice in which the sacred owl, in which the screech of night, complain, in which wild beasts shriek and yell, in which the serpent hisses, and the wailing of the waves dashed upon the rocks; the sounds, too, of the woods, and the thunders of the bursting cloud. Of objects so many there is the voice in

[148]

one. Then afterwards in a Haemonian chaunt she unfolds the rest, and her voice penetrates to Tartarus:

"Eumenides, and Stygian fiends, and penalties of the guilty, and Chaos, eager to confound innumerable worlds and thou, Ruler of the Earth, whom the wrath of the Gods, deferred for lengthened ages, does vex; Styx, and the Elysian fields, which no Thessalian sorceress is deserving of; Persephone, who dost detest heaven and thy mother, and who art the lowest form of our Hecate, through whom the ghosts and I have the intercourse of silent tongues; thou porter, too, of the spacious abodes, who dost scatter our entrails before the savage dog; and you, Sisters, about to handle the threads renewed, and thou, O ferryman of the burning stream, now, aged man, tired with the ghosts returning to me; listen to my prayers, if you sufficiently I invoke with mouth accursed and defiled, if, never fasting from human entrails, I repeat these charms, if full oft I have given you the teeming breasts, and have smothered your offerings with warm brains; if any infant, when I have placed its head and entrails on your dishes, had been destined to live; listen to my entreaty. A soul we ask for, that has not lain hid in the caves of Tartarus, and accustomed long to darkness, but one just descending, the light but lately withdrawn; and which still delays at the very chasm of pallid Orcus. Although it may listen to these spells, it shall come to the shades once again. Let the ghost of one but lately our soldier repeat the destinies of Pompey to the son of the chieftain, if the civil warfare deserves well at your hands."

When, having said these things, she lifted up her head and her foaming lips, she beheld the ghost of the extended corpse standing by, dreading the lifeless limbs and the hated place of its former confinement. It was dreading to go into the gaping breasts, and the entrails torn with a deadly wound. Ah wretch! from whom unrighteously the last privilege of death is snatched, to be able to die! Erichtho is surprised that this delay has been permitted by the Fates, and, enraged with death, with living serpents she beats the unmoved body; and through the hollow clefts of the earth, which with her charms she opens, she barks forth to the shades below, and breaks the silence of the realms:

"Tisiphone, and Megaera, heedless of thy voice, are ye not driving the wretched soul with your ruthless whips through the void space of Erebus? This moment under your real name will I summon you forth, and, Stygian bitches, will leave you in the light of the upper world; amid graves will I follow you, amid funereal rites, your watcher; from the tombs will I expel you, from all the urns will I drive you away. And thee, Hecate, squalid with thy pallid form, will I expose to the Gods, before whom in false shape with other features thou art wont to come, and I will forbid thee to conceal the visage of Erebus. I will disclose, damsel of Enna, under the boundless bulk of the earth, what feasts are detaining thee, upon what compact thou dost love the gloomy sovereign, to what corruption having submitted, thy parent was unwilling to call thee back.

"Against thee, most evil ruler of the world, into thy burst caverns will I send the sun, and with sudden daylight thou shalt be smitten. Are you going to obey? Or will he have to be addressed, by whom never, when named, the shaken earth fails to tremble, who beholds the Gorgon exposed to view, and with his stripes chastises the quailing Erinnys, who occupies depths of Tartarus by you unseen; in whose power you are, ye Gods above; who by the Stygian waves forswears."

Forthwith the clotted blood grows warm, and nourishes the blackened wounds, and runs into the veins and the extremities of the limbs. Smitten beneath the cold breast, the lungs palpitate; and a new life creeping on is mingled with the marrow so lately disused. Then does every joint throb; the sinews are stretched; and not by degrees throughout the limbs does the dead body lift itself from the earth, and it is spurned by the ground, and raised erect at the same instant. The eyes with their apertures distended wide are opened. In it not as yet is there the face of one living, but of one now dying. His paleness and stiffness remain, and, brought back to the world, he is astounded. But his sealed lips resound with no murmur. A voice and a tongue to answer alone are granted unto him.

"Tell me," says the Thessalian witch, "for a great reward, what I command thee; for, having spoken the truth, by the Haemonian arts I will set thee free in all ages of the world; with such a sepulchre will I grace thy limbs, with such wood will I burn them with Stygian spells, that thy charmed ghost shall hearken to no magicians. Of such great value be it to have lived once again;

neither charms nor drugs shall presume to take away from thee the sleep of Lethe prolonged, death being bestowed by me. Obscure responses befit the tripods and the prophets of the Gods; well assured he may depart whoever asks the truth of the shades, and boldly approaches the oracles of relentless death. Spare not, I pray. Give things their names, give the places, give the words by which the Fates may converse with me."

She added a charm as well, by which she gave the ghost the power to know whatever she consulted him upon. Sad, the tears running down, the corpse thus said:

"Called back from the heights of the silent shores I surely have not seen the sad threads of the Destinies; but, what from all the shades it has been allowed me to learn, fierce discord agitates the Roman ghosts, and impious arms disturb the rest of hell. Coming from different spots, some chieftains have left Elysian abodes, and some the gloomy Tartarus; what fate is preparing these have disclosed. Sad was the countenance of the spirits of the blessed. The Decii I beheld, both son and father, the souls that expiated the warfare, and Camillus weeping, and the Curii; Sulla, too, Fortune, complaining of thee. Scipio is deploring his hapless descendant, doomed to perish in the Libyan lands. The elder Cato, the foe of Carthage, bemoans the destiny of his nephew who will not be a slave.

"Thee, Brutus, first Consul, the tyrants expelled, alone rejoicing did I behold among the pious shades. Threatening Catiline, his chains burst asunder and broken, exults, the fierce Marii, too, and

[150]

NAVAJO EXORCISM

A Navajo group, showing a masked performer representing a god. He is exorcising the evil spirits from the victim. A boy is being initiated by a goddess who is whipping him with yucca leaves. Close by stands the Talking God, ready to sprinkle the youth with cornmeal to signify his holy condition. From Arizona.

Courtesy of The American Museum of Natural History, N. Y.

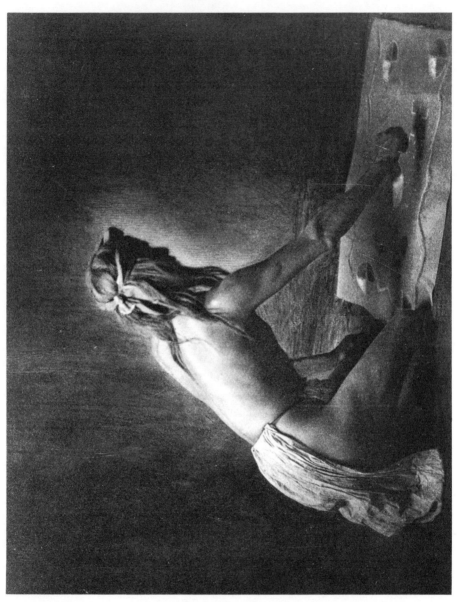

APACHE MEDICINE MAN
Courtesy of The American Museum of Natural History, N. Y.

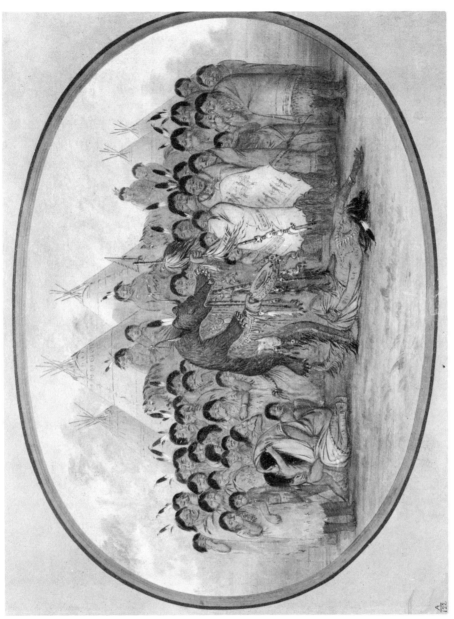

BLACKFOOT INDIAN CEREMONY OF 'WITCH DOCTOR.'
(Painting by George Catlin)
Courtesy of The American Museum of Natural History, N. Y.

MAGIC AND SPELLS

THIS series of three prints, which seems to represent straight magic to us now, probably stood for a fairly critical sort of scientific exposition in its own era, which was about 1600. (Don't look now, but much of the best scientific theory of today will seem similarly magical in time.)

The prints are the work of Raphael Custodis, a German who lived in Augsburg, and died in Frankfurt in 1651. He came from a family of printers, his father being Dominick Custodis, born 1650, a son of Peter Balten; Dominick took the name Custodis in 1584. The plates are marked "Stephan Michelspacher Ex.", but we have not so far been able to throw any light on him.

In the prints there are references to the elements then recognized, Earth, Air, Fire, and Water, also to Ammonium, Sulphur, Bismuth, and Vitriol; the disciplines of Astronomy, Philosophy, and Alchemy are happily linked.

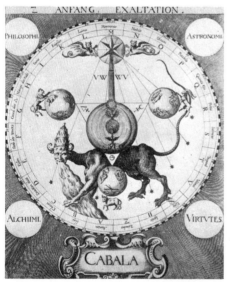

OCCULT DIAGRAMS
These diagrams illustrate alchemical and occult mysteries.

the Cethegi with their bared arms. I beheld the Drusi exulting, names beloved by the populace; the Gracchi, exorbitant with their laws, and who dared such mighty exploits. Hands, bound with the eternal knots of iron, and in the dungeon of Dis, clap in applause, and the guilty multitude demands the fields of the blessed. The possessor of the empty realms is opening the pallid abodes, and is sharpening rocks torn off, and adamant hard with its chains, and is preparing punishment for the conqueror. Take back with thee, O youth, this comfort, that in their placid retreat the shades await thy father and thy house, and in the serene quarter of the realms are preparing room for Pompey.

"And let not the glory of a short life cause thee anxiety; the hour will come that is to mingle all chieftains alike. Make ye haste to die, and proud with your high spirit go down though from humble graves, and tread under foot the ghosts of Romans deified. It is sought to know which tomb the wave of the Nile, and which that of the Tiber is to wash, and only is the combat among the chieftains as to their place of burial. Seek not thou to know thy own destiny; the Fates, while I am silent, will declare; a prophet more sure, Pompey himself, thy sire, will declare all things to thee in the Sicilian fields; he, too, uncertain whither he shall invite thee, whence warn thee away, what regions to bid thee avoid, what Constellations of the world. Wretched men, dread Europe, and Libya, and Asia; according to your triumphs does Fortune distribute your sepulchres. O wretched house, nothing throughout the whole earth wilt thou behold more safe than Emathia."

After he has thus revealed the Fates, gloomy with speechless features he stands, and demands of death once again. Magic incantations are needed, and drugs, that the carcase may fall, and the Fates are unable to restore the soul to themselves, the law of hell now once broken. Then, with plenteous woods she builds up a pile; the dead man comes to the fires; the youth placed upon the lighted heap Erichtho leaves, permitting him at length to die; and she goes attending Sextus to his father's camp.

The heavens wearing the aspect of light, until they brought their footsteps safe within the tents, the night, commanded to withhold the day, afforded its dense shades.

Lucan (39-65 A.D.), Roman poet. Author of epic poem *Pharsalia*.

SEXTUS: son of Pompey, who is in conflict with Julius Caesar, in the Roman Civil War. THESSALIAN WITCH: Thessaly, a region in ancient Greece, was notorious for witchcraft. PROPITIATING ENTRAILS: the reference is to the Roman sacrificial rites that involved examination of animal entrails.

Ancient Witches

Are there not indeed legends about Medea of Colchis, and others, particularly Italian Circe, kin to the deities?

Pliny the Elder (23-79 A.D.), Roman encyclopedist. Author of *Natural History*.

MEDEA: witch famous in Greek and Roman mythology. CIRCE: witch famous among Greeks and Romans. Appears in Homer's *Odyssey*.

A Changeling

When I was yet a long-hair'd Boy, for even then I liv'd a pleasant Life, I had a Minion, and he dy'd: He was (so help me Hercules) a Pearl, a Paragon, nay Perfection it self: But when the poor Mother lamented him, and we also were doing the same, some witches got round the House on a sudden, you'd have taken them for Hounds hunting a Hare. We had then in the House a Cappadocian, a tall Fellow, stout and hardy, that would not have stept an inch out of his way for Jupiter. He boldly drew his Sword, and wrapping his Coat about his left Arm, leaped out of the House, and as it might be here, (no hurt to the thing I touch) ran a Woman clean through. We heard a pitiful Groan, but not to Lye, saw none of them. Our champion came in and threw himself on a Bed, but all black and blue, so he had been trosh'd with Flails; for it seems some ill Hand had touched him. We shut the Door, and went on with our Mourning; but the Mother taking her Son in her Arms, and stroaking him, found nothing but a Bolster of Straw; it had neither Heart, Entrails, nor any thing, for the Fairies belike had stolen him out of his Cradle, and left that of Straw instead of him. Give me Credit, I beseech ye, Women are craftier than we are, play their Tricks by Night, and turn every thing Topsy-turvy. After this our tall Fellow never came to his Colour again, but in a few days died Raving-mad.

Petronius (1st century A.D.), Roman novelist. Author of *The Satyricon*, translated by Burnaby, 1694.

Appearance of Witches

With flowing hair and barefooted, as is the custom.

Statius (c. 45-96 A.D.), Roman poet. Author of epic *Thebais*.

A Witch Who Kept an Inn

Meroe, an old witch, owned an inn. Aristomanes, a character in the *Metamorphoses,* describes her:

She is capable of bringing down the sky, suspending the earth, making springs dry up, sweeping away mountains, conjuring the spirits of the dead. She can weaken the gods, put out the stars, light up Hell itself.

When a neighboring innkeeper would not return her love, she changed him into a frog. A lawyer who prosecuted her she turned into a ram.

Apuleius (born 123 A.D.), Roman novelist. Author of *Metamorphoses,* a picaresque novel pervaded by witchcraft.

Pamphila the Witch

Beware of the evil arts and the sinister wiles of Pamphila, wife of Milo. She is a witch of the first rank and is reputed to be an adept in every necromantic spell.

Apuleius (born 123 A.D.), Roman author of *Metamorphoses*, a picaresque novel pervaded by witchcraft.

The Magician as Priest

If, as I read among very many writers, what the Persians call magician is what we call priest, what crime is it, I ask you, to be a magician and to have a thorough knowledge and understanding and skill in the laws of ceremonials, the proper form of sacred rites, the ordinances of religious practices?

Apuleius (2nd century A.D.). Roman novelist. Author of *De Magia*.

Imperial Magic

He had about him every kind of magician and used their services daily.

Lampridius (3rd century A.D.), Roman historian.

The reference is to the Emperor Caracalla (188-217 A.D.).

The Lamia

They are wont to lust not for love but for flesh: and they particularly seek human flesh and by arousing sexual desire they seek to devour whom they wish.

Philostratus (3rd century A.D.), *Life of Apollonius of Tyana*.

LAMIA: a demon who stole children and sucked their blood. The ancient Greeks considered the lamia bisexual.

Lamia

The lamias that, according to legend, are accustomed to steal children and tear them apart.

Isidore of Seville (7th century), *Etymologiae*.

Proper Place for Magic

The places best fitted for exercising and accomplishing Magical Arts and Operations are those that are concealed, removed and separated from the habitations of men; wherefore desolate and uninhabited regions are most appropriate, such as the borders of lakes, forests, dark and obscure places, old and deserted houses, whither rarely and scarce ever men do come; mountains, caves, caverns, grottos, gardens, orchards; but best of all are crossroads, and where four roads meet, during the depth and silence of the night.

Key of Solomon, mediaeval grimoire.

Advice to Apprentices in Magic

O men! Weak mortals! Tremble for your boldness at the thought of possessing such profound knowledge.

Transport your spirit beyond your sphere, and learn from me that before any undertaking you must be firm and steadfast and attentive in observing scrupulously all disadvantage, confusion, and total loss. On the other hand, if you observe scrupulously what I say, you will come forth from your lowliness and poverty, completely successful in all your enterprises.

Arm yourself therefore with intrepidity and prudence, wisdom and virtue, that you may undertake a vast and mighty task, in which I have spent sixty-seven years, laboring night and day, in order to attain success in this great aim.

You must then do exactly what is indicated, as follows:

[153]

You will spend an entire quarter of the moon without frequenting the society of women or wantons, in order not to succumb to defilement.

Then you will begin your quarter of the moon at the moment that the quarter begins, promising Great Adonai, who is the chief of all the spirits, to take only two meals a day, or every twenty-four hours of the said quarter of the moon; which you will take at noon and midnight; or if you prefer at seven in the morning and seven at night, at the same time offering this prayer before taking your meals during the said quarter:

I implore you, great and mighty Adonai, master of all spirits, I implore you, great and mighty Adonai, master of all spirits, I implore you, O Eloim, I implore you, O Jehovam, O mighty Adonai! I offer you my soul, my heart, my vitals, my hands, my feet, my sighs, and my being. O great Adonai! Deign to be auspicious!

The Great Grimoire.

This invocation appeals only to the Beneficent Spirit.

How to Transport Witches

The fat of young children, and seethe it with water in a brazen vessel, reserving the thickest of that which remaineth boiled in the bottom, which they lay up and keep, until occasion serveth to use it. Then put hereunto Eleoselinum, Aconitum, Frondes populeas, Mountain parsley, Wolves-bane, leaves of the poplar and soot.

Mediaeval magic recipe.

Witches and Fiends

Midnight hags,
By force of potent spell, of bloody characters
And conjurations horrible to hear,
Call fiends and spectres from the yawning deep,
And set the ministers of hell to work.

Authorship uncertain.

Magic Cat

And the men were thrown into a sledge drawn by a discoloured cat; and the cat in its rapid course bore them off to the extreme limits of Pohjola, as far as the vast deserts of Lapland, where the horse's footsteps no longer resounds, and the mare's foal finds no pasture. Thus Lemminkainen mocked at young men, old men, and men in the prime of life, by means of his incantations.

Kalevala, Finnish Epic.

In this capacity, the witch assumed the form of a cat, or used the cat as an intermediary.
LEMMINKAINEN: a sorcerer.
POHJOLA: the Finnish region of darkness and evil spirits.

Witches Sell Favorable Wind to Seamen

In Ireland and in Denmark both
Witches for gold will sell a man a wind,
Which in the corner of a napkin wrapp'd,
Shall blow him safe unto what coast he will.

Sumner, *Last Will and Testament,* 12th century.

Welsh Soothsayers

Among these Welsh people there are—and you will not find them elsewhere—certain men called Awenithion, that is, inspired. When consulted on some doubtful issue, they immediately go into a frenzy as though beside themselves and finally become prophetic. They do not however utter the desired answer forthwith: but through much devious circumlocution, through a spate of talk, trivial and meaningless rather than coherent, yet expressed altogether in ornate language, lastly in some verbal byway, the seeker who observes the reply carefully will find a clear answer.

And so finally they are roused by others from this ecstatic state as though from a deep sleep, and are forcibly brought back to consciousness almost by violence. Now you will find two remarkable characteristics about them. After their reply, unless violently aroused and awakened, they do not usually become inspired after such a frenzy. Once awakened, they will recall nothing about what was uttered by them in their trance. Thus if they happen to be consulted on this point or any other and have to reply, they will explain in quite other, different terms: perhaps they speak through inspired and possessed spirits, though in ignorance. These gifts generally come to them in sleep through visions. For some believe that, as it were, sweet milk or honey is poured into them: while others think that a card with writing on it is placed on their mouths.

Description of Wales, by Geraldus Cambrensis (1146-c. 1223).

Luciferans

They worship Lucifer and believe him to be the brother of God, wrongly cast out of heaven, and that they will reign with him. They sacrifice children to him.

Anonymous, 14th century.

The Luciferans were a mediaeval Satanic sect, prevalent in the thirteenth century. They sacrificed to demons with nocturnal rites.

Infernal Punishment

He wished to see too far before him, he
  now looks behind and goes backward.
Behold Tiresias, who changed his aspect,
  when he of male was made woman.
Of a truth he knew the play of magic
  frauds.
See the wretched women who left the
  needle, the shuttle, and the spindle,
  and made themselves divineresses.
They wrought witchcraft with herbs and
  images.

Dante Alighieri (1265-1321), Italian poet. Author of *The Inferno*. Translated by J. A. Carlyle.

Dante sees the Diviners, Augurs, Sorcerers, etc. coming slowly along the bottom of the Fourth Chasm. By incantations and evil practices they have pried into the Future. Among these are Amphiaraus, Tiresias, Aruns the Tuscan, Manto, daughter of Tiresias, Eurypylus, Greek augur, Michael Scot, Guido Bonati of Forli, 13th century Italian astrologer, Asdente, shoemaker and diviner of Parma, hags who concocted philtres and practiced magic.
HE WISHED: Amphiaraus, ancient Greek diviner.
TIRESIAS: prophet of Thebes.
OF A TRUTH: Michael Scot, thirteenth century physician and astrologer to Emperor Frederick II.

[155]

Occult Cat Worship

In some other regions the devil appears to them in the shape and form of a cat, and they kiss him individually under the tail.

14th century Latin tract.

THEM: i.e., the Waldensians, a secret mediaeval occult sect.

Magic Carpet to Italy

But it now waxing late, and the necromancer desiring dispatch, a physician came with a certain draught, and telling him that it was to fortify his spirits, he made him drink it off, when he was immediately cast into a profound sleep. He was then, by Saladin's order, laid upon that magnificent bed, on which was set a most beautiful crown, of prodigious value, written upon in such a manner, as to shew that it was designed by Saladin as a present to Torello's lady. On his finger he put a ring, wherein was a carbuncle, that appeared like a flaming torch, the value of which was not to be estimated. To his side was a sword girt with such ornaments, that the like was scarcely ever seen. About his neck was a kind of solitaire, not to be equalled for the value of the pearls, and other precious stones, with which it was embellished. And lastly, on each side were two great basins of gold, full of double ducats, with many strings of pearl, rings, girdles, and other things too tedious to mention, which were laid all round him. When this was done, he kissed Torello once more, as he lay upon his bed,

commanding the necromancer then to use all possible expedition. Instantly the bed, with Torello upon it, was carried away in presence of them all, leaving them in discourse about it, and set in the church San Pietro di Pavia, according to his own request, where he was found by the sacrist, fast asleep, with all these jewels and other ornaments, in the morning when it rung to matins.

Boccaccio (1313-1375), *The Decameron*, Tenth Day, Nov. 9.

Intercourse of Men with Succubi

Many persons of both sexes, forgetful of their own salvation, have abused incubi and succubi.

Bull of Pope Innocent, 1484.

Anthropophagy in Witchcraft

There are some witches who, contrary to the inclination of human nature, even of wild beasts, devour their own young and are accustomed to eat them up.

Malleus Maleficarum, 15th century.

Power of Witches

Thus by their own power and more so through witchcraft they can do harm to all men.

Institor and Sprenger (15th century), *Malleus Maleficarum.*

Riding through the Air

Wherefore it seems that we must accept the depositions and confessions of those who admit that they are transported by demons not only at night but also by day from place to place.

Jean Vineti (15th century), *Tractatus contra daemonum invocatores.*

Lustful Witches

In conclusion, women act through carnal desire, which is insatiable in their case: hence, to sate their lust, they have dealings even with demons.

Kramer and Sprenger (15th century), *Malleus Maleficarum.*

Intercourse between Men and Spirits

We have heard of demons as incubi and succubi and that their intercourse is fraught with danger.

Walter Mapes (15th century), *De Nugis Curialium.*

Magic Powers

There is a persistent belief that some beings can change into others—which is a false assertion—as women changed into cats or men into wolves or some other animal or those who ride with Herodias.

Fra Pacifico da Novaro (15th century), *Somma Pacifica.*

HERODIAS: another name for Diana, the moon goddess.
The references here are to lycanthropy, the cat-witch, and levitation.

Academy of Witchcraft

There is another spot, thrice one hundred arms long, where a swarm of old hags teach alas! how many maidens. A thousand old witches, as instructors do, reveal the rites that must be learned: how to achieve their wishes by yielding to Venus: how to anoint themselves and produce thunder in the sky; how to blight crops and vines by hailstorm; how to change their bodies into different forms.

Girolamo Folengo, *Maccaronea,* 1519.

Appearance of Witches

They are deformed, anemic, and rather swarthy, revealing the black bile in their looks.

Jerome Cardan, *De Rerum Varietate,* 1557.

The mediaeval painters, and, later Goya, paint the witch as a voluptuous, seductive creature.

Witches' Food

Witches eat human flesh, especially the flesh of children and publicly drink their blood. But if they cannot procure children, they exhume human corpses from the grave or take off from gibbets the bodies of hanged men.

Jean Bodin, *De Magorum Daemonomania.* Paris, 1580.

[157]

Power of Witch

There was a current belief that:

Witches could sail in an eggshell, a cockle or mussel-shell, through and under the tempestuous seas.

Reginald Scott, *The Discoverie of Witchcraft,* 1584.

Confession of Witch

This aforesaid Agnis Sampson, which was the elder witch, was taken and brought to Haliriud-House, before the king's majestie, and sundry other of the nobilitie of Scotland, where she was straytly examined, but all the perswasions which the king's majestie used to hir, with the rest of his councell, might not provoke or induce her to confesse any thing, but stoode stiffely in the deniall of all that was layde to her charge; whereupon they caused her to bee conveyed away unto prison, there to receive such torture as hath beene lately provided for witches in that country. Item. The sayde Agnis Sampson was after brought againe before the king's majestie and his councell, and being examined of the meetings and detestable dealings of those witches, shee confessed that of Allhollon-Even, shee was accompanied, as well, with the persons aforesaid, as also with a great many other withches to the number of two hundreth, and that all they went together to sea, each one in a riddle or cive, and went in the same very substantially, with flaggons of wine, making merrie and drinking by the way in the same riddles or cives, to the kirk of North-Barrick, in Lowthian, and that after they had landed, tooke handes on the lande, and daunced this reill, or short daunce, singing all with one voice:

Commer, goe ye before, commer, goe ye;
Gif ye will not goe before, commer, let me.

Newes from Scotland, 1591.

Raising a Storm with a Cat

John Fian, alias Cunninghame, master of the school at Saltpans, Lothian, ever nearest to the devil, at his left elbow . . . chases a cat in Tranent. In which chase he was carried high above the ground, with great swiftness, and as lightly as the cat herself, over a higher dyke. Asked to what effect he chased the creature, he answered that in a conversation held at Brumhoillis, Satan commanded all that were present to take cats: like as he, for obedience to Satan, chased the said cat, to raise winds for destruction of ships and boats.

Newes from Scotland, 1591.

Definition of a Witch

A witch or hag is she which being eluded by a league made with the devil through his persuasion, inspiration, and juggling, thinketh she can design what manner of things soever, either by thought or imprecation, as to shake the air with lightnings and thunder, to cause hail and tempests, to remove green corn or trees to another place, to be carried of her familiar which hath taken upon him the deceitful shape of a goat, swine, calf, etc. into some mountain far distant, in a wonderful space of time. And sometimes to fly upon a staff or fork, or some other instrument. And to spend all the night after with her sweetheart, in playing, sporting, banqueting, dalliance, and diverse other devilish lusts, and lewd desports and to show a thousand such monstrous mockeries.

William West, 1594.

Prevalence and Power of Witches

By their incantations and unhallowed sorceries they have defiled almost the entire world. Men and beasts perish by the wickedness of these women. Nor does anyone conceive that the source is witchcraft. Many people suffer chronic and serious illnesses without realizing that they have been bewitched.

Abbot Johann Trithemius (16th century), *Antipalus Maleficiorum*.

Homage to Hecate

Witchcraft celebrates
pale Hecate's offerings.

William Shakespeare (1564-1616), *Macbeth*.

HECATE: goddess of Lower Regions and patroness of witchcraft.

Power of Witch

A witch; and one so strong
She could control the moon—make flows
and ebbs.

William Shakespeare, *The Tempest*.

Love of Magic

He surfets upon cursed Necromancie:
nothing so sweet as Magicke is to him;
which he preferres before his chiefest
blisse,
and this the man that in his study sits.

Christopher Marlowe (1564-1593), English dramatist. Author of *Dr. Faustus*.

THE MAN: Dr. Faustus himself.

Power of Magician

Faust: How am I glutted with conceit
of this.
Shall I make spirits fetch me what
I please.
Resolve me of all ambiguities?
Performe what desperate enter-
prise I will?
I'll have them flye to India for
gold.
Ransacke the Ocean for Orient
Pearle,
And search all corners of the
new-found-world
For pleasant fruites, and Princely
delicates.
I'll have them read me strange
Philosophy,
And tell the secrets of all forraine
Kings.

Christopher Marlowe (1564-1593), English dramatist. Author of *Dr. Faustus*.

Recipe for Aerial Travel for Witches

There take this unbaptized brat:
Boil it well—preserve the fat:

[159]

You know 'tis precious to transfer
Our 'nointed flesh into the air,
In moonlight nights, on steeple tops.

> Thomas Middleton (1580-1627), Elizabethan dramatist, author of *The Witch*.

The speaker is Hecate, witch-goddess of the Underworld.

Witch Cat

The Devil presented himself at the Sabbat in the form of a huge black cat.

> Henri Boguet, *Discours des Sorciers*, Lyons, 1590.

The occasion was the testimony of a witch, Rolande de Vernois.

Witch Changed into Cat

In good sooth, I may tell it to you as to my friend, when I go but into my closet I am afraid, for I see now and then a hare, which by my conscience giveth me is a witch or some witch's spirit, she stareth so upon me. And—There is a foule great cat sometimes in my barne which I have no liking unto.

> *A Dialogue of Witches and Witchcraft*, George Gifford, 1608.

Witch into Cat

A hag whose lies shoot poison—that has become an ould witch, and is now turning into a gib-cat.

> John Marston (c. 1575-1634), *The Fawne*.

GIB-CAT: an emasculated he-cat.

Locale for Witchcraft

I remember hearing that there were witches there and demons and nocturnal spirits, where those who dare can see demons and address them and learn the magic arts.

> Aeneas Sylvius, Pope Pius II (16th century), *Epistulae*.

WITCHES THERE: i.e, on a hill called Mons Veneris, putatively associated with magic practices.

Test for Witchcraft

It is a certain rule Witches deny their Baptism when they make Covenant with the Devil, water being the sole element thereof, and when they are heaved into the water it refuseth to receive them but suffers them to float.

> King James I, *Daemonologie*, 1597.

Familiars

I have heard old bedlams
Talk of familiars in the shape of mice,
bats, ferrets, weasels, and I wot not what,
that have appear'd, and suck'd, some say, their blood.

> John Ford (1586-1640) and Thomas Dekker (c. 1572-c. 1632), *The Witch of Edmonton*.

Outwitting Witches

Threatening or beating witches is the best way to remove spells cast by them.

> Guazzo, *Compendium Maleficarum*, 1608.

AMULET
This amulet, dating in the end of the Middle Ages, is a charm against sickness.
Bibliothèque Nationale, Paris.

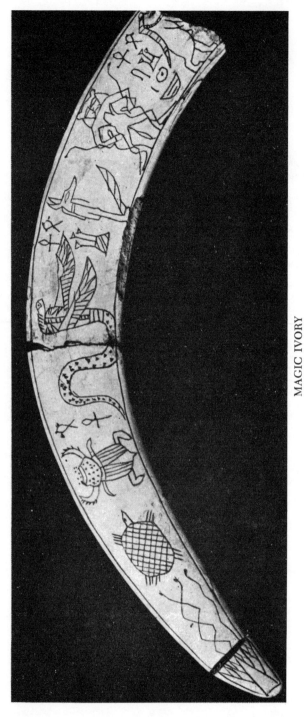

MAGIC IVORY

An Egyptian charm to protect against the bites of injurious animals. Middle Empire.
Louvre, Paris.

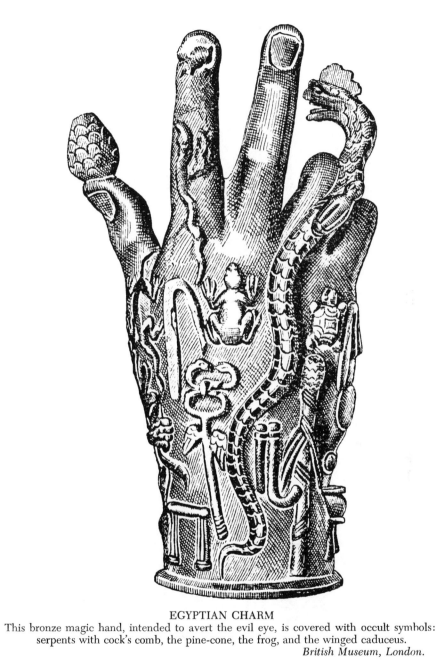

EGYPTIAN CHARM
This bronze magic hand, intended to avert the evil eye, is covered with occult symbols:
serpents with cock's comb, the pine-cone, the frog, and the winged caduceus.
British Museum, London.

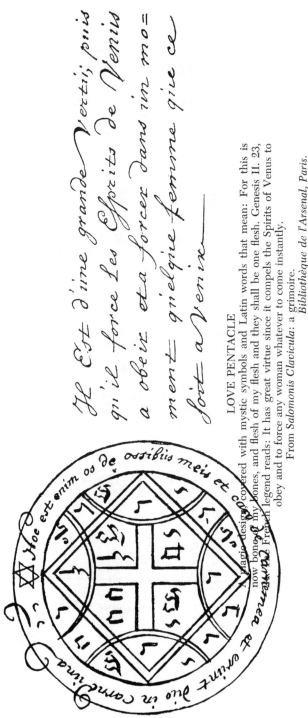

Il Est d'une grande vertu; puis
qu'il force les Esprits de Venus
a obeir et a forcer dans un mo=
ment quelque femme que ce
soit a venir———

Hoc est enim os de ossibus meis et caro
de carne mea; nunc vocabitur virago.

LOVE PENTACLE

A magic design covered with mystic symbols and Latin words that mean: For this is
now bone of my bones, and flesh of my flesh and they shall be one flesh. Genesis II. 23,
The French legend reads: It has great virtue since it compels the Spirits of Venus to
obey and to force any woman whatever to come instantly.

From *Salomonis Clavicula:* a grimoire.

Bibliothèque de l'Arsenal, Paris.

Cat as Familiar

Elizabeth Francis, a witch tried at Chelmsford in 1556:

learned this arte of witchcraft of hyr grandmother, whose nam mother Eue. Item when shee taughte it her, she counseiled her to renounce God and His Worde and to geue of her bloudde to Sathan (as she termed it) wyche she delyuered her in the lykenesse of a whyte spotted Catte, and taughte her to feede the sayde Catte with breade and mylke, and she dyd so, also she taughte her to cal it by the name of Sathan and to kepe it in a basket. Item that euery tyme that he did any thynge for her, she sayde that he required a drop of bloude, which she gaue him by prycking herselfe sometime in one place and then in an other. When shee had kept this Cat by the space of XV or XVI yeare, and as some saye (though untruly) being wery of it, she came to one mother Waterhouse her neyghbour she brought her this cat in her apron and taught her as she was instructed by her grandmother Eue, telling her that she must cal him Sathan, and geue him of her bloude and breade and milke as before.—Mother Waterhouse receyued this cat of this Frances wife in the order as is before sayde. She (to trye him what he coulde do) wyld him to kyll a hog of her owne, which he dyd, and she gaue him for his labour a chicken, which he fyrste required of her and a drop of her blod. And this she gaue him at all times when he dyd anything for her, by pricking her hand or face and putting the bloud to hys mouth wyche he sucked, and forthwith wold lye downe in hys pot againe wherein she

kepte him. Another tym she rewarded hym as before, wyth a chicken and a droppe of her bloud, which chicken he eate up cleane as he didde al the rest, and she cold fynde remaining neyther bones nor fethers. Also she said that when she wolde wyl him to do any thynge for her, she wolde say her Pater noster in laten. Item, this mother Waterhouse confessed that shee fyrst turned this Cat into a tode by this means, she kept the cat a great while in woll in a pot, and at length being moued by puertie to occupie the woll, she praied in the name of the father and of the sonne and of the holy ghost that it wolde turne into a tode and forthwith it was turned into a tode and so kept it in the pot without woll.

Thomas Cooper, *Witches at Chelmsford,* 1617.

Succubus

So Men (they say), by Hell's Delusions led,
Have ta'en a Succubus to their bed.

Abraham Cowley (1618-1667), English poet, *The Mistress.*

SUCCUBUS: a female demon that copulated with human males.

The Incubus

Belial, the dissolutest Spirit that fell,
The sensualist, and, after Asmodai,
The fleshliest Incubus.

John Milton (1608-1674), English epic poet. Author of *Paradise Regained.*

[161]

Devil as Cat

The Devil did appear in the form of a Pretty hansom Young Man first, and since Appeareth, to her in the form of a blackish Gray Cat or Kitling, that it sucketh of a Tett which Searchers since saw in the place She mentioned.

Samuel Petto, (17th century), *A Faithful Narrative*, 1652.

The occasion was the trial for witchcraft of Abre Grinset, a Suffolk witch, in 1665.

Power of Magician

Well! If there be any truth in the History, the Magicians were not only couzeners and Hocus-Pocus Men: there was something done that was extraordinary beyond Man's Art and Contrivance, or the effects of ordinary Nature. And therefore must have either God or some Spirit or Daemon, one or more for the Authour. The former no one faith, the Hand of God in this was only permissive. Therefore it is plain the magicians did this by spirits, creatures of the Invisible world.

Joseph Glanvil, *Saducismus Triumphatus*, 1681.

A Witch Trial

The Tryal of Bridget Bishop, alias Oliver, at the Court of Oyer and Terminer, held at Salem, June 2, 1692.

She was indicted for Bewitching of Several Persons in the neighbourhood, the Indictment being drawn up, according to the Form in such Cases usual. And pleading, Not Guilty, there were brought in several persons, who had long undergone many kinds of Miseries, which were preternaturally inflicted, and generally ascribed unto an horrible witchcraft. There was little occasion to prove the witchcraft, it being evident and notorious to all beholders. Now to fix the witchcraft on the Prisoner at the Bar, the first thing used was the Testimony of the Bewitched; whereof several testifi'd, that the Shape of the Prisoner did oftentimes very grievously Pinch them, Choak them, Bite them, and Afflict them; urging them to write their names in a Book, which the said Spectre called, ours . . .

One, Deliverance Hobbs, who had confessed her being a witch, was now tormented by the Spectre, for her Confession. And she now testifi'd, That this Bishop tempted her to sign the Book again, and to doing that she had confes'd. She affirm'd, That it was the Shape of the Prisoner, which whipped her with Iron Rods, to compel her thereunto. And she affirm'd, That this Bishop was at a General Meeting of the Witches, in a Field at Salem-Village, and there partook of a Diabolical Sacrament in Bread and Wine then administered . . .

John Londer testify'd, that upon some little Controversy with Bishop about her Fowls, going well to Bed, he did awake in the Night by Moonlight, and did see clearly the likeness of this Woman grievously oppressing him; in which miserable condition she held him, unable to help himself, until near Day. He told Bishop of this; but she deny'd it, and threatened him very much. Quickly after this, being at home on a Lord's day, with the doors shut about him, he saw a Black Pig approach him; at which, he going to kick, it vanished away. Immediately after, sitting down, he saw a black Thing jump in at the window, and come and stand before him. The Body was like of a Monkey, the Feet like a Cock's, but the Face most like a man's. He being so extremely affrighted, that he could not speak; this Monster spoke to him, and said, I am a messenger sent unto you, for I understand that you are in some Trouble of Mind, and if you will be ruled by me, you will want for nothing in this world. Whereupon he endeavoured to clap his hands upon it; but he could feel no substance; and it jumped out of the Window again; but immediately came in by the Porch, tho' the Doors were shut, and said, You had better take my Counsel! He then struck at it with a stick, but struck only the Ground-sel, and broke the stick: the Arm with which he struck was presently disenabled, and it vanished away. He presently went out at the Back-door, and spied this Bishop, in her Orchard, going towards her House; but he had not power to set one foot forward unto her. Whereupon, returning into the House, he was immediately accosted by the Monster he had seen before; which Goblin was now going to fly at him; whereat he cry'd out, The Whole armour of God be between me and you! So it sprang back, and flew over the Apple-tree, shaking many Apples off the Tree, in its flying over. At its leap, it flung Dirt with its feet against the Stomach of the Man; whereupon he was then struck Dumb, and so continued for

three days together. Upon the producing of this Testimony, Bishop deny'd that she knew this Deponent: Yet their two Orchards joined; and they had often had their little Quarrels for some years together.

Cotton Mather (1663-1728), Boston minister, participant in Salem, New England, witch hunts. Author of *The Wonders of the Invisible World.*

Bridget Bishop was hanged for witchcraft on June 10, 1692.

Witch into Cat

Robert Downer testified:

That this Prisoner being some Years ago prosecuted at Court for a Witch, he then said unto her, He believed she was a Witch. Whereat she being dissatisfied, said, That some She-Devil would shortly fetch him away! Which words were heard by others, as well as himself. The Night following, as he lay in his Bed, there came in at the Window, the likeness of a Cat, which flew upon him, took fast hold of his Throat, lay on him a considerable while, and almost killed him. At length he remembered what Susanna Martin had threat'ned the Day before; and with much striving he cried out, Avoid, thou She-Devil! In the Name of God the Father, the Son, and the Holy Ghost, Avoid! Whereupon it left him, leap'd on the Floor, and flew out at the Window. And there also came in several testimonies, that before ever Downer spoke a word of this Accident, Susanna Martin and her Family had related, How this Downer had been handled!

The Wonders of the Invisible World,
by Cotton Mather.

The occasion was the trial for witchcraft of Susanna Martin, 1692.

Names of Witches' Familiars

In mediaeval and later records of witch trials and in magic manuals occur these names of domestic animals and other small creatures—hares, toads, moles —considered to be familiars of the witch:
Makeshift, Thief of Hell, Rago, Swein, Greedigut, Rapha, Littleman, Volon, Josaphat, Rory, Tissy.

Familiars

Teaz'd with their cries her choler grew
And thus she sputter'd. Hence ye crew.
Fool that I was to entertain
Such imps, such fiends, a hellish train!
Had ye been never hous'd and nurst
I, for a witch had n'er been curst.
To you I owe, that crouds of boys
Worry me with eternal noise;
Straws laid across my pace retard,
The horse-shoe's nailed (each threshold's guard)
The stunted broom the wenches hide,
For fear that I should up and ride;
They stick with pins my bleeding seat,
And bid me show my secret teat.
Thomas Gay, Fables, 1726.

The reference is to an old hag of wicked fame, who mumbled forth her backward prayers. Saying prayers backward was associated with Satanic practices.
A HELLISH TRAIN: the witch's familiars: dogs, cats, hares, toads, or other animals.
BROOM: the reference is to the witch riding on her broomstick to a Sabbat assembly.
PINS: a reference to sympathetic magic involving an image representing the witch.

Power of Witch

The auld uncanny matrons
Grew whiles a hare, a dog, or batrons,
To get their will o' carles sleepan,
Wha hae nae staulks o' rountree keepan,
Ty'd round them when they ride or sail,
Or sew't wi' care in their sark-tail.

Ebenezer Picken (1769-1816), Scottish poet, *Poems,* 1830.

BATRONS: cat.
ROUNTREE: rowan-tree, used in witchcraft for apotropaic purposes.
SARK-TAIL: shirt-tail.

Occult Christening of Cat

Eftir thay had drukkin togidder a certaine space, in thair devillische maner, tuik ane katt, and drew the samyn nyne tymes throw the said Beigis cruik; and thaireftir come with all thair speed to Seaton-Thorne, be-north the zet. And thay thaireftir past altogidder, with the Devill, to the irne zet of Seatoun, where of new thay tuik ane cat, and drew the samyn nyne tymes throw the said Irne-zett. And immediatlie thaireftir came to the barne foiranent George Feudaris dur, where thay christened the said catt, and callit hir Margarit. And thaireftir come all bak agane to the Deane-fute, where

[164]

first thai convenit, and cuist the kat to the Devill.

Criminal Trials in Scotland, Robert Pitcairn, Edinburgh, 1833.

IRNE-ZETT: iron gate.

Raising a Storm with a Cat

And within aucht dayes eftir the said Bill was delyverit, the said Agnes Sampsoune, Jonet Campbell, Johnne Fean, Gelie Duncan, and Meg Dyn baptesit ane catt in the wobstaris hous, in maner following: Fyrst, Twa of thame held ane fingar, in the ane syd of the chimney cruik, and ane other held ane other fingar in the other syd, the twa nebbis of the fingars meting togidder; than thay patt the catt thryis throw the linkis of the cruik, and passit itt thryis under the chimnay. Thare-eftir, att Begie Toddis hous, thay knitt to the foure feit of the catt, foure jountis of men; which being done, the sayd Jonet fechit it to Leith; and about mydnych, sche and the twa Linkhop, and twa wyfeis callit Stobbeis, came to the Pierheid and saying thir words, 'See that thair be na desait amangis us'; and thay caist the catt in the see, sa far as thay mycht, which swam owre and cam agane; and thay that wer in the Panis, caist in ane other catt in the see att xj houris. Eftir which, be thair sorcerie and inchantment, the boit perischit betwixt Leith and Kinghorne.

Criminal Trials in Scotland, by Robert Pitcairn, Edinburgh, 1833.

The storm was raised when King James and Queen Anne were sailing home from Denmark: sixteenth century.

Transformation from Witch to Cat and Vice Versa

To change into cat:

I shall goe intill ane catt,
With sorrow, and sych, and a blak shott;
And I sall goe in the Divellis nam,
Ay will I com hom againe.

To change back into human form:

Catt, catt, God send thee a blak shott.
I am in a cattis liknes just now,
Bot I sal be in a womanis liknes ewin now.
Catt, catt, God send thee a blak shott.

Criminal Trials in. Scotland, Robert Pitcairn, Edinburgh, 1833.

The formulas, each to be repeated thrice, were revealed by Isobel Gowdie, a seventeenth century Scottish witch.

Transformation of Witches

There, accompanied with thy devilish companions and faction, transformed in other likeness, some in hares, some in cats, and some in other similitudes, ye all danced about the Fish Cross.

Criminal Trials in Scotland, Robert Pitcairn, Edinburgh, 1833.

The reference is to the Fish Cross in Aberdeen, Scotland, where Bessie Thom, a professed witch, performed ritual dances. The incident occurred in 1596, when the witches involved were charged with sorcery.

Tibetan Sorcery

"Doubtless," said we, "some grand solemnity calls you together?"

[165]

"Yes, tomorrow will be a great day: a Lama Boktè will manifest his power: Kill himself, yet not die."

We at once understood what solemnity it was that thus attracted the Ortous-Tartars. A Lama was to cut himself open, take out his entrails and place them before him, and then resume his previous condition. This spectacle, so cruel and disgusting, is very common in the Lama-series of Tartary. The Boktè who is to manifest his power, as the Mongols phrase it, prepares himself for the formidable operation by many days fasting and prayer, pending which, he must abstain from all communication whatever with mankind, and observe the most absolute silence. When the appointed day is come, the multitude of pilgrims assemble in the great court of the Lama-sery, where an altar is raised in front of the Temple-gate. At length the Boktè appears. He advances gravely, amid the acclamations of the crowd, seats himself upon the altar, and takes from his girdle a large knife which he places upon his knees. At his feet, numerous Lamas, ranged in a circle, commence the terrible invocations of this frightful ceremony. As the recitations of the prayers proceed, you see the Boktè trembling in every limb, and gradually working himself up into phrenetic convulsions. The Lamas themselves become excited: their voices are raised; their song observes no order, and at last becomes a mere confusion of yelling and outcry. Then the Boktè suddenly throws aside the scarf which envelopes him, unfastens his girdle, and seizing the sacred knife, slits open his stomach, in one long cut. While the blood flows in every direction, the multitude prostrate themselves before the terrible spectacle, and the enthusiast is interrogated about all sorts of hidden things, as to future events, as to the destiny of certain personages. The replies of the Boktè to all these questions are regarded, by everybody, as oracles.

When the devout curiosity of the numerous pilgrims is satisfied, the Lamas resume, but now calmly and gravely, the recitation of their prayers. The Boktè takes, in his right hand, blood from his wound, raises it to his mouth, breathes thrice upon it, and then throws it into the air, with loud cries. He next passes his hand rapidly over his wound, closes it, and everything after a while resumes its pristine condition, no trace remaining of the diabolical operation, except extreme prostration. The Boktè once more rolls his scarf round him, recites in a low voice a short prayer then; all is over, and the multitude disperse, with the exception of a few of the specially devout, who remain to contemplate and to adore the blood-stained altar which the Saint has quitted.

M. Huc, *Travels in Tartary, Thibet and China during the years 1844-5-6.*

BOKTE: a Tibetan saint-sorcerer.

Power of Witch

The witches' circle intact, charms undisturbed
That raised the spirit and succubus.

Robert Browning (1812-1889), English poet, *The Ring and the Book.*

SUCCUBUS: female demon that copulated with human male.

[166]

Lilith, the Night Demon

Of Adam's first wife, Lilith, it is told
(The witch he loved before the gift of
  Eve,)
That, ere the snake's, her sweet tongue
  could deceive,
And her enchanted hair was the first
  gold.

> D. G. Rossetti (1828-1882), English
> poet.

LILITH: in Assyrian demonology, a female
demon. In Talmudic tradition, Adam's first
wife, who bore him demons.

Freya's Cats

Then came dark-bearded Niord, and after
  him
Freya, thin-robed, about her ankles slim
The grey cats playing.

> William Morris (1834-1896), *Lovers
> of Gudrun.*

FREYA: Scandinavian goddess of love, also
equated with queen of the Lower Regions.
Her familiars are cats.
NIORD: Scandinavian god.
In Scandinavian demonology, witches held
weekly assemblies on Friday, Freya's sacred
day.

African Witchcraft — Twentieth Century Style

In a native plantation in Uganda, in
1955, the owner was charged with kid-
napping and killing two girls. He was
further accused of boiling them and using the bones of hands and feet to banish evil spirits from his sick wife.

In 1957, pupils at a native school in
Uganda, who had been teasing one of
the girls, fell into sudden trances, swing-
ing among the trees and acting like mon-
keys. The girl involved, at a price, called
off the spell. Pupils who did not pay remained under the spell.

A witch-doctor, under escort of the
authorities, visited the girl's home, where
strange magic accessories were found.
The parents were sentenced to five years'
imprisonment, while the girl was given
twelve strokes of the cane.

> News Items.

Witch a la Mode

Why do they call me a witch?
Remember my father was an alchemist.
I live alone, preferring loneliness
To the companionable suffocation of an
  aunt,
I shall amuse myself with simple
  experiments
In my father's laboratory. Also I speak
French to my poodle. Then you must
  know
I have a peacock which on Sundays
Dines with me indoors.

> Christopher Fry, *The Lady's Not for
> Burning.*

POODLE, PEACOCK: suggest familiars of the
mediaeval witch.

Witchcraft in 1957

Angoon, on Admiralty Island, off the
coast of Alaska, has a population of a

[167]

few whites and some four hundred Tlingit Indians. In 1957 the death of a Tlingit Indian child was the occasion for a sequence of magic rites. Cats and dogs were burnt in sacrificial ceremonies, while two young Indian girls, 'mediums for the witches,' were beaten with 'devil clubs'—bundles of thorns. Several villagers too were denounced to the United States authorities for practicing witchcraft.

News Item.

Chapter VII

Lycanthropy, Vampires, Voodoo

SECTION OF A MAGICAL SCROLL, WRITTEN WITH HUMAN BLOOD
(16th century)

Bodleian Library.

GREEN DRAGON
The Green Dragon, an aid to call on the Spirit Birto.
(16th century)

British Museum.

A DORÉ LUCIFER

Lucifer is one of the multiple names of Satan. As Lucifer the Light-bearer he has his home in the East. Dante's description is highly imaginative. Milton too, in his *Paradise Lost*, describes the Archfiend—as Mulciber.

Cassell and Co., Ltd., London.

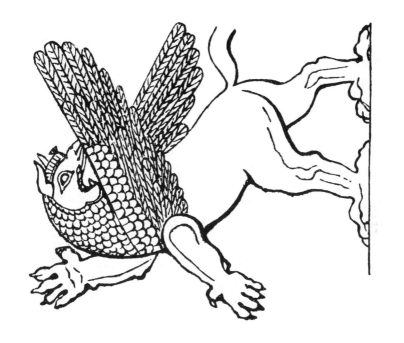

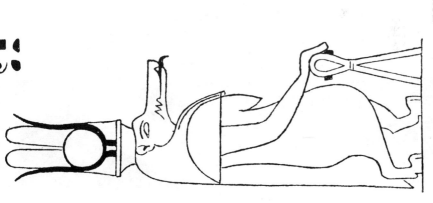

EGYPTIAN AND ASSYRIAN DEVILS

Symbolic representations of the Devil: sometimes in the form of a known animal, and on occasion in partly human, partly animal shape.

THE ABOMINATION OF SORCERERS
Notice the animals and objects, of magic significance, around the occultists: the circle, the skull, crossbones, the familiars, the attendant spirits in animal form.
(Painting by Jaspar Isaac, 16th century artist)

Chapter 7

LYCANTHROPY
VAMPIRES
VOODOO

Introduction

The most awesome phase of magic is possibly illustrated by lycanthropy. Lycanthropy is the changing of a human being into a wolf. The creature, turning from man into wolf and back into human form, is known as a werewolf. The werewolf appears in every culture, in every age. The ancients from Homer to Pomponius Mela, from Varro and Vergil to Apuleius, Strabo, and Solinus, testify to the prevalence of lycanthropy. In sixteenth century France the reality of lycanthropy was confirmed by royal decrees against the practice.

In some countries the change from man to animal involves another creature, indigenous to the respective country. In Malaya, for example, the human being turns into a tiger; in Iceland, into a bear; in Africa, into a tiger or hyena or leopard; in India, into a tiger or leopard. Such transformations come under the head of therioanthropy.

Akin to the werewolf, in certain respects, is the vampire. A vampire is a creature, sometimes a live human being, sometimes a monstrosity compounded of human and animal elements, sometimes a revived dead spirit, in material shape, that draws and drinks human blood, often to the point of the victim's death.

The vampire is involved in legend and fact, in myth and history, merging into horrendous records, sometimes remarkably circumstantial, of the prevalence of the phenomenon and the tragic culmination caused by the apparition.

In Assyrian demonology, the Ekimmu was a vampire demon. In Hindu mythology, Ralaratri was both a witch and a vampire. Katakhanes is a Cin-

[171]

galese variant, while the Burmese have their swawmx. The ancient Greeks knew a bisexual demon called a Lamia, that stole children and sucked their blood. In Solomonic legend, Ornias was a vampire demon. A Slavic expression for a vampire is Vikodlak. In Poland the vampires are Upirs, and in contemporary Greece, in remote valleys and clustering villages, they still appear, unquestioned and accepted, as Brucolacas.

In nineteenth century Gothic fiction, in the Frankenstein cycle, in the more popular periodicals that constituted the reading matter of the Victorian masses, the vampire was the grim protagonist, from *Varny the Vampire* down to *Dracula*.

Voodoo is a magic cult associated with the West Indies, notably Haiti. It derives primarily from ophiolatry—the cult of the serpent—that was rife in Africa, among the Ashanti. Transmitted by African slaves to the Western World, it assumed accretions and variations and expanded into erotic dance rhythms, to the accompaniment of equally erotic drum tattoos. Features of the voodoo ritual are occult chants, sacrifices of chickens and goats. These practices are still in vogue in remote areas of Haiti. Within living memory, voodoo has involved ophiolatry, anthropophagism, and human sacrifice.

A recurrent figure in voodoo is the zombie. A zombie is a human being whose soul has been extracted by a wizard. The body, exhumed after burial, is given a semblance of life. A zombie can participate, according to voodoo, in normal human activities, but under particular circumstances must return to the grave. The two mentors are the mamaloi, the priestess-magician and the papaloi or hounga, her male counterpart, who operate in the houmfort, the voodoo temple.

Similar to voodoo is obeah or obi, a cult prevalent particularly in Jamaica, West Indies. It contains elements of ophiolatry in its rites. A feature is the use of corpses, a practice that links Obeah with Satanic operations.

A necromantic offshot of voodoo is mialism, practiced in Jamaica and involving intercourse with the spirits of the dead.

Lycanthropic Items

The term werewolf is derived from Latin vir, a man, and wolf.

In ancient Greece, in the Peloponnese, the Arcadians were dedicated to a god-wolf called Zeus Lukaios—the Wolf Zeus.

In China and Japan, since the eleventh century, the equivalent of werewolf was the werefox.

In Germanic folklore, the transformation into a wolf is achieved by assuming a wolf's pelt.

In France, during the sixteenth and seventeenth centuries, endemic lycanthropy was prevalent in rural areas.

Sorcerers in Brittany, in the eighteenth century, were believed to assume the wolf shape or to clothe themselves in wolf pelt when going to a Sabbat.

In Ossory, Ireland, certain men, whenever they bit, changed into wolves.

According to early travelers, certain Irish races chose wolves as godfathers, prayed to them in sickness, and used their teeth as periapts.

In certain Irish families, lycanthropy was prevalent for generations. Laignech Fáelad could assume wolf-form at will and kill herds of cattle.

In Irish and Welsh folk ballads a common theme is the transformation into wolf-shape of children or wives, at the hands of a stepmother or a husband respectively.

In Greece and Rome, and in the Middle East and Europe, personal or clan or tribal names often contained a base meaning wolf. Autolycus, Lycomedes, Lycurgus, Lycaon in Greece, and Lupus, Lupicinus, Lupianus in Latin, were names associated with the root wolf. Hyrkodes, wolf-like, was the name of a Bactrian king. Adolf contains the word wolf. Ze'eb, the Wolf, was a Midianite prince. It is still a common Semitic appellation. Mustapha Kemal, first President of the new Turkey, was called Ata-turk, the Grey Wolf.

After World War I, in Germany, a secret terrorist movement was formed, called Organization Werewolf, whose operations were semi-military.

In Africa, particularly in the French and Belgian Congo regions, secret brotherhoods of 'leopard-men' masqueraded until quite recently as wolves, mangling victims with wolfish ferocity. So also the Isawiyya sects throughout all North Africa and Syria.

In Sweden and Estonia, there are still prevalent folklore beliefs in female werewolves.

In France, the werewolf is a loup-garou; in Denmark, a vaerulf; in Italy, a lupo-manaro; in Armenia, a mardagail.

Greek Werewolf

It was the custom of the Arcadians to shed human blood in their solemn sacrifice to Lycaean Zeus. Once a certain Daemoetas of Parrhasia tasted the entrails of a child who had been slain for sacrifice and immediately turned into a wolf. Ten years later the same man regained his human form and won the wrestlers' prize at the Olympic Games.

Agriopas, Greek author of *Olympionicae.*

Roman Wolf-Youths

The ancient Palatine town, surrounded by human herds, is purified by naked youths in wolf-skins.

M. T. Varro (1st century B.C.), Roman lexicographer. Author of *De Lingua Latina*.

The reference is to the Lupercalia, a Roman fertility festival, held annually on February 15.

A Shepherd Werewolf

Often have I seen Moeris turn into a wolf and hide in these woods: often too have I seen him summon the spirits from the depths of the tomb and transfer crops elsewhere.

Vergil (70-19 B.C.), Roman poet, *Eclogues*.

The transference of crops from one owner to another was a common magic practice.

King Lycaon Changed into Wolf

Don't worry, gods, he certainly paid the penalty. Still, I shall tell what the crime was, what the punishment was. The infamy of the times had reached our ears. Hoping to prove this false, I descended from high Olympus and as a god roamed over the lands in human guise. It would be tedious to mention how much evil I found everywhere. The report was less than the actual truth. I had crossed the mountain ranges of Maenalus, shaggy with the lairs of wild beasts, and the pine groves of cold Mt. Lycaeus and Cyllene. Then I proceeded to the abode and the inhospitable palace of the Arcadian tyrant Lycaon, when the late dusk was deepening into night. I gave the sign: a god had come. And the people began to pray. At first Lycaon mocked the devout prayers. Presently he said: "I shall find out by a simple test whether this person is a god or a mortal. And the truth will be beyond doubt."

At night he prepared to destroy me, sleep-laden, by sudden death. This test of the truth appealed to him. Not content with this, with a sword he cut the throat of a certain hostage sent from the Molossians, and boiled in hot water the limbs still warm with life and also cooked them over a fire. No sooner had he set them on the table, than I with avenging flame overthrew the house upon its master, and his equally guilty household. In terror Lycaon fled, and reaching the solitude of the country he howled wolfishly and vainly tried to speak. In his greed for his usual kill he turned upon the cattle and now he lusted for blood. His garments changed to shaggy hair, his arms to legs. He became a wolf, retaining traces of his former shape. His gray hair remained the same, his expression as fierce as ever. His eyes gleamed likewise, while the wildness of his appearance was unchanged.

Ovid (43 B.C.-17 A.D.),Roman poet. Author of *Metamorphoses*.

The narrator of Lycaon's impiety is Jupiter, king of the gods.
MOUNT OLYMPUS: home of the ancient Greek and Roman divinities.

A Greek Werewolf

One of the clan of a certain Anthius, chosen by ballot of the family, is led to a certain pool in the region of Arcadia, and having hung his clothing on an oak tree, swims across the water and goes away into the wilds, and is transformed ito a wolf, and consorts with the rest of his kind for nine years. If during this time he has kept himself from man, he returns to the same pool, and when he has swum across it, recovers his shape, with the decay of nine years added to his former appearance; also (this is more fabulous) he takes again the same clothing.

Pliny the Elder (23-79 A.D.), Roman Encyclopedist. Author of *Natural History*.

Roman Werewolf

Bold enough to impose laws on the enchanted moon and to change skin by appearing as a wolf at night.

Propertius (c. 50-16 B.C.), Roman elegiac poet.

ENCHANTED MOON: a reference to the witches' power to draw down the moon from the skies.

Roman Werewolf

We ambled off at cock-crow. The moon was shining bright as day. We reached the spot where the wood leads among the graves. My man went off behind a tombstone. I sat down and sang. Then, looking round for my friend, I found he had undressed, and laid all his clothes on the roadside. My heart was in my mouth, and I stood stock still like a dead man. He made a ring round his clothes and suddenly changed into a wolf. Don't think I'm joking. When he turned into a wolf, he began to howl and ran off into the wood. When I went to pick up his clothes, they had turned to stone. I drew my sword and slashed at the shadows all the way home until I came to my sweetheart's house. I looked like a ghost, sweat poured down, my eyes were glazed like a dead man's. My Melissa said: "If you'd come a little earlier, you could have helped us: for a wolf attacked all the flock. A slave pierced him in the neck with a spear." When I got home, I found my friend lying stretched out on a bed, like an ox, and a doctor was tending his neck. I then realized that he was a werewolf, and afterward I couldn't have eaten a morsel of bread with him, not on my life.

Petronius (1st century A.D.), Roman novelist. Author of *The Satyricon*. The present story is being told by a guest, Niceros, at Trimalchio's banquet.

There was a belief that wounds inflicted on a person while in animal form remained on a human body after transformation to human shape. This phenomenon, current in mediaeval demonology also, is known as repercussion.

An Irish Werewolf

An Irish priest was met by a wolf in Meath and desired to come to see his dying wife. There were natives of Ossory, whose people had been cursed for their wickedness by St. Natalis, and were compelled to take two by two a wolf-shape for seven years, returning to their own form at the end of that time. The priest was persuaded to give the she-wolf the sacrament, for the other turned her skin down a little, showing that she was an old woman.

> Giraldus Cambrensis (1147-c.1220), Welsh historian. Author of *Topographia Hibernica.*

SEVEN YEARS: in magic rituals, the number seven possessed mystic implications.

Welsh Vampire

I know of a strange portent that occurred in Wales. William Laudun or Landun, an English knight, strong of body and of proven valour, came to Gilbert Foliot, then Bishop of Hereford, now of London, and said: "My Lord, I come to you for advice. A Welshman of evil life died of late unchristianly enough in my village, and straightway after four nights took to coming back every night to the village, and will not desist from summoning singly and by name his fellow-villagers, who upon being called at once fall sick and die within three days, so that now there are very few of them left." The Bishop, marvelling, said: "Peradventure the Lord has given power to the evil angel of that lost soul to move about in the dead corpse. However, let the body be exhumed, cut the neck through with a spade, and sprinkle the body and the grave well with holy water,

and replace it." When this was done, the survivors were none the less plagued by the former illusion. So one night when the summoner had now left but few alive, he called William himself, citing him thrice. He, however, bold and quick as he was, and awake to the situation, darted out with his sword drawn, and chased the demon, who fled, up to the grave and there, as he fell into it, clave his head to the neck. From that hour the ravage of that wandering pestilence ceased, and did no more hurt either to William himself or to any one else.

> Walter Map (c. 1140-c. 1209), English Chronicler. Author of *De Nugis Curialium.*

Soldier Turned Werewolf

I know one thing, that among our fellow-citizens it is common knowledge that, in the course of human destinies, certain men are transformed into wolves during the changes of the moon. For we know that in Auvergne, in the bishopric of Clermont, Ponce de Chapteuil, a noble, in time disinherited Raimbaud de Pinetum, a very active, trained military man.

This man became a wanderer and a refugee over the face of the earth. Like a wild beast he prowled through the byways and forests, for one night, smitten by a great dread, he had been turned into a wolf and had at the same time lost his senses. He caused such havoc that he forced many farmers to abandon their homes. In his wolf form he devoured children: and he mangled old

[176]

folk with his wolfish fangs. At last he was severely wounded by a woodman, and lost one foot by a stroke of the axe: and so he resumed his human shape. Then he admitted in public that he had decided to sacrifice one leg, because by amputating it he had got rid of his misfortune. For they say that amputation of a limb frees such men from their calamitous condition.

Otia Imperialia—Leisure Hours of an Emperor, by Gervase of Tilbury, an English scholar who in the third century wrote the *Otia Imperialia* for the Emperor Otto IV.

Livonian Werewolf

In Livonia a servant, whose power as a werewolf was disputed, went to the cellar and soon after came out as a wolf. The dogs bit out one of its eyes, and next day the man appeared with one eye.

Olaus Magnus, mediaeval chronicler.

Norse-Werewolves

On the feast of the Nativity of Christ, at night, such a multitude of wolves transformed from men gather together in a certain spot, arranged among themselves, and then spread to rage with wondrous ferocity against human beings, and those animals which are not wild, that the natives of these regions suffer more detriment from these, than they do from true and natural wolves.

Olaus Magnus, mediaeval chronicler.

Norse Werewolf

Then avenged will be
The death of Helgi
When thou, as a wolf,
Wanderest in the woods,
Knowing nor fortune
Nor any pleasure,
Having no meat
Save rivings of corpses.

Norse poem, *Helg Hundingsbana.*

Norse Werewolf

When this peril Finn saw,
That witchcraft did him harm,
Then he changed himself into a werewolf:
He slew many thus.

Son of Finnur. Faroe Islands Saga.

Norse Werewolf

Thou thyself hast eaten wolves' meat and murdered thy brother. Thou hast often sucked wounds with cold mouth and slunk, loathsome to all men, into the dens of wild beasts.   *Völsunga Saga.*

Vigfusson-Powell, Corpus Poet. Boreale. Oxford, 1883.

THOU: that is, Sinfiötli, a werewolf.

A Scottish Vampire

In the northern regions of England also we learn that a similar and equally strange phenomenon occurred at the

[177]

same time. There is a fine town at the mouth of the River Tweed, called Berwick, a royal burgh of the King of Scotland. There, a poor man, but an evil one, as was later on clearly evident, having been duly laid to rest after his death, used to leave his tomb at night, with the Devil's aid, as the belief was: and, to the accompaniment of a retinue of loud-barking dogs, roamed through the countryside, inspiring great terror among the inhabitants. This went on for a good many days, and no one dared to venture out of doors after dark, while everyone dreaded an encounter with the ominous monster. The elders and the common people held a meeting on what was to be done, for they were afraid that the ignorant among them, if ineffective action were taken, would soon be sucked of their blood by the dead monster. The more cautious, however, prudently considered that possibly, if a remedy were applied too late, the infected air, tainted by continual contact with the plague-bearing corpse, would result in widespread disease and death. It was evident therefore that precautions must be taken in line with numerous occurrences in similar cases. They therefore summoned ten daring young men to exhume the foul corpse and cut it limb for limb and reduce it to burning and fuel of fire. When this was done, the plague was stayed. For the monster itself, while it was driven around by the Devil, as has been said, declared to certain people whom it chanced to meet that as long as it was not consumed by fire the people would have no rest. So, when it was burned, peace indeed seemed to have been granted to the people, but a plague came later and destroyed most of the people of that region. For although it spread at the same time to all parts of England, it did not rage so disastrously anywhere else.

Historia Rerum Anglicarum. William of Newburgh (1136-c. 1198), author of this History of England, was canon of the Augustinian priory of Newburgh, in Yorkshire, England.

Imaginative Lycanthropy

Pescara:
> Pray thee, what's his disease?

Doctor:
> A very pestilent disease, my lord.
> They call it licanthropia.

Pescara:
> What's that?
> I need a dictionary to't.

Doctor:
> I'll tell you:
> In those that are possess'd with't
>   there oreflowes
> Such mellencholly humour, they
>   imagine
> Themselves to be transformed into
>   woolves,
> Steale forth to church-yards in the
>   dead of night,
> And dig dead bodies up: as two
>   nights since
> One met the duke, 'bout midnight
>   in a lane
> Behind St. Markes church, with the
>   leg of a man
> Upon his shoulder; and he howl'd
>   fearefully:

[178]

Said he was a woolffe: onely the
difference
Was, a woolffes skinne was hairy
on the outside,
His on the in-side: bad them take
their swords,
Rip up his flesh, and trie . . .

John Webster (c. 1580-c. 1625),
English dramatist. Author of *Duchess of Malfy*.

German Werewolf

At Bamberg, Peter Stumpf was condemned to death for intimacy with a succubus for more than twenty-eight years. This demon had given him a girdle. When he put it on, it appeared to him and to others that he had changed into a wolf. He tried to devour two of his daughters-in-law.

Francesco Guazzo. *Compendium Maleficarum,* 1608.

Vampire in Silesia

Johannes Cuntius, a citizen and alderman of Pentach, in Silesia, when about sixty years of age, died somewhat suddenly, as the result of a kick from his horse. At the moment of his death a black cat rushed into the room, jumped on to the bed, and scratched violently at his face. Both at the time of his death and that of his funeral a great tempest arose—the wind and snow 'made men's bodies quake and their teeth chatter in their heads.' The storm is said to have ceased with startling suddenness as the body was placed under the ground. Immediately after the burial, however, stories began to circulate of the appearance of a phantom which spoke to people in the voice of Cuntius. Remarkable tales were told of the consumption of milk from jugs and bowls, of milk being turned into blood, of old men being strangled, children taken out of cradles, altar-cloths being soiled with blood, and poultry killed and eaten. Eventually it was decided to disinter the body. It was found that all the bodies buried above that of Cuntius had become putrefied and rotten, but his skin was tender and florid, his joints by no means stiff, and when a staff was put between his fingers they closed around it and held it fast in their grasp. He could open and shut his eyes, and when a vein in his leg was punctured the blood sprang out as fresh as that of a living person. This happened after the body had been in the grave for about six months. Great difficulty was experienced when the body was cut up and dismembered, by the order of the authorities, by reason of the resistance offered; but when the task was completed, and the remains consigned to the flames, the spectre ceased to molest the natives or interfere with their slumbers or health.

Henry More, *Antidote against Atheism* (early 17th century).

St. Patrick and Werewolves

St. Patrick cursed a certain race in Ireland, with the result that they and their descendants became wolves at a certain time every seventh year, or for seven years on end.

W. Stokes, *Religion of the Celts,* 1873.

SEVENTH YEAR: in magic, seven had mystic implications.

Chinese Were-Tiger

When he wishes to eat people he puts off his clothes and is changed into a striped tiger. He then advances with a great roar, and the traveller is instantly torn to pieces.

N. B. Dennys. *Folk-lore of China,* 1876.

A Variant Baluch Werewolf

The black takes the form
of a beautiful woman at
night and hugs men to
death.

M. L. Dames, *Folklore* 13, 1902.

The reference is to the folklore of Baluchistan, now part of Pakistan.

The Cult of Obeah

As a fact, Obeah is rather to be ranked, it seemed to me, with those ancient Eastern mysteries, at once magical and profligate, which troubled society and morals in later Rome.

Charles Kingsley, *At Last: A Christmas in the West Indies,* 1871.

OBEAH—or OBI: a magic cult, similar to Voodoo, prevalent in Jamaica and other islands of the West Indies. Obeah contains features of ophiolatry, and at one time used corpses in its rites.

Obeah or Fetish-Worship

It appears to me, on closer examination, that it is not a worship of natural objects; not a primaeval worship; scarcely a worship at all; but simply a system of incantation, carried on by a priesthood, or rather a sorcerer class; and this being the case, it seems to me unfortunate that the term Fetish-worship should have been adopted by so many learned men, as the general name for the supposed primaeval Nature-worship. The Negro does not, as the primaeval man is supposed to have done, regard as divine (and therefore as Fetish, or Obeah) any object which excites his imagination: anything peculiarly beautiful, noble, or powerful; anything even which causes curiosity or fear. In fact, a Fetish is no natural object at all: it is a spirit, an Obeah, Jumby, Duppy, like the "Duvvels" or spirits of the air, which are the only deities of which our Gipsies have a conception left. That spirit belongs to the Obeah, or Fetish-man; and he puts it, by magic ceremonies, into any object which he chooses. Thus anything may become Obeah, as far as I have ascertained. In a case which happened very lately, an Obeah-man came into the country, put the Obeah into a fresh monkey's jaw-bone, and made the people offer to it fowls and plantains, which of course he himself ate. Such is Obeah now; and such it was, when the Portuguese first met with it on the African coast four hundred years ago.

Charles Kingsley, *At Last: A Christmas in the West Indies,* 1871.

CAGLIOSTRO

Count Alessandro Cagliostro (1745-1795) was an Italian alchemist and magician whose real name was Giuseppe Balsamo. Fleeing periodically from the scenes of his many crimes, he roamed over Europe, acquiring great wealth through the sale of magic elixirs and potions. He experienced so many adventures that his name became legendary. His last years were spent in imprisonment, in the fortress of San Leo. Among his recorded feats are the production of a diamond by alchemy and the exorcism of a dead woman. He also founded a secret society called The Egyptian Lodge, noted for its occult séances.

THE SPELL OF THE BOW
The witch has shot a peasant in the foot with a magic hazel wand. The victim has taken off his shoe as his foot as begun to swell. If the peasant yields to the witch, the spell will be lifted.
Ulrich Molitor was a medieval demonographer.

WITCH MILKING AN AXE

A witch could perform all kinds of thaumaturgic acts. Here is one extracting milk from the handle of an axe.

(A German woodcut of the sixteenth century)

DR. FAUSTUS

Dr. Johannes Faustus was a noted medieval occultist. A legend credited him with selling his soul to Mephistopheles, the Archfiend. Christopher Marlowe, the Elizabethan dramatist, presents the story in *Dr. Faustus*. Note the magician's familiar, the cat, and also the elemental spirits in the scene.

Chapter VIII

Manuals of Magic

Chapter 8

MANUALS OF MAGIC

Introduction

A great and to some degree untapped material dealing with various manifestations of witchcraft is incorporated in folklore and old ballads, in religious hymns, in legends and antique chronicles, in poems and plays. But apart from all such dispersed matter, ranging over many centuries and as many different countries, there is a coherent and well attested body of magic ritual known as grimoires—manuals widely popular in the Middle Ages. Written by practicing wizards, or attributed pseudepigraphically to prominent magicians or cryptic warlocks such as King Solomon, Pope Honorius, Cagliostro, Dr. John Dee, Paracelsus, Albertus Magnus, they have made their weird impact among all social levels, in village and court, farm and boudoir, throughout the breadth of the European continent, and in adapted versions, among the Middle Eastern countries.

These goetic guides cover necromancy and divination, alchemy and astrology, levitation and a vast array of demoniac skills, from comparatively harmless charms for specific diseases through more hazardous love philtres and extending to sacrificial rites involving human beings. All these handbooks have this element in common, that they present sober and at least hypothetically effective directions toward the desired magical consummation. And if the magical consummation is not attained, the implication is that ritually the thaumaturgic performance was not rigorously fulfilled. And always, the onus of such scrupulous adherence to the prescriptions of the ritual devolved upon the practitioner: so that the efficaciousness of the rite itself was never brought into question.

[183]

Memory Training

And if the heart, eye or braine of a Lapwing or black plover be hanged upon a mans necke, it is profitable against forgetfulness and sharpeneth mans understanding.

Albertus Magnus, *Book of the Marvels of the World.*

Summoning the Spirits

I conjure thee, Spirit, by the Living God, by the true God, by the blessed and omnipotent God: He who created the Heavens, the Earth, the Sea, and all the things that are in them, from out of nothing.

In the Name of Jesus Christ, by the power of the Holy Sacraments and of the Eucharist, and in the power of this Son of God who was crucified, who died, and who was buried, for our sake: He who rose once again, on the Third Day, and who is now seated at the right of the Supreme Creator, and from where He will come to be a judge over the living and over the dead; and likewise by the priceless love of the Holy Spirit, the Perfect Trinity:

I conjure thee into this circle, O accursed spirit, thou, who hast dared to disobey God. I exorcise thee, Serpent, and I order thee to appear immediately, in human form, well-shaped, in body and soul, and to comply with my commands without deception of whatsoever kind, and without either mental reservation: and this by the Great Names of God, the God of Gods and the Lord of all Lords:

Adonay, Tetragrammaton, Jehova, Tetragrammaton, Adonay, Jehova, Otheos, Athanatos, Ischyros, Agla, Pentagrammaton, Saday, Saday, Saday, Jehova, Otheos, Athanatos, Aliciat Tetragrammaton, Adonay, Ischyros, Athanatos, Sada, Sady, Sady, Cados, Cados, Cados, Eloy, Agla, Agla, Agla, Adonay, Adonay:

I conjure thee, O evil and accursed Serpent, to appear at my wish and pleasure, in this place and before this Circle, immediately, alone and without any companion, without any ill-will, delay, noise, deformity or evasion. I also exorcise thee by the ineffable names of God, namely, Gog and Magog, which I am not worthy to speak. Come here, come here, come here. Satisfy me and my commands, without evasion or lie. If thou does not this, Saint Michael, the invisible Archangel will soon strike thee in the deepest pit of Hell.

Come then, and obey me, and accomplish my desire.

Grimoire of Honorius the Great, attributed to Pope Honorius III.

Make Yourself Invisible

Abac, Aldai, Iat, Hibac, Guthac, Guthor, Gomeh, Tistator, Derisor Destatur: Come here all of you who like the places and times in which duplicity and trickery are done! And you, the masters of invisibility: come here, and deceive those who see things: that they may appear to see what they do not, and that they may hear what they hear not, and that their senses may be tricked, and that they may see what is not true!

[185]

Come then, here, and stay, and consecrate this spell, for God Almighty, the Lord, has assigned to you this function!

Key of Solomon, mediaeval grimoire.

The wording of this invocation implies its efficacy by means of some form of mass hypnosis.

A Stone of Many Purposes

Take the stone which is called Echites, and it is called of some Aquileus, because the Eagles put these in their nests. It is of purple colour, and it is found nigh the bankes of the Ocean Sea and sometime in Persia; and it alwaies containeth another stone in it which soundeth in it, when it is named.

It is said of ancient Philosophers, that childe, it letteth untimely birth, it mitigateth the peril of making afraid, and it is said to be good to them that have the fling skins; and as the men of Chaldee say and affirme, that if there be any poyson in thy meates if the aforesaid stone be put in, it letteth that meat be this stone, hanged upon the left shoulder, gathereth love between the husband and wife. It is profitable to women great with swallowed downe, and if it be taken out, meate is soone swallowed downe.

Albertus Magnus (c. 1206-1280), *Secrets of Albertus Magnus*—mediaeval magic manual.

Queer Bird

Casso is a beast that is knowne very well. It is called Rapa among the Chaldees, and of the Greeks Orgalo. Aaron sayeth of this: if the feete of it be borne of any man, he shall desire alwaies to go forth. Also he that beareth the feet of it shall alwaies overcome, and shall be feared of his enemies. And he saith that his right eye, wrapped in a wolves skin, maketh a man pleasant, acceptable and gentle. And if meate be made of the aforesaid things, or powder of it be given to any man in meate, the giver shall be greatly loved of him that receiveth it.

Albertus Magnus, *Secrets of Albertus Magnus,* mediaeval magic manual.

Lust Banished

Turtur, a Turtle, is a birde very well knowne. It is called Merlon of the Chaldees, of the Greeks Pilax. If the heart of this foule be borne in a Wolves skin, he that weareth it shall never have an appetite to commit lechery from henceforth.

Albert Magnus, *Secrets of Albertus Magnus,* mediaeval magic manual.

Invocation over Magician's Instruments

Dalmaley Lameck Cadat Pancia Velous Merroe Lamideck Caldurech Anereton Mitraton: Most Pure Angels, be the guardians of these instruments, they are needed for many things.

True Grimoire.

Herb of Venus

The seventh is the hearb of the planet Venus, and is called Pisterion, of some Hierobotane, id est, Sterbo columbaria et Verbena, Vervin.

The root of this hearb put upon the neck healeth the swine pockes, apostumus behinde the eares, and botches of the neck, and such as cannot keepe their water. It healeth cuts also, and swelling of the evil, or fundament, proceeding of an inflammation which groweth in the fundament.

It is also of great strength in veneriall pastimes. If any man put it into his house or vineyard, or in the ground, he shal have great store of increase.

Albertus Magnus, *Secrets of Albertus Magnus.*

How to Grow Tall

Camelus, the Camell, is a beast known well enough. It is called of the Chaldees, Ciboi, of the Greeks Iphim. If the blood of it be put in the skin of the beast called Stellio, and then set on any mans head, which is like a lizard, having on his backe spots like stars, it shall seeme that he is a Giant, and that his head is in heaven.

Albertus Magnus, *Secrets of Albertus Magnus.*

Fishing Made Easy

Foca, a Porpaise, is a fish well knowne, of the Chaldees it is called Daulumber, of the Greeks Labor: this fish is of divers natures. If the tung of it be taken and put with a little of the heart of it in water, for a surety fishes will gather there together.

Albertus Magnus, *Secrets of Albertus Magnus.*

Magic Properties of Raven

Cornus, called of some a Raven, and of others a Crow. The vertue of this foule is marvellous, as Euar and Aaron rehearse. If her egges be sodden, and put againe in the next, the Raven goeth soone to the red sea, in a certain Isle, where Aldoricus or Alodrius is buried. And she bringeth a stone wherewith she toucheth her egges, and all the egges be as rawe again.

It is a marvellous thing to stire up sodden egges. If this stone be put in a ring, and the leafe of the Lawrell tree under it, and if a man be found in chains, or a doore shut, be touched therewith, he that is bound shall be loosed, and the doore shall be opened.

Albertus Magnus, *Secrets of Albertus Magnus.*

Things to Come

Mustella the wesell is a beast sufficiently known. If the heart of this beast be eaten yet quaking, it maketh a man to know things to come.

Albertus Magnus, *Secrets of Albertus Magnus.*

[187]

Names Invoked in Roman Necromancy

Cerberus	Hecate
Chaos	Mercury
Charon	Persephone
Demogorgon	Pluto
Earth	Styx
Elysium	The Fates
	The Furies

Mediaeval Grimoire.

Understanding Bird Language

Associate with two fellowes in the twenty-eighth day of October, and goe into a certaine wood with dogges as to hunt. And cary home with thee the beast which thou shalt find first. Prepare it with the heart of a foxe, and thou shalt understand the voice of birds and beasts. And if thou wilt also that any other understand, kisse him, and he shall understand.

Albertus Magnus, *Book of the Marvels of the World.*

Love Charm

If thou wilt that a woman bee not visious nor desire men, take the private members of a Woolfe, and the haires which doe grow on the cheekes or eyebrowes of him, and the haires which bee under his beard, and burne it all, and give it to her to drinke, when she knoweth not, and she shal desire no other man.

Albertus Magnus, *Book of the Marvels of the World.*

Effects of Magic on Animals

And Aristotle said in the *Booke of Beastes:* if any man put wrought ware upon the hornes of a cows calfe, it will goe with him wheresoever he will without labor.

And if any man anoint the hornes of kine with ware and oyle, or pitch, the paine of their feet goeth away.

And if any shall anoint the tungs of oxen with any tallow, they neither taste nor eat meat, but they shall die for hunger, except it be willed away with salt and vinegar.

And if any man anoint the nether parts of a Cocke with oyle, he neither wil nor may tread a henne.

If thou desire that a Cocke grow not, anoint his head and forehead with pyle.

Albertus Magnus, *Book of the Marvels of the World.*

Talisman for Victory

The fourth hearb is named Aquillaris, of the Chaldees; it springeth in the time in which the Eagles build their nests. It is named by the Greeks Vallias, of the Latins Celidonia, and of the Englishe man Celindine. This hearb springeth in the time which Swallows and also the Eagles make their nests.

If any man shal have this hearb with the heart of a Mole he shal overcome all his enemies, and all matters in suite, and shal put away all debate.

Albertus Magnus, *Secrets of Albertus Magnus.*

Magic Herb

The second is the hearb of the Sun, which is called Poligonia, or Coraligiola.

[188]

This hearb taketh name of the Sunne: for it engendereth greatly, and so this hearb worketh many wayes.

Others call this hearb Alchone, which is the house of the Sun: This hearb healeth the passions and griefes of the hart and stomach. He that toucheth this hearb hath a vertue of his signe or planet. If any man drink the juyce of it, it maketh him to do often the act of generation. And if any man beare the roote thereof, it helpeth the grief of the eies. And if he beare it with him before he have any griefe, there shal come to him no griefe of his eyes. It helpeth them also that be vexed with the phrensie, if they beare it with them in their breast.

Albertus Magnus, *Secrets of Albertus Magnus.*

Lock-Breaking by Magic

This hearb Missell toe, with a certaine other hearbe, which is named Martegon, that is Silphion or Laserpitium, as it is written in the Almans language, it openeth all lockes.

Albertus Magnus, *Secrets of Albertus Magnus.*

How to Know the Future

Take the stone which is called Bena, which is like a Beastes tooth, and put it under thy tongue. And as Aaron and the old philosophers say, as long as thou doest hold it thou mayest conjecture and tell of things to come, and thou shalt not erre in any wise for judging.

Albertus Magnus, *Magical Stones.*

How to Become Invisible

Take the stone which is called Ophethalminus, and wrap it in the leafe of the Laurell or Bay tree. And it is called Lapis Obtelmicus, whose colour is not named, for it is of many colours, and it is of such vertue, that it blindeth the sights of them that stand about. Constantinus carrying this in his hand, was made invisible therewith.

Albertus Magnus, *Magical Stones.*

CONSTANTINUS: Roman Emperor, 4th century A.D.

Chastity Test

Take the stone which is called Magnes, in Englishe the loadestone, it is of sadde blew colour, and it is found in the sea of Inde, and sometime in the parts of Almaine, in the province which is called Caste Fraunce.

Lay this stone under the head of a wife. And if she be chaste, she will embrace her husband. If she be not chaste, she will fall forth of her bed.

Albertus Magnus, *Magical Stones.*

Conjuration of a Girl

I salute thee and conjure thee, O beautiful Moon, O most beautiful Star, O brilliant light which I have in my hand. By the air that I breathe, by the breath within me, by the earth which I am touching: I conjure thee. By all the names of the spirit princes living in you. By the ineffable Name On, which created everything! By you, O resplendent

[189]

Angel Gabriel, with the Planet Mercury, Prince, Michiael, and Melchidael.

I conjure you again, by all the Holy Names of God, so that you may send down power to oppress, torture and harass the body and soul and the five senses of (victim), she whose name is written here, so that she shall come unto me, and agree to my desires, liking nobody in the world, for so long as she shall remain unmoved by me. Let her then be tortured, made to suffer. Go, then, at once! Go, Melchidael, Baresches, Zazel, Firiel, Malcha, and all those who are with thee! I conjure you by the Great Living God to obey my will, and I promise to satisfy you.

True Grimoire.

Preparations for this conjuration involve waxing or waning moon, occult inscription on virgin parchment, and lighted taper.

Chastity Test

Take the stone called Galeritis, which is the same that is called Catabres, and it is found in Lybia, Britannia, the most noble Isle of the world (wherein is contained both countries, England and Scotland). It is of double colour: black, and the colour of saffron, and it is found gray coloured, turning to paleness. It healeth the dropsie, and it bindeth the bellies that are loose. And as Avicenna saith, that if the stone be broken and washed, or be given to a woman to be washed, if she be not a virgin, she will shed her water, if she be a virgin the contrary.

Albertus Magnus, *Magical Stones.*

Conjuration of Lower Infernal Powers

Osurmy: delmusan: atalsloym: charusihoa: melany: liamintho: colehon: paron: madoin: merloy: bulerator: donmedo: hone: peloym: ibasil: meon: alymdrictels: person: crisolay: lemon sessle nidar horiel peunt: halmon: asophiel: ilnostreon: baniel: vermias: slevor: noelma: dorsamot: Ihavala: omor: frangam: beldor: dragin: Venite.

True Grimoire.

Conjuration of Lucifer

Lucifer, Ouyar, Chameron, Aliseon, Mandousin, Premy, Oriet, Naydrus, Esmony, Eparinesont, Estiot, Dumosson, Danochar, Casmiel, Hayras, Fabelleronthou, Sodirno, Peatham, Venite, Lucifer. Amen.

True Grimoire.

Invocation over Goat Skin Used in Magic Writing

Adonay, Dalmay, Lauday, Tetragrammaton, Anereton, and all you, Holy Angels of God, come and be here, and deign to infuse into this skin the power that it may be correctly conserved, so that all that is written upon it may become perfected.

True Grimoire.

Similarly, incense, ink, water, salt and other items associated with occult rites were exposed to invocation before being put to use.

OCCULT ALPHABETS

Magic formulas, symbols, and esoteric designs were from the earliest times associated with the occult arts. In the illustration some of the characters have Hebraic names. From *Magus*, an early nineteenth century exposition of magic.

MAGIC CIRCLE

The magic circle, drawn around the sorcerer, symbolized the boundary that separated the demon from the magician. Within the circumference of the circle were inscribed various cryptic formulas and figures. In the illustration the necromancer is invoking spirits.

(XVI century MS.)

British Museum, London.

THE BATTLE BETWEEN MAN AND EVIL

A symbolic illustration of Evil as a cosmic force embattled against man. This is an ancient Manichean concept too, predicating two principles, Good and Evil, everlastingly at war with each other.

William Blake was an English nineteenth century mystic and artist.

SATAN

Various names and attrributed have been assigned to the Archfiend. In the Middle Ages the most popular conception of Satan was in the form of a goat. Satan itself means *adversary*. Diabolus means *two morsels* 'For he kills two things, the body and the soul.' Demon means *cunning over blood*. Belial signifies *without a master*, while Beelzebub connotes *Lord of flies*. As Lucifer, Satan is the Light-bearer.

(Gostave Doré was a nineteenth century French artist)

Chapter IX

Who is Who in Witchcraft

Chapter 9

WHO IS WHO IN WITCHCRAFT

Introduction

Ancient and mediaeval chronicles, histories and oral legends have preserved the names and sometimes the biographies and influences of those who were adepts or active in the Black Arts. The information may be brief, a fragmentary allusion, a provocative reference, as if the name were so notorious that further elaboration was unnecessary. In other instances, both the personality himself and his life, crammed with occult performances, have entered into the history of witchcraft. This Who's Who embraces such figures, along with demonographers and others associated in any degree with the Black Arts, and summarizes their achievements or contributions and their significance.

[193]

Abaris

A legendary figure, identified by some authorities as a Scythian magician. He lived without food, and practiced transvection through the air by means of a golden arrow. Traditionally, he was reputed to be the master of Pythagoras, the Greek philosopher.

Adamantius

Jewish physician who lived in Constantinople in the fourth century A.D. Author of treatise on occult significance of physiognomy.

Agamede

Witch mentioned in Homer's *Iliad.*

Agonaces

Ancient magician. According to tradition, he lived 7000 B.C., and taught witchcraft to Zoroaster.

Agrippa

Agrippa von Nettesheim (1486-1535). Henry Cornelius Agrippa von Nettesheim, commonly called Agrippa, was versatile in many directions: as physician, soldier, occultist. He experienced fame and oblivion, riches and poverty, royal, diplomatic and military favor. His travels included France, Italy, England, and Belgium, but in Brussels he was imprisoned for debt. His *Magnum opus* is *The Occult Philosophy,* which defends magic as a composite of scientific knowledge, religious doctrine, and occultism.

Agrusadapariksay

Ancient esoteric Hindu treatise on occultism.

Albertus Magnus
(1206-1280)

Bishop of Ratisbon, he became interested in the occult arts; experimented with alchemy and magic, and produced amazing phenomena. A prolific writer, he was the author of a study of alchemy, containing directions for the practicing alchemist. Reputedly, he achieved the transmutation of metals by means of the philosopher's stone. He was also credited with power over atmospheric conditions and with the fashioning of an android, an automaton capable of speech.

Alexander the Paphlagonian
2nd century A.D.

Magician. Native of Abonotica. Established oracle under his own direction. Success continued for twenty years. Consulted by Emperor Marcus Aurelius.

Allen, Jonet

Scottish witch. Burned, 1661.

Amalaric, Madeleine

French sorceress of sixteenth century. Executed on charge of causing death of eleven persons.

Anania

Johannes Laurentius Anania. Sixteenth century demonographer. Author of *De Natura Daemonum*—On the Nature of Demons: published in Venice, 1581.

Ansuperomin

Sorcerer who flourished in reign of Henry IV of France. Known for participation in Sabbat assemblies.

Anthony, Francis

Seventeenth century quack physician and alchemist. Claimed ability to dissolve gold into a universal remedy.

Apollonius of Tyana

Greek philosopher who flourished in the first century A.D. In quest of occult science, he traveled as far as India, lecturing on occult subjects, relating his encounters with demons and vampires. His reputation as a wizard became so widespread that in Asia Minor temples were dedicated to him as a supreme almost divine thaumaturgist. In Rome, he was brought to trial for practicing divination. During the Middle Ages Apollonius' reputation became legendary, while he himself acquired the distinction of the Archmagician.

Apuleius

Roman philosopher and occultist of the second century A.D. Accused of securing a wife by magic means, he defended himself in a speech, still extant, in which he discusses occult techniques. He is also the author of the *Metamorphoses,* or The Golden Ass, a picaresque novel crammed with magic practices and occult rites.

Apusorus of Media

Ancient Chaldean magician.

Arabantiphocus

Ancient Babylonian magician.

Arnold of Villanova

Thirteenth century physician, occultist, and alchemist. Traveled in Europe and Africa. Credited with transmutation of metals and converse with Satanic powers. In his medical practice he employed occult conjurations, mystic symbolism, and magic potions.

Arnuphis

Egyptian sorcerer who flourished in second century A.D.

[196]

Artemidorus

Oneirologist who flourished in 2nd century A.D. Author of *De Somniorum Interpretatione Libri Quinque*. This treatise was popular, in several translations, as late as the eighteenth century.

Artephius

Hermetic and mystic who flourished in 12th century. Reputedly lived more than a thousand years, with the help of demons. Author of *The Art of Prolonging Life*, written, according to tradition, at age of 1025.

Ascletarion

Sorcerer who predicted that the Roman Emperor Domitian's body would be devoured by dogs. After Domitian's death the prediction was fulfilled.

Ashmole, Elias

English alchemist, 17th century.

Astrampsychos

Ancient Chaldean magician.

Avenar

Jewish astrologer, 5th century A.D. Calculated the advent of Hebraic Messiah.

Bacis

Ancient Greek seer of Boeotia. Mentioned by Cicero.

Bacon, Roger

(1214-1294)

English Friar, scientist, and philosopher. As the result of his investigations and experiments, he accepted 'natural magic', i.e. the phenomena that occur within mathematical and physical areas. But he attacked human superstitions and delusions, and rejected the Black Arts, including incantations, invocation of spirits, spellbinding. Despite this attitude, Bacon was widely known as a magician.

Balcoin, Marie

French witch in reign of Henry IV, condemned to stake for witchcraft.

Barchusen, Johann Conrad

Eighteenth century alchemist. Author of alchemical treatise.

Basilides

Founder of a sect of Gnostics. Flourished in Alexandria in second century A.D.

Bavan, Madeleine

Seventeenth century French witch. Notorious for participation in Sabbat rite.

Becher, J. Joachim

Eighteenth century German chemist and alchemist.

Beckford, William

Eighteenth century English writer. Author of *Vathek*. Less known are his interests in Oriental magic and demonology.

Belephantes

Chaldean astrologer. According to the Greek historian Diodorus Siculus, he predicted that the entry of Alexander the Great into Babylon would be fatal to the Emperor: as was the case.

Benedict IX

Pope reputed to have been adept in sorcery and incantations.

Berosus

Astrologer of Greek island of Cos, flourished in first century A.D. Many grimoires were ascribed to his authorship.

Beuther, David

Seventeenth century alchemist. Reputed to possess secret of making gold, imprisoned to extract his secret. Released, he poisoned himself to protect secret.

Biscar, Jeannette

French sorceress. In goat form, she was conveyed to a Sabbat by the Devil himself.

Bocal

Priest—sorcerer who flourished in the reign of Henry IV of France. Charged with participation in Black Mass, he was condemned to death.

Bodin, Jean

French lawyer: died, 1569. Demonographer, author of *De la Démonomanie des Sorciers*.

Bogomils

Children of Satanaël. Mediaeval Satanists who inhabited Central European regions.

Boguet, Henri

French demonographer, 17th century. Author of *Discours des Sorciers*.

Bolingbroke, Roger

Fifteenth century wizard. Notorious for his demoniac conjurations, astrological and magic performances. Having attempted to kill Henry VI of England by witchcraft, he was hanged in London.

Bonatti, Guido

Italian astrologer and magician, 13th century. Reputed to have made an apothecary wealthy by fashioning a wax image of a ship endowed with magic properties.

Bragadini, Mark Antony

Sixteenth century Italian alchemist. Beheaded for boasting of transmutation of metals by demoniac aid.

Bulwer Lytton
(1831-1891)

English novelist who interested himself in thaumaturgic studies. Associated with the French demonographer Eliphas Lévi. Author of occult novel entitled *The Coming Race.*

Cagliostro
(1745-1795)

Count Alessandro Cagliostro, originally, Giuseppe Balsamo. Italian magician and alchemist. After committing numberless crimes in Sicily, he fled from the island. After a sequence of travel and adventure throughout Europe, pervaded by practice in sorcery and alchemy with his wife Lorenza Feliciani, he was persona grata among the distinguished families of the Continent. By the sale of love philtres, magic elixirs, and similar concoctions, he amassed great wealth. Again and again involved in scandals, he was compelled to travel from one country to another, acquiring a legendary reputation. His declining years were spent, in imprisonment, in the fortress of San Leo. Reputedly, he was successful in necromancy and the manufacture of diamonds by alchemy. He was also the founder of an occult society called The Egyptian Lodge.

Calmet, Augustin
(1672-1756)

French Benedictine monk. Author of a book on witchcraft, lycanthropy, and demonology.

Cardan, Jerome

Most prominent intellectual personality of his age. French scientist and astrologer. Author of *De Subtilitate*, 1550. In Books 18 and 19 he discusses philtres, charms, and demons.

Casanova, Giacomo
(1725-1798)

Italian adventurer. Noted especially for his amorous encounters. Also practiced witchcraft, and divination, for which he used a cryptogram called a Kabbala. Possessed the grimoire The Key of Solomon, which involved him in charges by the Inquisition. Associated with occult treasure hunts and conjurations of spirits.

[199]

Catalin

Wizard noted in Irish magic legend.

Cellini, Benvenuto
(1500-1571)

Italian goldsmith and sculptor. In his autobiography he describes his personal attendance at a conjuration performed in Rome.

Cham-Zoroaster

According to legend, the first magician to appear after the Flood.

Chymierastes, J. C.

Eighteenth century alchemist.

Cobham, Eleanor

Fifteenth century. Wife of Humphrey, Duke of Gloucester. Accused of witchcraft and necromancy. Associated with Margery Jourdain, called the Witch of Eye. Banished for life to Isle of Man.

Craca

Mediaeval witch who changed food into stone. Mentioned by Danish chronicler Saxo Grammaticus.

Crollius, Osvaldus

Seventeenth century alchemist. Follower of Paracelsus.

Crowley, Aleister
(1875-1947)

Scottish Satanist and occultist. Founder of cult based on mystic principles, in violent opposition to Christianity. In London he established a Satanic temple, and another one in Italy. Women were involved obscenely in his occult practices. He edited an esoteric journal, published poetry, and wrote a treatise *Magick in Theory and Practice,* published in Paris, 1929. He claimed to be a reincarnation of Edward Kelley, the associate of Dr. John Dee the occultist. A black magic ritual was performed over his grave by his devotees. He is the protagonist of W. Somerset Maugham's novel *The Magician.*

Dashwood, Sir Francis

Occultist, 18th century. Organizer and Superior of a lewd Satanic circle known as the Medmenham Franciscans.

Dee, Dr. John
(1527-1608)

English scholar and mathematician. Studied in Europe. Interested in alchemy, astrology, and arcane lore. Involved in imprisonment for casting horoscopes and practicing enchantment against Mary, Queen of England. As a government agent, he was later sent on service to Europe, where he became associated with Edward Kelley, magician, in necromantic acts, including crystalomancy.

A WITCHES' HOUSE

In this sixteenth century woodcut, witches are making preparations to attend the Sabbat, their seasonal assembly. One witch is flying through the chimney. Another is already mounted on her broomstick. Witches were credited with the power of levitation, flight or movement through the air.

A KNIGHT VISITS A WITCHES' HOUSE

The usual reason for a knight to consult a witch was to secure a love potion.
Olaus Magnus was a sixteenth century Swedish chronicler.

OLD-MAID WITCH

The illustration represents a witch spinning, an occupation often associated with magic rites, spells, and incantations.

(Engraving by Holbein, sixteenth century German artist)

SYMBOLISM OF THE OPERATIONS OF THE PHILOSOPHER'S STONE
The Alchemic Sublimation. One of the aims of the medieval alchemists was the transmutation of base metals into gold.
(From *Figures d'Abraham Juif*: a medieval grimoire)
Bibliothèque Nationale, Paris.

Author of *Liber Mysteriorum*—Book of Mysteries. His speculum or mirror, one of his magic properties, is now in the British Museum.

Delrio, Martin

Sixteenth century Spanish demonographer. Notorious for the prosecution of sorcerers. Author of *Disquisitionum Magicarum Libri Sex*, published in Louvain, 1599.

Diodorus of Catania

Ancient sorcerer, noted for his power of fascination. Buried alive in an oven.

Dipsias

Witch skilled in herbal lore, necromancy, whirling magic wheels, flying. Mentioned by Roman poet Ovid.

Earl of Bothwell

Scottish noble, 16th century. Grand Master of a sodality or coven of witches.

Elich, Philip Ludwig

Sixteenth century German demonographer. Author of *Daemonomagia*, published in Frankfurt, 1607.

Epimenides

Ancient Cretan philosopher, also reputed magician.

Erichtho

Witch skilled in necromancy and all phases of the Black Arts. She appears in the Roman epic poem *Pharsalia*, by Lucan (39-65 A.D.).

Faustus, Dr. Johannes

Mediaeval German magician. Prolific author of books on witchcraft. Reputed to have been the greatest necromancer of his age. His occult performances became incorporated into legendary tales and grimoires. Rembrandt has an etching of Faust, represented as engaged in magic operation.

Fian, John

Scottish schoolmaster and sorcerer. Burned at Edinburgh, 1591.

Flamel, Nicholas

French alchemist who flourished in the 16th century.

Flaque, Louis Eugène

French sorcerer and Kabalist who flourished in the nineteenth century.

Fludd, Robert

(1574-1637)

English mystic and Kabalist. Author of *Mosaical Philosophy* and *Summum Bonum*, treatises in defence of the Black Arts.

[201]

Forman, Dr.

Seventeenth century astrologer and magician. Practiced image magic at court of King James VI of Scotland.

Gafferel, Jacques

(1601-1681)

French magician who acted as librarian to Cardinal Richelieu.

Gaufridi, Louis

Wizard known as the Prince of Sorcerers. Executed in 1611, in France.

Gerbert, Pope Sylvester II

Reputed to have been proficient in magic. Inventor of a bronze head that gave oracular responses. Also practiced necromancy.

Gilles de Rais

French nobleman, 15th century. After squandering fortune, he attempted to retrieve his wealth by magic and necromantic means, for which he was executed.

Glanvil, Joseph

(1636-1680)

English minister of religion. Demonographer. Author of treatise on witchcraft, published in 1668.

Gnostics

Adherents of a doctrine composed of Babylonian, Persian, Egyptian, and Christian elements, along with occult features. Long considered as sorcerers.

Gobryas

Ancient Chaldean magician.

Gowdie, Isobel

'Queen of Scottish witches' flourished in 17th century, at Auldearne. Reputedly bore on her shoulder the Devil's Mark. Made voluntary confession of witchcraft, 1662.

Graterakes, Valentine

Seventeenth century Irish physician who used occult means in his medical practice.

Gregory VI

Pope reputed to have been skilled in sorcery.

Grierson, Isobel

Scottish witch. Burned at stake; ashes scattered to the winds, 1607.

Grillando, Paolo

Italian judge, 16th century. Author of a treatise on sorcerers, divination, and analogous occult practices.

Gross, Allison

In Scottish ballad, an ugly witch who cast spells on persons resistant to her will.

Grossetête, Robert

Also called Robert of Lincoln, 13th century. Prominent in mathematical sciences. Also had reputation for magic. Invented head of brass that uttered oracular prophecies.

Guazzo, Francesco Maria

Italian priest and demonographer, 17th century. Author of *Compendium Maleficarum*, Witches' Manual.

Guibourg

Eighteenth century French abbé who was involved in the occult practices of Madame de Montespan: executed.

Guido de Monteroquer

Demonographer. Author of *Manipulus Curatorum*, 1333.

Guillaume de Paris

Mediaeval magician. With demoniac aid, he fashioned articulate statues.

Hacks, Charles

German physician of nineteenth century. Reputed author, under pseudonym of Dr. Bataille, of *Le Diable au dix-neuvième siècle—The Devil in the Nineteenth century*, recounting personal occult experiences and the prevalence of Satanism.

Hakim

Also known as Mocanna. Follower of Mohammed who assumed miraculous powers. Created a moon that rose out of a sacred well and diffused its beams for miles around. Tradition that he dissolved in a bath prepared with his own ingredients, leaving nothing but a lock of his hair.

Harries, Dr. John

Nineteenth century Welsh physician and diviner. Possessor of an infamous *Book of Magic*.

Hecate

In Greek and Roman mythology, a triple goddess, patroness of witchcraft. First mentioned by the Greek poet Hesiod. Represented as being accompanied by dead souls, while dogs howl at her nocturnal approach. Called by the Greek dramatist Queen of the Ghost-World. Her statues were of triple form: as Selene, the moon, in heaven; Artemis, the huntress, on earth; Persephone, queen of hell. She was associated with unspeakable rites and sacrifices. Her emissaries were The Silent Watchers of the Night, Empusas, foul female demons, and a ghastly ghoul called Mormo.

Hermes Trismegistus

Hermes Thrice Greatest. The designation of Thoth, Egyptian god, as the master of alchemical art. Reputedly, he originated works on alchemy, astrology, and magic.

Hermotimus

Also called Hermodorus of Clazomene, ancient Greek reputed to have faculty of leaving his body and returning at will.

Hildebrand, Pope Gregory VIII

Pope reputed to have been skilled in sorcery and necromancy.

Hu-Jum-Sin

Chinese alchemist and occultist.

Iamblicus

(250-325 A.D.)

Neoplatonist philosopher. Author of *The Mysteries of the Egyptians, Chaldeans, and Assyrians,* a defense of witchcraft, still extant.

Iannes et Iambres

Egyptian magicians at court of Pharaoh who competed with Moses' occult skill.

Idris

In Welsh legend, a magician-giant. His name is topographically commemorated in Cader-Idris, the Chair of Idris, a hollow area on a Welsh mountain peak.

Imhetep

Egyptian magician-priest of Memphis.

Isaac of Holland

Alchemist who flourished in the fifteenth century A.D.

Jechiel, Rabbi

Physician and Kabalist who lived in reign of Saint Louis of France. He possessed a magic lamp that required no replenishment: also a nail that produced flaming agony in his enemies.

John XX

Pope reputed to have been skilled in magic.

Johnson, Margaret

Seventeenth century witch of Lancashire. Charged with converse with the Devil, who usually came to her in the form of a cat.

Julianus

Ancient magician, also known as Theurgus, the Necromancer. Reputed to have banished plague from Rome by occult means.

Khamuas

Egyptian magician, son of Rameses II.

Khunrath, Heinrich

German physician and alchemist, flourished in 16th century.

Knights Templar

In Middle Ages, an association of knights, farmers, and men in holy orders, under Cistertian-reformed Benedictine rule. In the 14th century, they were charged with Satanic practices.

Koh Hung

(4th century A.D.)

Chinese magician. Author of *Pao Poh-Tsze*, a manual on charms.

Kramer, Heinrich

Co-author, with Jacob Sprenger, both Dominicans, of *Malleus Maleficarum*—The Witches' Hammer, published in 15th century. This book, containing rules for detecting witches, constituted the ecclesiastical basis for discovering and punishing magic practices.

Kyteler, Lady Alice

Irish witch of the fourteenth century. Charged with sorcery and poisoning her four husbands. The record of her trial is extant.

Lamont, Marie

Scottish witch. Tried in 1662. Confessed to Sabbat meetings, service with the Devil, and transformation into cat.

L'Ancre, Pierre de

Demonographer, died 1630. Instrumental in condemning to death many victims on charge of sorcery. Author of *Le Livre des Princes* and *L'Incrédulité et Mescréance du Sortilège*, Paris, 1622.

La Voisin, Catherine

French witch, fortune-teller, and dispenser of love philtres, 17th century. She was involved in the occult and Satanic practices of Madame de Montespan.

Libanius

Magician who, during a siege of the city of Ravenna, in Italy, by the Roman Emperor Constantius, overpowered the enemy forces by magic means.

Libo Drusus

Roman necromancer. Mentioned by the Roman historian Tacitus.

Lilith

In Assyrian demonology, a female demon. In Talmudic legend, Adam's first wife. Represented as winged, with dishevelled hair.

Lotapes

Ancient wizard. Attached to Pharaoh's court.

[205]

Lully, Raymund

(1235-1315)

Spanish alchemist and Kabalist. Reputed to have transmuted base metal into gold, called after him aurum Raymundi.

Marmarus of Babylonia

Ancient Babylonian magician.

Martines de Pasqually

Hermetic and mystic who flourished in France in the 18th century.

Mary the Jewess

An alchemist who belongs to the fourth century A.D. Her name is still associated with the term bain-marie, used in chemistry.

Master John

Necromancer who flourished in the 14th century. Involved in plotting the death of Edward II of England by Black Magic.

Maternus, Julius Firmicus

Roman writer, 4th century A.D. Author of treatise, in eight books, on astrology and magic, entitled *Mathesis*.

Medea

In Greek and Roman mythology, witch whose powers embraced rejuvenation, invisibility, skill in drugs, philtres, herbal lore.

Megain, Perrenon

French witch of the 17th century.

Melampus

Ancient Greek writer. Author of two treatises on divination.

Merlin

Wizard associated, in the Middle Ages, with Arthurian cycle. Reputedly born of nightmare demons.

Meroë

Thessalian witch who appears in the *Metamorphoses*, novel pervaded by witchcraft, written by Roman novelist Apuleius (c. 123 A.D. Date of death uncertain).

Mme. de Montespan

A mistress of Louis XIV of France. In order to retain the king's dying love, she practiced occult and Satanic rites, participating in an obscene Amatory Mass, in the concoction of philtres, and, according to historical chronicles, in child sacrifice as well. Among her accomplices were a certain Abbé Guibourg, Lesage, an alchemist, and Catherine La Voisin, a notorious witch.

Mora, Pietro

Milanese physician of 17th century. Also Satanist, alchemist, wizard, astrologer.

Nectanebus

King of Egypt in fourth century B.C. A noted magician, he was skilled in concocting philtres, in astrology, divination, and the casting of runes. He made wax figures of his forces and of enemy forces, and by observing their movements in a bowl of Nile water, he forecast his own victory. In another instance, he succeeded in circumventing disaster by a timely escape.

Nider, Johannes

(17th century)

Demonographer. Author of *Formicarius,* published in 1691. Book 5 deals with witchcraft.

Nostradamus

(1503-1566)

French physician, astrologer, and seer, whose actual name was Michel de Notre-Dame. Author of *Centuries,* series of poetic predictions that foretold personal and national events whose oc-

currence coincided remarkably with his prognostications. Attached to court of Catherine de Medici, where he continued his cryptic predictions, including his own death.

Oenothea

Ancient priestess-witch, mentioned by the Roman novelist and occultist Apuleius.

Osthanes

According to the Roman Encyclopedist, Pliny the Elder (1st century A.D.), Osthanes was the first writer on magic. He accompanied Xerxes in his expedition against Greece.

Pamphile

Witch who appears in the *Metamorphoses* of Apuleius, the Roman novelist.

Pamphilos

Chaldean magician. Mentioned by medical writer Galen, 2nd century A.D.

Paracelsus

(c. 1490-1541)

German physician, magus, and astrologer, whose actual name was Theophrastus Bombast von Hohenheim. Traveled throughout Europe, practicing medicine, occultism, alchemy, prognostications. Wrote on sylphs, salamanders, nymphs: incorporating mystic elements into Germanic folk legends.

Noted for his magic speculum used in divination, for making which he offered detailed instructions.

Pazalas

Ancient Chaldean magician, to whom were attributed, later, collections of prophecies and charms.

Pendragon, Uther

Warlock who appears in Welsh legend.

Perkins, William
(1558-1602)

Cambridge Puritan, of Christ's College, Author of *A Discourse of the Damned Art of Witchcraft*. Valuable source for study of witchcraft in seventeenth century England. Illustrates influence of Puritan pulpit in disseminating fear of the Black Art.

Peter of Abano
(c. 1250-1310)

Italian physician. As a young man, he was initiated into occult lore by a sorcerer. Traveled in Europe, performing thaumaturgic feats. Charged by Inquisition with practicing Black Arts, he was sent to prison, where he died. Author of *The Elements of Magic* or *The Heptameron*.

Porta, Giovanni Battista della
(1538-1615)

Italian physician, interested in witchcraft. Author of *Natural Magic*, in twenty books, dealing particularly with alchemy. Founded in Naples Academy of the Secrets of Nature.

Postel, Guillaume de
(1510-1581)

French astrologer, Kabalist. In Paris, became professor of Oriental languages and mathematics. Traveled and lectured, claiming to have received revelation in the stars. Imprisoned by Inquisition. After escaping, he returned to his professorship. Forced to flee to convent, where he died. Author of *The Key of Things Kept Secret from the Foundation of the World*.

Priests of Sekhnet

Ancient Egyptian priest—magicians.

Pythia

Ancient Greek priestess—prophetess. Medium for oracular utterances of the gods while in a trance induced by incense fumes.

Richelieu, Duc de
(1585-1642)

Armand Jean du Plessis de Richelieu. Apart from his prominence as a statesman, he engaged in magic arts.

Ripley, George

English occultist and alchemist of 15th century. Reputed to have achieved transmutation of metals.

Rocail

Reputedly younger brother of Seth, son of Adam. By magic means, erected a palace peopled with statues that performed functions of human beings.

Sabellicus, Georgius

Magician and necromancer, 15th century. Self-styled The Most Accomplished, a second Faustus, the spring and center of necromantic art, astrologer, magician, consummate in cheiromancy, and in agromancy, pyromancy, and hydromancy inferior to none that ever lived.

Sadur and Ghadur

According to Arab legend, two magicians who challenged Moses' magic skill.

Sagana

Roman witch. Mentioned by Roman poet Horace. Associated with witch Canidia.

Saint-Germain

In the 18th century, the Count of Saint-Germain was a Man of Mystery. Attached to court of Louis XV of France. Claimed to be 2000 years old. Known to speak and write a dozen Oriental and western languages. Adept in alchemy. Reputed to have achieved invisibility, and to have corresponded, after his putative death, with French nobility. Author of occult book entitled *La Très Sainte Trinosophie*—The Most Holy Triple Philosophy.

Salvius Julianus

Roman Emperor of 2nd century A.D. Adept in magic.

Sammonicus, Quintus Serenus

Roman physician of the 3rd century A.D. Employed magic in his medical practice.

Sampson, Agnes

"Wise wife of Keith." Notorious Scottish witch of the sixteenth century.

Schröpfer, Johann Georg

(1730-1774)

German necromancer. Practiced witchcraft against his personal enemies and initiated many followers into occult arts. Died a suicide.

Scot, Michael

(c. 1175-1232)

Scottish magician. Attached to court of Emperor Frederick II. Author of many books on necromancy, incantations, alchemy, divination, oneiroscopy. Acquired legendary reputation for skill in wizardry and his occult experiences. Mentioned by Dante.

Setnau Kha-em-Uast

Ancient Egyptian prince, skilled in occult practices.

Sibly, Ebenezer

English physician, 18th century. Author of *New and Complete Illustration of the Occult Sciences*, published in 1790. The book confirms a belief in occult powers and demoniac forces.

Simon Magus

A sorcerer.
But there was a certain man, called Simon, which beforetime in the same city used sorcery, and bewitched the people of Samaria.

Acts of the Apostles 8

A pupil of Dositheus. According to legend, he had the power of levitation and of mass hypnotism. He reappears in Irish folklore as Simon the Druid. Justin Martyr (105-165 A.D.) refers to him:

A certain Simon, a Samaritan of Gitton, who in the reign of Claudius Caesar performed works by the magic arts of demons.

Sinclair, George
(1654-1696)

Scottish professor of mathematics and philosophy. Author of *Satan's Invisible World Discovered*.

Sinistrari, Ludovico Maria d'Ameno
(1622-1701)

Italian demonographer. Author of *De La Démonalité et des animaux incubes et succubes*. Translated into French in 1876.

Smith, Isobel

Scottish witch. Tried for witchcraft, 1629.

Solomon

In the history of witchcraft, the Arch Magician.

In the centuries that followed the death of King Solomon, and particularly in those mediaeval ages steeped in mystic lore and arcane experimentations, the Biblical monarch had lost his ethnic identification, his territorial exclusiveness. He had become less of a monarch, more of a potent necromancer. He had become, in fact, a legendary figure, dominating the entire cosmos, associated with dark forces, sometimes malefic, always effectual. In his *Antiquities of the Jews*, that strange personality, Josephus, in the first century A.D., had already alluded to the King's expertness in exorcism, his intimacy with the demons of the Infernal Regions, his amazing control of the interterrestrial elements. King Solomon's name, his attributes, the symbols of his office and his exploits had become absorbed into the magic folklore of Ethiopia, into the gnomic traditions of China, into the legends of India and the Ukraine,

MATTHEW HOPKINS, WITCH-FINDER

A seventeenth century English lawyer who launched a wide campaign for the extermination of witches. It was said that he was instrumental in the execution of thousands of witches.

SATAN AS A GOAT

In medieval witchcraft, the Archfiend Satan is represented as a goat to whom homage is paid by all the practitioners of the Black Art.

SATAN IS BOUND FOR A THOUSAND YEARS

Satan is here represented in a characteristic form: partly human, and winged

SATAN INSPIRES IDOLATRY

Witchcraft was believed to be a survival of ancient pagan rites. Hence in the Middle Ages it
was pursued with bitter enmity by the Church.
Witchcraft was in essence associated with the
Antichrist.

DIABOLUS IS OVERTHROWN

Diabolus is Satan as a devourer of two things,
body and soul.

THE WITCH OF ENDOR

Saul before the witch, who exorcised the spirit of David.
(Painting by Salvatore Rosa, 17th century Italian artist.)

Louvre, Paris.

Bulgaria and Malaya, Ireland and Estonia. Firdausi, the Persian poet, wrote a poetic life of Solomon, called Suleimen Nameh. Other Persian writers, as well as Turkish and Arab—among them Ishag ibn Ibrahim, Ahmad el Kermani, Jalal-ud-din, and Saas-ed-din—have enriched the Bible narrative with fabulous tales of Solomon's power over gnomes and undines, salamanders, and elves. Even the Koran finds occasion to hint at the necromantic activities of the monarch, mentioning that the Djinn worked under Solomon's supervision.

King Solomon's seal and his lamp, his magic cauldron and his very throne, guarded by sculptured lions that could shriek and howl, have been the age-old theme of numberless Asian tales, still bruited in the dusty caravanserais, in the teeming bazaars.

King Solomon was still functionally a king, but he was predominantly an arch thaumaturgist. It was rumored and written secretly and in furtive scrolls that the power of the king was derived from sinister, evil sources; that, somehow and at some unknown time, Solomon had abandoned his ancient tribal god and had wantonly attached himself to false, seductive pagan deities, to Ashtoreth, that obscene divinity, to Milcom of the Ammonites, to Chemosh the Moabite god. Furthermore, apocryphal texts and dark tradition asserted that Solomon was ultimately punished for his pagan blasphemies by being condemned to be eaten by 10,000 ravens every day, everlastingly.

He was now pictured, by the people of many disparate nations, as equipped with a magic carpet that transported his entire armies through the air. He was represented as conversant with the tongues of the birds and the beasts of the fields. He comprehended the humming of insects, could interpret the rustle of forest leaves, the sounds made by undersea creatures. He was a supreme polyhistor, who had embraced every area of knowledge. He was a mighty alchemist. He was master too of the demon world that built his Temple. The Djinn, through the agency of the arch fiend Asmodeus, brought him the Shamir. It was a tiny worm, no bigger than a barley grain, created in the twilight of the Friday in the week of Creation; and it helped to build the Temple without the use of tools. Lastly, Solomon was the putative author of numberless works on divination and goety, on astrology and necromantic rites.

Both in the West and in the Orient King Solomon had assumed a universal personality, lordship of the occult realms. He was the final reference, the arbiter of witchcraft, for all the warlocks and Satanists, for the alchemists and exorcists of the middle centuries. According to the most famous necromancers of those dramatic and restless times, Solomon's Lamp was the palpable means by which the spirits of the Infernal Regions—Abigor and Alastor, Baalzephon, Lucifuge Rofocale, and Zapan—could be invoked. Quite recently, one of the romantic "thrillers" by Sax Rohmer made the motif of the plot revolve around the Seal of Solomon, the long lost talismanic periapt that gave unlimited power to its possessor. It was in the form of two interlaced triangles, a supremely effective instrument of wizardry, recommended by the celebrated Peter of Abano for summoning spirits. In mediaeval woodcuts and similar illustrations of magic rites, the Seal of Solomon appears prominently, unfailingly, an essential element in the successful consummation of alchemical transmutations of metals, planetary augury, and spell-binding. Solomon's Mirror, also, which was actually a polished plate, was one of the basic accessories of the sorcerers engaged in their cryptic divinatory rituals.

In the eleventh century the name of Solomon had acquired a sinister significance, anathema to the ecclesiastical authorities. A certain Leontius of Constantinople, for example, in a public sermon, declared that the King had dominion over demons; while Gregentius, an Archbishop, asserted that Solomon enclosed demons in urns, sealed the urns, and buried them in the ground.

From the time of his very birth, that provoked the Demon Iblis into a passion at the thought of the coming ascendancy of this supermundane being, King Solomon's legendary life was a sequence of momentous episodes based on his magic skills, his divinatory powers, his necromantic wizardry.

Asmodeus, king of the demons, offered to show Solomon a fantastic creature. He drew out of the depths of the earth a two-headed monster, one of the descendants of Cain who lived in a world of their own. The creature settled in Jerusalem, had normal children, except the seventh, who, like his father, had two heads. On the death of the father, the two-headed son claimed two shares of the inheritance. But Solomon, inspired by demoniac ingenuity, blindfolded the monstrosity and poured boiling water over one head. The two heads in unison shrieked their duality, and the inheritance was consequently rightly divided.

By means of the Philosopher's Stone Solomon was able to secure dominion over the Djinn, subduing them to such a degree that they dined with him daily, seated at iron tables. But even Solomon had to be careful. He always drank out of crystal cups, for he found that when his glance was obscured by a metal vessel, the demons stuck out their tongues at him in derision.

Once Solomon chained the powerful demon Sachra Elmarid to a mountain side, to assert his dominance. In every commentary, too, in every Black Book of Magic, the feats of the King are multiplied and heightened, so that the mystic Kabala and the Asiatic apologues all merge into a tumultuous laudation of the supreme adept, no longer a Semite, but common to all mankind, a monarch turned Promethean, but also, on occasion, diverted from beneficent deeds and associating in tenebrous ways with malefic powers.

The Magic Carpet of Solomon transcended all the unbridled imagination of the Arabian Nights. It was sixty miles long, sixty miles wide. The material was of green silk, interwoven with gold, ornamented with rich and intricate designs. The entire royal army was carried on it, along with slaves, kitchen apparatus, stables, for horses and camels. At the king's summons the carpet appeared at the city gate. When he had seated himself, the prince of men, Ramirat the prince of demons, the lion prince of beasts, and the eagle prince of birds installed themselves around the monarch. Overhead flew every kind of bird, in dense formation, as a protective screen against the sun. At the king's command, the wind raised the carpet and swept it over any desired region, while the magician-king gazed down upon all living things under his dominion.

In these aerial flights he experienced encounters. He met birds that spoke. He discovered in labyrinthine castles long-imprisoned images that shrieked their hostility and dread of Solomon. He came upon apes dressed like men and living in houses.

In the Middle Ages many grimoires and other types of magic manuals were, in spite of doubtful reliability and unwarranted authenticity, current as the work of Solomon himself. There was, to begin with, the Testament of Solomon, attributed to some period between the second and the fifth century A.D., yet referable, in the popular and even the demonographers' view, to the king himself. There was, of course, no other means of identification of the origin, authorship, or validity of the Testament; which implies that the book was normally accepted at its face value. It is a corpus of magic lore, the final source of consultation for all practitioners, every thaumaturgic adept. The Testament is in the form of a putative autobiographical narrative, each section introduced with: I, Solomon. It reveals the mysteries of demonology, explaining Solomon's techniques, how he achieved his secret knowledge, the visit of the Witch Queen of Sheba, and similar apocryphal but widespread features of his turbulent life.

Solomon's ring, again, engraved with the mystic pentalpha, was a means of subduing all the infernal demons. An obscure manual, called Lemegeton or the Lesser Key of Solomon, which is preserved in manuscript form in the British Museum, describes in minute detail the hierarchy of these infernal powers, consisting of seventy-two demons of varying ranks and functions.

But possibly the greatest of all the Solomonic treatises is the Clavicle or Key of Solomon, the source of all mediaeval magic. It was in the hands not only of sorcerers, but, as late as the seventeenth century, of scholars, courtiers, and physicians. It presents directions on conjuration; on how to become invisible; how to discover hidden treasure. It is black magic incarnate, hinting at macabre and blasphemous performances, calling for the fat of a dead man as an ingredient in weird concoctions, or demanding winding sheets for sinister rites.

The Solomonic legends are by no means dead. They vary in tone and motive, and assume protean forms. They go deeply underground; but they reappear in every age, refreshed and once again challenging after their long hibernation.

Sons of Cham-Zoroaster

Four sons of Cham-Zoroaster were: Cush, Mizraim, Phut, Canaan, who each controlled magic in his respective territory—Africa, Egypt, the desert tribes, Phoenicia.

[213]

Sprenger, Jacob

Co-author, with Heinrich Kramer, both Dominicans, of *Malleus Maleficarum*— The Witches' Hammer, published in 15th century. This book, containing rules for detecting witches, constituted the ecclesiastical basis for discovering and punishing magic practices. The Malleus went through many editions, in German, French, Italian.

Stevenote de Audebert

French witch who, at her trial in 1616, produced a contract she had made with Satan.

Style, Elizabeth

English witch who, in 1664, publicly confessed, at her trial, to a pact made with the Devil.

Tarmoendas

Ancient Assyrian magician.

Tchatcha-em-ankh

Egyptian priest—magician of the 4th millennium B.C. By magic incantations he raised the water level of a lake.

Theodoris of Lemnos

Greek witch. Mentioned by the orator Demosthenes, 4th century B.C., who states that she was condemned to death for enchantment. The Greek historian Herodotus mentions that Lemnos was notorious for sorcery.

Tiresias

Ancient Greek soothsayer afflicted by gods with blindness, but endowed with prophetic gift. Understood language of birds, art of divination, necromancy.

Trithemius, Johannes
(1462-1516)

German Abbot of Spanheim. Friend of Agrippa. Author of works on alchemy and magic and *Liber Octo Quaestionum*, which classifies demons. Reputed to have exorcised Mary of Burgundy, wife of Emperor Maximilian.

Tuchet, Eleanor

Wife of prominent lawyer, 17th century. Professed prophetic faculty with aid of spirits. Author of *Strange and Wonderful Predictions*.

Vellada

Ancient priestess—prophetess of Germany. Mentioned by the Roman historian Tacitus.

Weishaupt, Adam

Illuminatus, adept in magic practices, 18th century.

Wierus, John

(1516-1588)

Surnamed Piscinarius, German magician who was a pupil of Agrippa. Author of *De Praestigiis Daemonum et incantationibus ac veneficiis,* a treatise on demoniac activities, incantations and sorceries by aid of philtres and similar means.

Zaratus of Media

Ancient Chaldean magician.

Zlito

Sorcerer of 14th century. Attached to court of King Wenceslaus of Bohemia. Reputed to have had skill in levitation.

Chapter X

*Goetic diversions - Divination
Astrology - Levitation
Alchemy*

Chapter 10

GOETIC DIVERSIONS — DIVINATION
ASTROLOGY — LEVITATION
ALCHEMY

Introduction

Stemming from the Black Arts, and involving goetic premises, assuming the techniques and conditions of occult practices are alchemy, divination, astrology, and levitation.

In the course of time, alchemy, which in its beginnings implied conjurations, merged into valid scientific procedures. Primarily, it was enwrapped in thaumaturgy. It aimed at unique, non-normally attainable consummations by the urgent means of goetic devices in which, however, the motif was entirely rational in its objective. Alchemy, in short, was the quick road toward the manipulation and control of matter. But it was always a road, darkly meandering, that never reached a terminus.

Divination is associated with occult powers, secretive experiments that attempt, with reputed success, to break through the barriers of cosmic design, the architectonics of nature. Divination predicates investigation of the future, discovery of the unknown, recovery of hidden objects, and the interpretation of dreams, or oneiroscopy. Its methods are varied, and range over the entire field of magic apparatus. Animals and insects may be used as the bearers of occult messages. The spirits may be consulted. Entrails of animals are observed. The flights of birds have their specific denotation. Objects and living beings, grimaces and laughter, the wearing of clothes and the flicker of flame, serpents and twigs, the navel, eggs and ashes betoken, in the sphere of divination, a particular portent, an accredited omen. Aeromancy is a method that

[219]

observes atmospheric conditions. Alectryomancy employs a cock that pecks grain placed on letters of the alphabet. This practice is dramatically described in Thornton Wilder's *The Ides of March*. Messages, enclosed in balls of dough, become prophetic of the future. This method, known as aleuromancy, is still in use among the Chinese. Salt is used in alomancy, while wheat or barley cakes, used in a kind of trial by ordeal in the Middle Ages, constituted alphitomancy. The caul on a child's head, at birth, was examined in amniomancy. The Roman Emperor Julian, the Apostate, is said to have consulted the intestines of sacrificed children: a method known as anthropomancy. Even objects that lie about haphazardly were fit for mantic purposes. The practice was called apantomancy.

Sitting on a shield, within the magic circle, and pronouncing conjurations, the karcist falls into a trance during which he makes mantic revelations. This is aspidomancy. Knucklebones are used in astragalomancy; in axinomancy, an axe; in belomancy, arrows; in bibliomancy, chapters or lines in a book, selected at random, are consulted. When the wizard burned branches of brier and vervain, on which were inscribed questions to be answered, the procedure was called botanomancy. The very fact that each specific method, or variant, had a name, testifies to the prevalence and widespread recognition of divinatory practices. The prophetic inspiration of Brizo, a goddess of sleep, gave rise to brizomancy. Capnomancy involves wreaths of smoke: catoptromancy, a lens or mirror: a technique known to the Greeks and Romans, and practiced by the Incas and the Dyaks of Borneo. An exhaustive listing would become overwhelming. Let there be mentioned hepatoscopy and critomancy, daphnomancy and empyromancy, ichthyomancy and lampadomancy, margaritomancy and molybdomancy. In essence, the purpose was always to interpret the futurity from the appearance or juxtaposition or action or condition or multiplicity of objects: leaves, entrails, fire, shoulder blades of animals, straws, the howling of dogs, wine, sounds of water, even the pace of a horse. It was, in short, a kind of frenzied prophecying run wild, bent desperately on utilizing every conceivable article, sound, sight, for proleptic visionary efficacy.

The study of the heavens is the oldest pastime of man. The ancient Chinese, the Chaldeans and Egyptians, the Hebrews and Greeks inquisitively surveyed the heavens. But with a purpose. To wrest from the myriad stars and planets, from the conjunction of certain constellations and the recurrence of planets in particular quarters, some coherent, rational pattern of the cosmic scheme. Astrology established various systems of relationships among the heavenly bodies, and from these relationships the adepts deduced corresponding relationships in the affairs of men. Such surveys and examinations, in the course

[220]

CRYSTALLOMANCY
A form of divination by means of crystal gazing.
(Painting by G. P. Jacomb-Hood, modern English artist.)

IDEALISTIC DEMONIAC CONCEPTION
The three demons in the illustration are reputedly powerful spirits in the Satanic hierarchy.

THE DEVIL PRESIDES AT A SABBAT

A Sabbat, or Sabbath, was a gathering of witches to do homage to their Master, the Satanic Archfiend. Satan, in these medieval assemblies, was represented, as he is in the illustration, in the form of a goat. In the foreground a child is being sacrificed. The illustration appears in Pierre de Lancre's *L'Incrédulité et Mescréance du Sortilège*, a seventeenth century work on demonography.

DEPARTURE FOR THE SABBAT

The Sabbat was an assembly of witches to do honor to the Master Fiend. Note the witch preparing an ointment to smear her body. Another witch is being anointed, to enable her to use levitation. A magic circle, mystically inscribed, a skull, familiars, spirits in animal form, surround the sorcerers.

(Teniers was a seventeenth century Dutch artist)

of the centuries, became so circumstantial, so minutely detailed and planned as to present a cohesive sequence, a formal astral design, a stellar pattern, whereby the future of human affairs, and the progression of the individual person, might be determined.

It was a spacious theory, a literally heavenly revelation: and the theory caught on, grew into an appreciable body of systematized knowledge, acquired profound practitioners, induced wide and continued credence among the peoples of all lands.

Hermes Trismegistus, Hermes the Thrice Greatest, the equated Thoth of the Egyptians, is the fountain head, the primary source of astral lore. Ptolemy the learned Egyptian produced his monumental texts on the subject, his Tetrabiblos in particular. Among the Romans, Firmicus Maternus published a treatise in eight books, still extant. Belephantes was known among the Chaldeans. In the fifth century A.D. appeared Avenar, a Jewish astrologer who studied the movements of the planets with a view to foretelling Messianic deliverers. The Middle Ages in Europe were aglow with notable astrologers: Dr. John Dee and Guillaume de Postel, Paracelsus and Nostradamus. And in India and China the kings themselves were equipped with the astrological faculties, and as kings-magicians-astrologers they held all past knowledge, and the misty future, in their omniscience.

The practice never died out, and man, panting to break through the obfuscating veil of dark futurity, at any risk, at any cost, searches for furtive means to read his destiny. Hence the contemporary scene, in every European country, in Africa orally, in the West similarly by oral and also written communication, remains absorbed in astrological anxieties; and passes on the knowledge of professional astrologers to eager clients, while the monthly horoscopes, in newspapers and periodicals, and in bulky manuals, entice the hapless human to creep toward the tempting or ominous fringe of the future.

Levitation is the self-raising of objects, or of the human body, into the air. This practice, which opposes the laws of gravitation, as all witchcraft opposes the physical laws, was uniformly attributed to witches. By transvection, riding on a broomstick or similar means of conveyance, they sailed through the skies on their nocturnal missions. Reputedly, in the seventeenth century, St. Joseph of Copertino, an Italian monk, flew, by means of auto-levitation, from the middle of a church to the tabernacle of the high altar, a distance of forty feet. In the mediaeval chronicles of witches on trial, their capacity for levitation is specifically recorded. The faculty is also known to be possessed by certain Tibetan priests.

[221]

Mystic Voice of the Gods: The Oracle

Among the ancient Greeks, the gods were real and manifest, endowed with human attributes, visible in human form. They dwelt in the clouds and the forests, in fields and valleys. They congregated on lofty Mount Olympus. They haunted rivers and springs and secluded fastnesses. Always, they were in contact with mortals, who were anxious to rend the veil of fate. Always, they communed and communicated with man. And man was invariably eager to discover the significance of those provocative communications, to pierce through into the will of the deities. When man was perplexed —and to the ancient Greeks all life was a sequence, with interludes, of hazards and alarms—he appeared for direction and spiritual guidance to these divinities.

The response of the god, at the instance of the beseeching visitant, was the oracle. The oracle was the voice of the deity, thundering upon man, steering him to a fated destination, at any given moment, through a dilemma, through the perils confronting him. Throughout Greece there were special shrines, dedicated to oracular revelations, associated with particular deities. Asclepius, god of healing, was consulted at valley-girt Epidaurus. Zeus, almighty ruler of the universe, had shrines at Olympia and Dodona, the latter nestling among the hills of Epirus. Apollo, the supreme god of prophetic utterance, dwelt at Argos, in Boeotia, at Didyma, and at Claros. Didyma, a few miles from Miletus, had a temple as early as the fifth century B.C., but it was destroyed during the invasion of the Persians. A century later, however, the cult of Apollo was restored, with the erection of the largest temple in all Greece. The sanctuary at Claros was likewise very ancient, dating back to proto-Hellenic times.

But of all such sanctified spots the most sacred, as well as the most frequented, was Delphi. Delphi was the omphalos or navel, the spiritual and geographical center of all Greece. It was a holy place from earliest antiquity. Here dwelt Phoebus Apollo. Here his priests watchfully guided worshippers. Here the voice of the divinity gave solace and tranquillity, decision and hope, to countless pilgrims. They were of all kinds, these suppliants, the frightened and the sick, Persian and Egyptian, Greek and foreign, an endless host of confused or questing humanity. The oracle was not confined to national or ethnic frontiers. For the voice of Apollo was universal, and his influence flowed beyond geographical barriers.

There were four major ways of divining the will of the gods. There was interpretation of dreams, through the agency of trained priests and diviners. There was the necromantic evocation of the spirits of the dead. Divination was also practiced by means of signs—such as the clashing of brazen cymbals, the rustling of oak leaves, the throwing of dice, drawing lots, and examination of the entrails of sacrificial victims. But the most widespread method was consultation of the oracle, the spoken will of the god.

There were, of course, techniques and rituals involving the approach of the god, the ministrations of the priests, the significance of the responses themselves. At Claros, for instance, the ritual of consultation had its own exclusive features. The mouthpiece of the god was the priest-prophet. He withdrew to a secluded grotto, where he drank the water of a sacred spring. Thereafter he pronounced the Apolline counsel in ambiguity-enfolded language. At Argos, the priestess, before making the divine pronouncement, drank the blood of a lamb. At Didyma, again, the priestess was seated on a wheel-shaped disc, and after bathing her feet and the hem of her robe in a spring, she inhaled the vapors issuing from it.

The procedure at Delphi, since it was the most impressive, the most celebrated of all oracular presentations, may be described as typical. The temple itself was highly ornamental in its architectural design. On the entrance walls texts were inscribed in gold lettering. According to tradition, these texts had been composed by the Seven Sages, ancient Greek philosophers. The texts included spiritual admonitions, among them the famous "Know Thyself." Within the temple stood a golden statue of Apollo himself, while around the spacious corridors were chapels, shrines, votive offerings, treasuries.

The god Apollo had, as his earthly counterpart, a young woman of honorable birth, who wore gold ornaments in her hair and flowing robes. In later times, the medium was a priestess over fifty years of age. The priestess was called a Pythia, in commemoration of Apollo's subjugation of a monstrous python.

After purification rites and due sacrifices, the suppliant made his request, either orally, or in writing. The priestess, directed by the attendant hierophants, went into a trance. This she did by inhaling the fumes from a flaming tripod. The fumes were probably hypnotic, issuing from hempen ingredients or from poppy leaves. When the fumes had penetrated, and the Pythia was no longer her normal self, she was said to have been entered by the god. The god now wrestled with her, as if she were a mare still chafing at the bit. She might writhe and contort herself, in a vain attempt to throw off the divine influence. But finally she succumbed, mastered by Apollo. In this frenzied state she now gave tongue to the god's decision. But she spoke in panting gasps, in staccato-fragmentary exclamations, in a frothing jumble of sounds and murmurings. The result was enigmatic and ambiguous to the votaries. But now the attendant priest stepped in. His function was to interpret the incoherent mouthings of the Pythia into a rational, meaningful sequence. Trained and experienced, he composed her utterances into versified form; or sometimes into subtle prose. If the omens were favorable, the Pythia performed her prophetic functions daily.

Yet there still remained a perplexity. Because the characteristic of the oracle was its invariable ambivalence. The oracle was never mistaken, because it was the voice of the god. But it was never, on the other hand, immediately and conclusively right, at first sight. It had cryptic undertones that held double meanings. For the oracle always offered two possible solutions, two possible prophetic confirmations, each containing a basis of truth. Which was the final, the completely true interpretation? On what did the essential interpretation depend? Who could discover that? The priest offered the oracle. The suppliant went off, to accept or carry out the implicit instructions of the god. If the result coincided with the manifest pronouncement of the divinity, most obviously, most evidently, the oracle was correct and valid. If the result was contrary to the petitioner's expectations or to the outcome of the question at issue, the petitioner had only to examine the oracle again. And this time, reading between the lines, and catching the subtle drift that branched into two opposing directions, he realized that the oracle spoke with a double tongue, that the oracle proposed two contingencies. And the event itself always demonstrated which meaning was the true, the valid meaning. Hence the oracle was always final, unquestionably impregnated with the divine truth. It was, it must be assumed, the foolhardiness or the imperceptive mind of the supplicant that had misread or misinterpreted the truth. For the truth, as the ancient Greeks were well aware, as the Orient is even now, is not one indivisible, homogeneous concept. It is a many-faceted thing, and derives its validity from man, not from itself.

Oracular responses have been preserved, through the ages, in literary texts and in inscriptions from Greece, Asia Minor, and elsewhere. Many are embedded in the works of antique Greek historians, such as Herodotus and Strabo, Plutarch—himself a priest of Apollo, and Pausanias. But there was always the fact of dubious oracles, for forged oracles frequently appeared. These forged oracles could, on account of their legendary re-

moteness, never be authentically verified. So that historical truth and imagination often conflicted.

In the course of time, collections of oracular confirmations were consulted, in temples and communal archives, on occasions of emergency. As a result, what had previously not appeared clear might on a second interpretation be fulfilled in a particular case. So that, in effect, the validity of the oracle was timeless, never in question, never impugned. It could be fulfilled, or would be fulfilled, at a given but indeterminate time, at the god's own discretion.

Now what types of questions, what problems, were submitted to oracular solution? Men came to seek counsel about marriage. Would it be favorable? Would there be children? Would married life be propitious? Or how might a commercial enterprise turn out? Would this mercantile venture be hazardous? All the puzzles and doubts that assail and beset the ordinary man in the routine of his daily life were the substance of oracular requests. Nothing was too enigmatic, nothing too personal, nothing too comprehensive to submit to the cosmic decision of Apollo. Towns and individuals, kings and communities, generals and peasants beseech answers. How shall plague be averted from the city? That question recurs with fatalistic insistence. How to survive famine that has devastated the crops? Is it advisable to found a particular colony, a new settlement in a strange land? Will this war be successful, and how long will it last? What is a cure for this sickness? The variety of appeals is infinite. A Greek tribal community wants to know why the fishing catch is so meager. One person asks for wages. A father begs for grandchildren. A remedy for madness is implored. How should a ghost be exorcised? Should the petitioner return home after a long absence? Give me, Apollo, a cure for poverty. Where should I settle, O Pythia? What career should I choose? What is my real parentage, asks a perplexed son. The Pythia must have been exposed to a battery of questions, answered from encyclopedic omniscience. Or her answers were of such a general nature as to suit the question itself.

And thus it actually was. For her answer came forth—final, infallible, true, but enigmatic. Croesus, wealthy king of Lydia in Asia Minor, was assaulted by the Persians. He sent to the Delphic oracle to find out the issue. A great kingdom would fall, declared the Pythia. Informed, Croesus was elated, because he envisioned the collapse of the Persian Empire. But it was his own kingdom that fell. And yet the oracle was true, and would have been true if the Persian Empire itself had fallen.

On another occasion, the oracle was asked how to find a treasure. Move every stone, answered the priestess, comprehensively. After a cosmic flood, Deucalion and his wife Pyrrha, sole survivors, asked the goddess Artemis to repeople the earth. The oracle replied: Depart from this temple and throw the bones of your great mother behind you. Deucalion interpreted the great mother as Mother Earth, and the bones as stones in the earth. They threw the stones behind them, and the stones turned into men and women. That, of course, is a mythological symbol, but it is a symbol that marks the essential truth of the oracle.

Again, the Spartans, at war with Arcadia, were told by the oracle that they would dance on conquered land, and piece it out among themselves. They did so, but with their own conquered land, and under conditions of bondage. The oracle is always final. The future is inescapable. But the key to that future, only the oracle held.

There is no real oral survival of the antique oracular techniques. But perhaps the consultation of the dark gypsy lady, equipped with crystal ball, comes closest in concept and intention to the Delphic oracle. In essence, however, there are procedures that offer similar results. Among the Persians, for instance, at the present day, the poetry of Firdausi is used in bibliomancy. It is regularly consulted, to find out what day is propitious for business, whether the next child will be a boy or a girl. Or one leafs through the Bible for advice. Or turns to the horoscope for what is virtually oracular pronouncements.

Oneiromancy in Egypt

And it came to pass in the morning that his spirit was troubled; and he sent and called for all the magicians of Egypt, and all the wise men thereof: and Pharaoh told them his dream but there was none that could interpret them unto Pharaoh.

Genesis 41.8.

Prognostication by Means of Arrows

For the King of Babylon stood at the parting of the way, at the head of the two ways, to use divination: he shook the arrows to and fro, he consulted the teraphim, he looked in the liver.

Ezekiel 21.21.

The name of the enemy was inscribed on the arrow. Shaking up the arrows in the quiver, the king directed the arrow at the enemy whose name was inscribed thereon. The technique is known as belomancy.

King Nebuchadnezzar's Dreams

Then the king commanded to call the magicians, and the astrologers, and the sorcerers, and the Chaldeans, for to shew the king his dreams. . . .

The Chaldeans answered before the king, and said, There is not a man upon the earth that can shew the king's matter: therefore there is no king, lord, nor ruler, that asked such things at any magician, or astrologer, or Chaldean.

Daniel 2.

Biblical Diviners

So the elders of Moab and the elders of Mid'ian departed with the fees for divination in their hand; and they came to Balaam, and gave him Balak's message. *Numbers* 22.7.

Jonah's Fate Decided by Lots

And they said every one to his fellow, Come, and let us cast lots that we may know for whose cause this evil is upon us. So they cast lots, and the lots fell upon Jonah. *Jonah* 7.

Biblical Diviners

And the Philistines called for the priests and the diviners and said, "What shall we do with the ark of the Lord? Tell us with what we shall send it to its place." *I Samuel* 6.2.

Divination by Balaam

And the elders of Moab and the elders of Midian departed with the rewards of divination in their hand; and they came unto Balaam and spake unto him the words of Balak.

And when Balaam saw that it pleased the Lord to bless Israel, he went not, as at other times, to seek for enchantments, but he set his face toward the wilderness. *Numbers* 22.24.

A Woman Diviner

A certain damsel possessed with a spirit of divination met us. *Acts* 16.16.

This occurred while Paul was at Philippi.

Chaldean Divination

More Credit, yet, is to Chaldeans giv'n; What they foretell, is deem'd to Voice of Heav'n.

Their Answers, as from Hammon's altar, come;

Since now the Delphian Oracles are dumb.

Juvenal (1st century A.D.), Roman Satirist. Translation by John Dryden.

CHALDEANS: Chaldea was anciently associated with magic.
HAMMON: Egyptian diety.
DELPHIAN ORACLES: prophetic utterances made by Sibyl in temple of Apollo at Delphi, in Central Greece.

Divination by Aid of Lamp

You go to a clean cell without light and you dig a new hole in an east wall, and you take a white lamp in which no minimum of gum water has been put, the wick being clean, and you fill it with genuine oasis oil, and you recite the spells of praising Ra at dawn in his rising, and you bring the lamp when lighted opposite the sun, and recite to it the spells as below four times, and you take it into the cell, you being pure, and the boy also, and you pronounce the spells to the boy, he not looking at the lamp, his eyes being closed, seven times. You put pure frankincense on the brazier and you put your finger on the boy's head, his eyes being closed. When you have finished you make him open his eyes towards the lamp: then he sees the shadow of the god about the lamps, and he inquires for you concerning that which you desire. You must do it at midday in a place without light. If it be that you are inquiring for a spirit damned, a wick of sail-cloth is what

you put in the lamp, and you fill it with clean butter. If it is some other business, a clean wick with pure genuine oil is that which you put in the lamp; if you will do it to bring a woman to a man, ointment of roses is that which you put in the lamp. You must lay the lamp on a new brick, and the boy also must sit on another brick with his eyes closed. You cry down into his head five times.

Demotic (Egyptian) Magic Papyrus. Translated by Griffith and Thompson.

Divination by means of lamp flames is known as Lampadomancy.

Man Has Power to Divine

There is, then, in the soul a power to presage which it has acquired from external sources and which has been made an integral part of it by the will of God.

Cicero (106-43 B.C.), Roman orator, statesman, philosopher. Author of *De Divinatione.*

Widespread Belief in Divination

So far as I am aware, there is not to be found anywhere a race of men, no matter how highly civilized and cultured, or, for that matter, how utterly savage and brutish, which is not firmly convinced that there are portents that point to coming events, and that certain persons are able to recognize these portents and to predict from them what the future holds in store.

Cicero (106-43 B.C.), Roman orator and philosopher. Author of *De Divinatione*, translated by H. M. Poteat.

Types of Diviners

And yet, there are certain rare spirits who have the power to rise above the demands of the flesh and with passionate concentration to devote themselves to the contemplation of the supernatural. Some of these men are able to prophesy, not under the inspiration of messages from on high, but by the employment of their own rational faculties. For instance, their knowledge of the laws of Nature makes it possible for them to predict coming events, such as great floods or the destruction of heaven and earth by fire, at some time in the future. Others, who spend their lives in the service of the state, as, for example, we know Solon of Athens did, have the vision to perceive the approach of despotism long before it actually arrives. We may declare that such men are 'farsighted,' that is, that they are able 'to see what is far away,' but there is no more reason why we should ascribe superhuman powers to them than to Thales of Miletus, who, in order to put to rout his detractors and to prove that even a philosopher could make money if he cared to do so, is said to have bought up the whole Milesian olive crop before the trees had begun to bloom. It is possible that he was so well informed upon the subject of olives that he knew the trees would produce abundantly. Incidentally, we are told that he was the first to predict the eclipse of the sun which occurred during the reign of Astyages.

Cicero (106-43 B.C.), Roman philosopher, author of *De Divinatione*.

Types of Divination Depend on Geographical Condition

I myself am of the opinion that the various races of men have been led to the choice of this or that type of divination by the very nature of their respective countries. The Egyptians and Babylonians, for instance, dwell upon level, far-spreading plains, with never a hill to cut off their view of the heavens; well, they have given themselves wholly to the study of the stars. The Etruscans, on the other hand, a profoundly religious folk and therefore punctilious and indefatigable in offering sacrifices, have always devoted their attention to the contemplation of entrails. And because the atmosphere of their part of Italy is thick and heavy, portents from the sky have appeared with great frequency; for the same reason amazing prodigies in the air and on the earth are constantly occurring, together with certain omens connected with the conception and birth of men and beasts. And so the Etruscans are the most adroit of all interpreters of portents. In fact, the peculiar force of each of these types of signs, as you often remark, is made quite plain by

[229]

the terms our canny forefathers employed for them. Thus, signs which 'make clear' are called ostenta; those which 'portend' are called portenta; those which 'point out' are called monstra; those which 'predict' are called prodigia. But the Arabians, Phrygians, and Cilicians spend most of their time pasturing their flocks and herds and roving the mountains and the plains, in winter and summer alike, and so they enjoy unusual opportunities for the study of the songs and the flights of birds; so do the Pisidians and our neighbors the Umbrians. Now the Carians—particularly the citizens of Telmessus, referred to previously —who dwell in a country which has a soil of unparalleled richness and fertility, in whose fecund depths strange things are germinated and come to birth, have diligently pondered those signs which 'make clear.'

Cicero (106-43 B.C.), Roman philosopher, author of *De Divinatione*.

Famous Chaldean Astrologer

Berosus was famous in astrology and on account of his divine predictions the Athenians publicly erected a statue to him, with a tongue of gold.

Pliny the Elder (23-79 A.D.), Roman encyclopedist. Author of *Natural History*.

Acquiring Power of Divination

If anyone swallows the heart of a mole, fresh from the body and still palpitating, he will receive the gift of divination, and a foreknowledge of future events.

Pliny the Elder (23-79 A.D.), Roman Encyclopedist. Author of *Natural History*.

Divination by Necromancy

But mingled with the timid multitude is Sextus, an offspring unworthy of Magnus for a parent, who afterwards, roving, an exile, on the Scyllaean waves, a Sicilian pirate, polluted his triumphs on the deep, who, fear spurring him on to know beforehand the events of fate, both impatient of delay and faint-hearted about all things to come, consults not the tripods of Delos, nor the Pythian caves, nor does he choose to enquire what sounds Dodona, the nourisher on the first fruits, sends forth from the brass of Jove, who from the entrails can reveal the fates, who can explain the birds, who can observe the lightnings of heaven and search the stars with Assyrian care, or if there is any method, secret, but lawful.

He had gained a knowledge of the secrets of the ruthless magicians detested by the Gods above, and the altars sad with dreadful sacrifices, and the aid of the shades below and of Pluto; and to him, wretched man, it seemed clear that the Gods of heaven knew too little.

The vain and direful frenzy the very locality promotes, and, adjoining to the camp, the cities of the Haemonian women, whom no power over any prod-

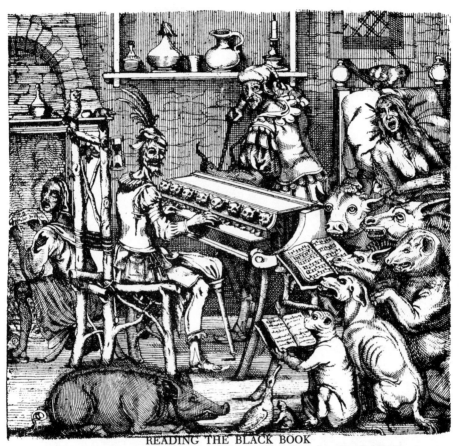

READING THE BLACK BOOK

The Black Book was a grimoire: a magician's manual used in the Middle Ages. Here a crippled magician is playing on an instrument from which protrude eight heads of cats, forming an octave. In the bed an old witch is singing, with a crow, her familiar, perched over her head. Another witch, crouching at the fireside, is singing and reading from a parchment. A cacophany of sound supplied by animals adds to the weird, demented, occult concert.

DOCTOR JOHN DEE

Doctor John Dee (1527-1608) was an English mathematician, astrologer, and necromancer. Imprisoned on charges of casting horoscopes and using enchantments against Queen Mary of England, he was later sent on government service to Europe, and became acquainted with Edward Kelly, a self-styled magician. Dr. Dee was the author of Liber Mysteriorum, *The Book of Mysteries*. A magic mirror, once Dr. Dee's property, is now in the British Museum.

SOVEREIGN OF THE INFERNAL HOSTS

In the infernal hierarchy Satan is the Supreme Demon, master of thousands of demoniac powers, potentates, and princelings, as well as numberless legions of minor spirits. Gustave Doré was a nineteenth century French artist.

MACBETH AND THE WITCHES
An early conception of the three witches in Shakespeare's *Macbeth*.

igy that has been invented can surpass, whose art is each thing that is not believed. Moreover, the Thessalian land produces on its crags both noxious herbs, and rocks that are sensible to the magicians as they chaunt their deadly secrets. There spring up many things destined to offer violence to the Deities; and the Colchian stranger gathers in the Haemonian lands those herbs which she has not brought.

The impious charms of the accursed nation turn the ears of the inhabitants of heaven that are deaf to peoples so numerous, to nations so many. That voice alone goes forth amid the recesses of the heavens, and bears the stringent words to the unwilling Deities, from which the care of the skies and of the floating heavens never calls them away. When the accursed murmur has reached the stars, then, although Babylon of Perseus and mysterious Memphis should open all the shrines of the ancient Magi, the Thessalian witch to foreign altars draws away the Gods of heaven.

Through the charms of the Thessalian witches a love not induced by the Fates has entered into hardened ears; and stern old men have burned with illicit flames. And not only do noxious potions avail; or when they withdraw the pledges swelling with its juices from the forehead of the mother about to show her affection. The mind, polluted by no corruption of imbibed poison, perishes by force of spells. Those whom no unison of the bed jointly occupied binds together, and influence of alluring beauty, they attract by the magic whirling of the twisted threads. The courses of things are stayed, and retarded by

lengthened night, the day stops short. The sky obeys not the laws of nature; and on hearing the spells the headlong world is benumbed; Jupiter, too, urging them on, is astounded that the poles of heaven do not go on, impelled by the rapid axles.

At another time, they fill all places with showers, and, while the sun is hot, bring down the clouds; the heavens thunder, too, Jupiter not knowing it. By those same words, with hair hanging loose, have they scattered abroad far and wide soaking clouds and showers. The winds ceasing, the sea has swelled; again, forbidden to be sensible of the storms, the south wind provoking it, it has held its peace; and bearing along the ship the sails have swelled against the wind. From the steep rock has the torrent hung suspended; and the river has run not in the direction in which it was descending. The summer has not raised the Nile; in a straight line the Maeander has urged on his waters; and the Arar has impelled headlong the delaying Rhone; their tops lowered, mountains have levelled their ridges.

Olympus has looked upwards to the clouds, and with no sun the Scythian snows have thawed, while the winter was freezing. Impelled by the stars, the shores protected, the charms of the Haemonian witches have driven Tethys back. The earth, too, has shaken the axle of her unmoved weight, and, inclining with the effort, has oscillated in her mid regions. The weight of a mass so vast smited by their voice, has gaped open, and has afforded a prospect through it of the surrounding heavens. Every animal powerful for death, and produced to do injury, both fears the Haemonian arts and supplies them with its deadly qualities. Them do the ravening tigers and the magnanimous wrath of the lions fawn upon with gentle mouth; for them does the serpent unfold his cold coils, and is extended in the frosty field. The knots of the vipers unite, their bodies cut asunder; and the snake dies, breathed upon by human poison.

What failing is this of the Gods of heaven in following after enchantments and herbs, and what this fear of disregarding them? Of what compact do the bonds keep the Deities thus bound? Is it obligatory, or does it please them to obey? For an unknown piety only do the witches deserve this, or by secret threats do they prevail? Have they this power against all the Gods of heaven, or do these imperious charms sway but a certain Deity, who, whatever he himself is compelled, can compel the world, to do? There, too, for the first time were the stars brought down from the headlong sky; and serene Phoebe, beset by the dire influences of their words, grew pale and burned with dusky and earthy fires, not otherwise than if the earth hindered her from the reflection of her brother, and interposed its shade between the celestial flames; and, arrested by spells, she endures labours so great, until, more nigh, she sends her foam upon the herbs situated beneath.

Lucan (39-65 A.D.), Roman poet. Author of epic poem *Pharsalia*.

The occasion is the consultation by Sextus, Pompey's son, of the oracle to discover the outcome of the Roman Civil War between Julius Caesar and Pompey.

Presumption of Diviners

Menippus: To think that men who creep upon this earth, and are not a whit wiser, or can see farther than ourselves, some of them old, blind, and lazy, should pretend to know the limits and extent of heaven, measure the sun's circuit, and walk above the moon.

Friend: These are, indeed, bold and presumptuous diviners.

Lucian (c. 120-c. 181 A.D.), Greek satirist. Author of *Dialogues*.

Divination with a Smile

Lycinus: I can tell you another scheme also, if you do not choose to have sacrifices and victims, or be at the great expense of a priest: and that is, to take some pieces of paper, with the names of all the philosophers upon them, throw these into an urn, and let a young lad, whose father and mother are both alive, take the urn, and draw out the first lot that comes to hand; whoever he is that is thus drawn, let him be your philosopher.

Hermotimus: This is all raillery, Lycinus, and does not become you.

Lucian (c. 120-c. 181 A.D.), Greek satirist. Author of *Dialogues*.

Priestess of Delphi

Lycinus: As they say of the priestess at Delphi, when she drinks of the second fountain, that she is immediately full of the god, and delivers her oracle to all that ask for it.

> Lucian (b. c. 120 A.D.), Greek satirist. Author of *Dialogues.*

The Pythia, the priestess of Delphi, before ascending the tripod, washed her whole body in the Castalia, a fountain at the foot of Mount Parnassus, and drank large draughts of the water that inspired her to prophecy.

Divination by Water

On the people of Tralles consulting magic in an enquiry concerning the issue of the Mithridatic War, a boy, while contemplating the reflection of an image of Mercury on some water, chanted the things which would come to pass in 160 lines of verse.

> Apuleius (c. 123 A.D. Date of death uncertain), Roman novelist. Author of *Metamorphoses*, pervaded by magic adventures; *De Magia.*

Divination by observation of a liquid surface is known as elaeomancy.

Finding an Object Magic

Fabius, having lost five hundred denarii, came to consult Nigidius. The latter, by means of incantations, inspired certain boys so that they were able to indicate to him where a pot containing a certain portion of money had been hidden in the ground, and how the rest had been dispersed.

> Apuleius (c. 123 A.D. Date of death uncertain), Roman novelist. Author of *Metamorphoses* and *De Magia.*

Boy Used for Divination

Therefore they have imputed that some boy, bewitched by incantation, with no witnesses present, in a secret spot, collapsed, unconscious. To make their story complete, they had to add that he had uttered many prophecies.

> Apuleius (2nd century A.D.), Roman novelist. Author of *De Magia*, in which he defends himself against charge of witchcraft.

Divination of Eastern Origin

For Numa himself, being not instructed by any prophet or angel of God, was fain to fall to hydromancy: making his gods (or rather his devils) to appear in water, and instruct him in his religious institutions. Which kind of divination, says Varro, came from Persia, and was used by Numa and afterwards by Pythagoras, wherein they used blood also, and called forth spirits infernal. Necromancy the Greeks call it; but necromancy or hydromancy, whether you like, there it is that the dead seem to speak.

> St. Augustine (354-430 A.D.), one of the Church Fathers. Author of *The City of God.*

NUMA: ancient King of Rome.
HYDROMANCY: a method of divination by gazing into water surfaces.
VARRO: Marcus Terentius Varro, Roman encyclopedist (1st century B.C.).
PYTHAGORAS: Greek philosopher (6th century B.C.).
NECROMANCY: evocation of the spirits of the dead.

[233]

Julian Practices Divination by Mirror

There was besides this folly in Julianus, that through the magicians he avoided very many things by which he thought that the hatred of the people would be softened down or the arms of the soldiers held in check. For they both sacrificed certain victims not consistent with Roman rites and chanted profane charms; and those things which they say are done at the mirror, in which blindfolded boys are said to see the future in a charmed whirl, Julianus did. And then the boy is said to have seen the decease of Julianus.

Scriptores Historiae Augustae (4th century A.D.).

JULIANUS (332-363 A.D.): Roman Emperor, "Julian the Apostate."
BLINDFOLDED BOYS: mediums.
Divination by means of mirrors is known as catoptromancy.

An Occasion for Sortilege

Then the aged Vainamoinen,
He the great primeval sorcerer,
Hastened alder-sticks to cut him,
And arranged the sticks in order,
And began the lots to shuffle,
With his fingers to arrange them,
And he spoke the words which follow,
And in words like these expressed him:
"Leave I ask of the Creator,
Seek an answer that misleads not.
Tell me, signs of the Creator,
Lots of Jumala, instruct me,

Where the sun is hidden from us,
Since no more as time elapses,
In the sky do we behold them?"

Kalevala, Finnish Epic.

Sortilege is the technique of divination by lots. It includes rhabdomancy, discovery of hidden objects with the aid of a rod, and belomancy, divination by means of arrows. The sorcerer, Vainamoinen, by means of alder-sticks, discovers the location of the sun and the moon.

Diviners

They are called scryers who by divining in bright and polished objects—such as gleaming swords, basins, cups, and various kinds of mirrors—satisfy the consultations of inquirers.

John of Salisbury (c. 1115-1180), author of *De Vestigiis Philosophorum*.

Chaldean Divination

Giovanni: My lady hath given the Chaldean her nativity, who is to consult with the ephemerides.

James Shirley, author of *The Sisters*, 1652.

CHALDEAN: in the seventeenth century, a general term for a magician. Anciently, Chaldea was the home of magic arts.
EPHEMERIDES: in astrology, tabulated position of heavenly body during successive days.

Astrology and Witchcraft

The plague created against Saistan is abundance of witchcraft, and that char-

[234]

acter appears from this, that all people from that place practice astrology: those wizards produce snow, hail, spiders, and locusts.

Great Bundahisn, Persian sacred text.

Fanciful Astrology

This Heaven, that's inhabited by twelve Gods, turns it self into as many Figures; and now 'tis Aries: He that's born under that Sign has much Cattle, much Wooll, and to that a Jolt-head, a Brazen-face, and will be certainly a Cuckold: There are many Scholars, Advocates, and Horned Beasts, come into the World under this Sign. We praised our Nativity-Caster's pleasantness, and he went on then again: The whole Heaven is Taurus, and wonder it e'er bore Foot-ball-Players, Herds-men, and such as can shift for themselves. Under Gemini are foaled Coach-Horses, Oxen calved, great Baubles, and such as can claw both sides are born. I was born my self under Cancer, and therefore stand on many Feet, as having large Possessions both by Sea and Land. For Cancer suits one as well as the other, and therefore I put nothing upon him, that I might not press my own Geniture. Under Leo, Spendthrifts and Bullies: under Virgo, Women, Runagates, and such as wear Iron Garters: under Libra, Butchers, Slip-slop-makers, and Men of Business: under Scorpio, Empoisoners and Cut-throats: under Sagittary, such as are Goggle-ey'd, Herb-women, and Bacon-stealers: under Capricon, poor helpless Rascals, to whom yet Nature intended

Horns to defend themselves: under Aquarius, Cooks and Paunch-bellies: under Pisces, Caterers and Orators: And so the World goes round like a Mill, and is never without its Mischief; that Men be either born or perish. But for that tuft of Herbs in the middle, and the Honey-comb upon it, I do nothing without just reason for it: Our Mother the Earth is in the middle, made round like an Egg, and has all good things in her self, like a Honey-comb.

Petronius (1st century A.D.) Roman novelist. Author of *The Satyricon.*
One of the chief characters is a wealthy parvenu who, at an elaborate banquet, explains the Signs of the Zodiac ignorantly.

Power of the Planets

It is certain that the Sun has the property of heating moderately and drying: these effects are more easily discerned on account of its magnitude. The Moon excels in humidity. Saturn causes cold and dryness. In Mars the property of dryness dominates. As for Mercury, its property is almost equally balanced, for dryness, because it never moves far from the Sun, and for moisture, because it is near the Moon.

Claudius Ptolemaeus (2nd century A.D.), author of *Tetrabiblos.*

Influence of Stars

Each month there is a spirit that goes forth and walks by night. These spirits that walk by night must be appeased. For the external influences act on man, in accordance with the stars.

> Kwang-Tchu (3rd century A.D.), author of *Treatise on Wandering Influences*.

The Theme of the Universe

This is the generation of the world, according to Aesculapius and Hanubius, to whom the mighty power of Mercury confided the secrets of this knowledge. They placed the Sun in the fifteenth part of the Lion, the Moon in the fifteenth part of Cancer, Saturn in the fifteenth part of Capricorn, Jupiter in the fifteenth part of Sagittarius, Mars in the fifteenth part of Scorpion, Venus in the fifteenth part of Libra, Mercury in the fifteenth part of Virgo, and Hora in the fifteenth part of Cancer. According to this generation, and according to these conditions of the stars, and according to the evidences relating to this generation, they claim that the destinies of man are in conformity with this aforesaid order, as it is written in the book of Aesculapius entitled Myriogenesis.

> Julius Firmicus Maternus (4th century A.D.), author of *Libri Matheseos*, a treatise on astrology.

Truth of Astrology

When Gordianus the Elder once consulted an astrologer about the birth of his son, it is said that the astrologer answered: "He will be the son of an Emperor, and himself an Emperor." And when the Elder Gordianus laughed, they say that the astrologer pointed to a constellation, and referred to ancient books, to confirm that he had spoken the truth.

> Capitolinus (4th century A.D.), Roman biographer.

GORDIANUS THE ELDER: i.e. Gordianus I, Roman Emperor (3rd century A.D.).

Elements of the Cosmos

The god who is the creator of man composed the body of man with a mixture of the four elements: fire, water, air, and earth, so that the conjunction of these elements may produce a being in the form of the divine imitation . . . For this reason, the five stars and also the sun and the moon sustain man by a fiery and perpetual movement, as if he were a microcosm.

> Julius Firmicus Maternus (4th century A.D.), author of *Libri Matheseos*, a treatise on astrology.

Mediaeval Astrologer

Mandrogerus: There are three kinds of slaves: the powerful planets, the importunate geese, the grim dog-heads. Their images are in all the temples and all the shrines. Win their good graces, and you will know no obstacles.

> *Querolus* (circa 5th century A.D.).

MANDROGERUS: astrologer and magician, one of the characters in this mediaeval play.

Magic in the Stars

And hee that beleeveth that the marvellousnesse of things be in stars of which al things like their marvellous and hid properties, may know that every thing hath his proper figure celestiall, agreeing to them, of which also commeth marvellousnesse in working. For every thing which beginneth, beginneth under a determinate ascendant and celestiall influence, and getteth a proper effect, or vertue of suffering or working a marvellous thing. And he that believeth of the marvellousnesse of things that come by amity and enmity, as buying and selling cannot be denied so to come, and thus universal everything is ful of marvellous things, after every way of searching the natures of them. And after that the Philosophers knew this, they began to prove and say what is in things.

Albertus Magnus (c. 1206-1280), *Book of the Marvels of the World.*

Chiromantic Symbolism

Subtle (alchemist):
The thumb, in chiromancy, we give
    Venus;
The fore-finger to Jove; the midst to
    Saturn;
The ring to Sol; the least to Mercury,
Who was the lord, sir, of his horoscope,
His house of life being Libra: which
    fore-showed
He should be a merchant, and should
    trade with balance.

Ben Jonson (1573-1637), *The Alchemist.*

Levitation

Magic Flight

Take the oak rod, turn in the direction in which you want to fly, and write the name of your destination on the ground.

Key of Solomon, mediaeval grimoire.

OAK ROD: the magician's potent wand.

Buddhist Levitation

In the third century B.C. Prince Mahendra, Buddhist, accompanied by disciples, went on a mission to Ceylon. He accomplished the journey by levitation, rising into the air and alighting in Ceylon on the Missa Mountain, where Buddhist temples were later established.

Levitation of Witches

In the middle of the fifteenth century, The Council of Ancyra made a resolution condemning women who rode abroad with Diana and Herodias.

DIANA, HERODIAS: synonyms for the Moon goddess, associated with Sabbat assemblies.

Flight through the Air

Demons can lead men through divers places, both by day and by night, sometimes flying and sometimes against their will.

Alfonso Tostato (15th century), *Commentary on Matthew.*

[237]

Saintly Levitation

St. Francis Xavier visited the East in 1541. Witnesses testified that on several occasions he levitated in the air.

Dramatic Transvection

Gayman:

By Magick Art I was conducted—I know not how
To an inchanted Palace in the Clouds.

Mrs. Aphra Behn (1640-1689), English dramatist. Author of *The Lucky Chance.*

Alchemy

Table of Emerald

Words of the arcana of Hermes, written on the Tablet of Emerald, found in his hands in the dark cave in which was found his body, that had been buried there.

It is true, and no falsehood, certain and veritable: What is inferior is like that which is superior. And what is superior is like that which is inferior, to perpetuate the miracles of things.

And just as all things stream from One, through the mediation of One, so all things created have been from this unique One, by adaptation.

The father is the Sun; the mother, the Moon. You shall separate the earth from fire, the subtle from the dense, gently, with great skill.

This is the strong force of all forces, which will vanquish all things subtle and penetrate all solids.

Egyptian text attributed wrongly to Hermes Trismegistus.

Alchemical Formula for Making Gold

Take the following ingredients: twenty parts of platinum, the same amount of silver, plus 240 parts of brass, and obtain also 120 parts of nickel.

Melt these items separately in different crucibles. They are then combined together when in the molten condition. This alloy is then poured into moulds to cool. Then use the metal.

Atharva Veda, Sanskrit Magic Text.

Enigma of the Philosopher's Stone according to Hermes and Agathodaimonos

I have nine letters. I am tetrasyllabic. Hearken to me.
The first three have three letters.
The rest contain the rest.
Five are aphonic.
The total number comes to twice eight hundred plus three and four times ten and three. Knowing what I am, you will know the divine Wisdom that is in me.

Manuscript in St. Mark's, Venice.

[238]

Alchemical Quiz

Dialogue between Subtle, alchemist, and
Face, housekeeper.

Subtle: Name the vexations, and the
martyrizations of metals in the work.
Face: Sir, putrefaction,
Solution, ablution, sublimation,
Cohabation, calcination, ceration, and
Fixation.
Subtle: This is heathen Greek to you,
now!—
And when comes vivification?
Face: After mortification.
Subtle: What's cohabation?
Face: 'Tis the pouring on
Your *aqua regis*, and then drawing him
off,
To the trine circle of the seven spheres.
Subtle: What's the proper passion of
metals?
Face: Malleation.
Subtle: What's your *ultimum suppli-
cium auri?*
Face: Antimonium.
Subtle: This is heathen Greek to you?
—and what's your mercury?
Face: A very fugitive, he will be gone,
sir.
Subtle: How do you know him?
Face: By his viscosity,
His oleosity, and his suscitability.
Subtle: How do you sublime him?
Face: With the calce of egg-shells,
White marble, talc.
Subtle: Your magisterium, now,
What's that?
Face: Shifting, sir, your elements,
Dry into cold, cold into moist,
moist into hot, hot into dry.

Subtle: This is heathen Greek to you
still!
Your *lapis philosophicus?*
Face: 'Tis a stone; a spirit, a soul, and
a body:
Which if you do dissolve, it is dissolved;
If you coagulate, it is coagulated;
If you make it to fly, it flieth.

Ben Jonson (1573-1637), *The Alchemist.*

Gold Galore!

And this be your elixir,
Your *lapis mineralis* and your lunary,
Give me your honest trick yet at primero,
Or gleek: and take your *lutum sapientis*,
Your *menstruum simplex!* I'll have gold
before you.

Ben Jonson (1573-1637), *The Alchemist.*

Alchemy in Action

Subtle (an Alchemist):
It is, of the one part,
A humid exhalation, which we call
Materia liquida, or the unctuous water;
On the other part, a certain crass and
vicious
Portion of earth; both which concorporate,
Do make the elementary matter of gold;
Which is not yet *propria materia*,
But common to all metals and all stones;
For, where it is forsaken of that moisture,
And hath more dryness, it becomes a
stone;
Where it retains more of the humid
fatness,
It turns to sulphur or to quicksilver,
Who are the parents of all other metals.

Nor can this remote matter suddenly
Progress so from extreme unto extreme,
As to grow gold, and leap o'er all the
means.
Nature doth first beget the imperfect,
then
Proceeds she to the perfect. Of that airy
And oily water, mercury is engendered;
Sulphur of the fat and earthy part; the
one,
Which is the last, supplying the place of
male,
The other of the female, in all metals.
Some do believe hermaphrodeity,
That both do act and suffer. But these
two
Make the rest ductile, malleable,
extensive.
And even in gold they are; for we do find
Seeds of them, by our fire, and gold in
them;
And can produce the species of each
metal
More perfect thence, than Nature doth
in earth.
Besides who doth not see in daily practice
Art can beget bees, hornets, beetles,
wasps,
Out of the carcases and dung of creatures;
Yea, scorpions of an herb, being rightly
placed?
And these are living creatures, far more
perfect
And excellent than metals.

Ben Jonson (1573-1637), *The Alchemist*.

Philosopher's Stone

This much concerning the revelation
of our stone is, we doubt not, enough

for the Sons of the Doctrine. The strength
thereof, shall never become corrupted
but the same, when it is placed in the
fire, shall be increased. If you seek to
dissolve, it shall be dissolved; but if you
would coagulate, it shall be coagulated.
Behold, no one is without it, and yet all
do need it! There are many names given
to it, and yet it is called by one only,
while, if need be, it is concealed. It is
also a stone and not a stone, spirit, soul,
and body; it is white, volatile, concave,
hairless, cold, and yet no one can apply
the tongue with impunity to its surface.
If you wish that it should fly, it flies; if
you say that it is water, you speak the
truth; if you say that it is not water, you
speak falsely. Do not then be deceived
by the multiplicity of names, but rest assured that it is one thing, into which
nothing alien is added.

Guglielmo Grataroli (16th century),
Turba Philosophorum.

Mystic Alchemy

I signify to posterity that I make philosophy near to the Sun and Moon. He,
therefore, that will attain to the truth
let him take the moisture of the Sun and
the Spume of the Moon.

Guglielmo Grataroli (16th century),
Turba Philosophorum.

The Mystery of Alchemy

O all ye seekers after the science, the
arcanum of gold and the art of the coin
is a dark vestment, and no one knows

WITCHES TRAMPLE ON THE CROSS

A medieval woodcut illustrating the power of the Archfiend. Witchcraft was believed to be a survival of ancient pagan cults and was consequently an enemy of the Church.

WITCHES SWEAR FEALTY TO THE DEMON

In the Middle Ages, witches were reputedly the servants of the Archfiend, who was, as here, represented in goat form. Sometimes, as in the illustration, he is also winged.

(A medieval woodcut)

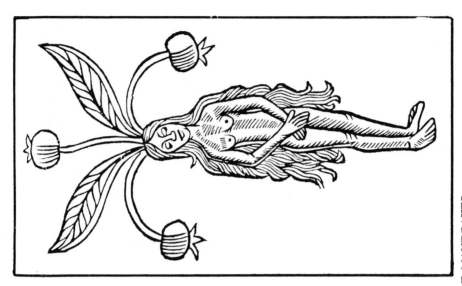

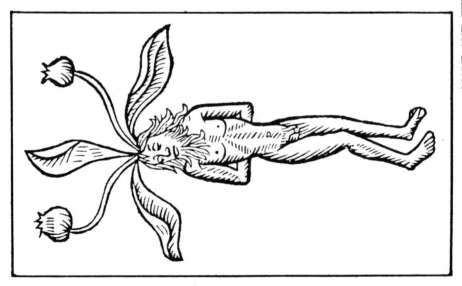

MALE AND FEMALE MANDRAKES
(Medieval woodcuts)

A mediæval death-bed

Condemned souls carried to their place of punishment

Satan in bonds

The Demon of the Treasure

The Trumpeter of Evil

The witch and the demon

MEDIEVAL CONCEPTION OF DEMONS

In the medieval demonology, demons are frequently represented in animal form, usually that of a goat; or, less frequently, as satyrs: winged, too, and partly human in appearance.

MEDIEVAL CONCEPTIONS OF THE DEVIL

In the Middle Ages, Satan was conceived as the Supreme Fiend, the essence of evil, Antichrist. He is protean in form, and everlastingly in quest of human souls.

what the Philosophers have narrated in their books without frequent reading, experiments, and questionings of the Wise. For that which they have concealed is more sublime and obscure than it is possible to make known in words.

Guglielmo Grataroli (16th century), *Turba Philosophorum.*

Making Gold

I counsel posterity to take the gold which they wish to multiply and renovate, then to divide the water into two parts.

Guglielmo Grataroli (16th century), *Turba Philosophorum.*

Chapter XI

Witchcraft versus the State

Chapter 11

WITCHCRAFT VERSUS THE STATE

Introduction

When the practices of magic, in all their irrational, phantasmal, and obfuscating variations, seeping through the tribal and communal activities, began to exercise increasingly malefic impacts, the state itself, the governing controls, stepped in. Magic never remained content with mere adumbrations, with ideological notions divorced from material reference, from physical limitations. It extended tangentially, intruding aggressively into alien fields and always engendering tumult and disaster, agonies and massacre. Even after the introduction of Christianity, according to St. Augustine, pagan customs survived in Britain; for as late as the seventh century, in 690, Archbishop Theodore of Canterbury forbade the offering of Satanic sacrifices, the eating in heathen temples, the use of spells and divination, the celebration of feasts in abominable places, and the dressing up in animal skins for occult rites.

When magic spawned from a palpable manifestation harmful to or affecting the individual only, into a subversive phenomenon involving large masses of people, then vigorous suppressive action had to be taken. The result was that from proto-history onward, from the time of Cham-Zoroaster, traditionally the first magician after the era of the Flood, royal decrees, imperial injunctions, state condemnations aimed at the confinement of witchcraft within a narrow, controlled circle: or, when the effects of wizardry tended to create confusion or havoc and destruction among the population, witchcraft was categorically outlawed, with resultant penalties of banishment and even death. Even association and contact, converse and acquaintance with practitioners of the Black Art were subject to such penalties. For witchcraft, in the course of time, and under political urgencies, not infrequently began to impair the powers of the state. It progressively spread into public policies, national issues, even interfering with royal successions. It encroached on established religious cults and hence competed, and sometimes with no little success, with the conventional, long-accepted order of priesthood. At times, too, the machinations of the wizard caught and held the personal interest of the ruling class, with consequent public danger of excessive, undue influences. Measures, therefore, had to be taken to safeguard the functions of empire, the stability of sovereignty, the perpetuity of traditional mores.

Furtive rites, obscene and blasphemous ceremonials, demoniac and unhallowed conjurations, the entire horrendous apparatus of the magic art, flowing beyond the cryptic, exiguous frontiers in which only the individual and the magus were involved, broke these barriers and, becoming a menace to the social frame, to political and social existence, had to be restrained. Magic, abandoning its mystic role, had stepped out too far: had stepped into actuality, into living, hazardous reality. Yet, despite all the prohibitions involving torture, banishment, and death, the practice, resilient like some baleful phoenix, uprose from its own apparent ashes, to renew, in a kind of perpetuating cycle, its weird and ominous operations.

Condemnation of witchcraft appears in the Bible, and extends into Roman imperial edicts, into the governmental machinery of the dual Roman Empire, into the dark Gothic and Hunnish ages. But the greatest anti-witchcraft operations were manifested during the broad span of the middle centuries, throughout Europe: involving witch-hunts and trials, prosecutions and persecution of Black Art adepts, by both state and ecclesiastical authorities. And during these centuries manifestos, exposés, voluminous treatises and demographic surveys and compendiums of wizardry, revelations of Satanic conclaves were published and studied voraciously. Usually, the authors of such works were exponents, who were also professed or reputed wizards, ecclesiastics, or lawyers in the capacity of persecutors. The interest in the subject, on account of its close, almost daily impingement on ordinary life, was so widespread that even kings displayed no slight awareness. King James VI, in fact, wrote a learned work on Demonology, while princelings and notabilities in various cultural areas were, from early days, credited with actual thaumaturgic powers, or were professed or putative magicians: among them the Emperor Nero, Fredegonde, the Frankish queen of the sixth century, Catherine de Medici and Cesare Borgia, Henry III and the Popes Leo the Great and Sixtus V, the Duc de Richelieu and Oliver Cromwell, the king-magicians of the antique Chinese

[246]

dynasties, as well as, apocryphally, Moses and King Solomon, Zoroaster, Aristotle, Alexander the Great, Virgil, St. Jerome, and Mohammed.

Mediaeval treatises on witchcraft fell into two distinctive categories: they were either expository, or violently condemnatory. Dominating the thirteenth century was Albertus Magnus, theologian turned scientific investigator, alchemist and mage, whose powers reputedly embraced the fashioning of an articulate android and who left behind a voluminous although in some cases a pseudepigraphic corpus of arcane writings.

The Irish *Book of Ballymote*, dating in the fourteenth century, is virtually a textbook on magic. In Toledo, Spain, in fact, magic was an academic study, taught by a professor of the art, the course lasting seven years. The *Antipalus Maleficiorum* is another treatise on magic by the demographer John Trithemius, a sixteenth century German abbot, and a friend of Agrippa von Nettesheim, himself credited with exorcism of Mary of Burgundy, wife of the Emperor Maximilian. Agrippa von Nettesheim, a diplomat, soldier, and occultist, produced *The Occult Philosophy*, substantially a defense of magic, a synthesis of Neoplatonic theory, Christian dogma, and Cabalistic mysticism. In the same century Giovanni Battista della Porta, a Neopolitan physicist, came out with a *Natural Magic*, while in France Guillaume de Postel, a Cabalist, was the author of *The Key of Things Kept Secret from the Foundation of the World*. In Germany, too, John Weyer, a pupil of the notorious Agrippa, was writing his *De Praestigiis daemonum et Incantationibus ac Veneficiis*—The Magic Activities of Demons, and incantations and sorceries, together with the *Pseudomonarchia Daemonum*, a catalogue of sixty demons and their functions.

Such works presupposed at least a belief in the efficacy of witchcraft, without the intrusion of the question of its spiritual or moral and ethical implications. To strip aside the arrogance of magic, on the other hand, was the avowed purpose of another group of demonographers. They accepted the fact of magic, the dark yet efficacious operations of witchcraft, but they damned them as originating by Satanic aid, and in collusion with demoniac agencies. These opponents, pursuing a vehement, merciless exposé and punishment of all warlocks and witches who, always fatally, encountered their investigations, were usually lawyers or churchmen. For they were the guardians of the safety of the religious and the political fabric, open to the continuous assault of witchcraft. Heinrich and Jacob Sprenger, German Dominicans, produced, in the craft. Heinrich Kramer and Jacob Sprenger, German Dominicans, produced, in the fifteenth century, the *Malleus Maleficarum*—The Witches' Hammer—that be-

and actually contained a body of rules for identifying the culprits. In 1580 Jean Bodin's *De la Démonomanie des sorciers* appeared in France. Nicholas Rémy published his *Demonolatria* in Lyons, in 1595. In 1599 the monumental attack on sorcery appeared—the *Disquisitionum Magicarum Libri Sex*—Six Books on Magic Questions—by Martin Delrio, the Spanish prosecutor of witchcraft. Shortly after, in 1608, Francesco Guazzo, an Italian priest, following the same lines, exposed magic practices in his *Compendium Maleficarum*, while Henri Boquet, in the same year, in France, published a *Discours des Sorciers*. All these works were written with one ad hoc purpose, to rout and punish witchery, to expose its anti-Christian and blasphemous ways, to exact the death penalty whenever possible.

It might be thought that, with the age of enlightenment and scientific progress that ushered in the nineteenth century, the Black Arts, crushed and forsaken, would revert to their hidden lairs, or mistily draw to a terminus. But Francis Barrett, professor of chemistry in London, gave new life and impetus to the subject by the publication of his comprehensive *The Magus*, that ranges over demoniac ways, exorcisms, necromancy, conjurations and periapts. In France, somewhat later in the century, Alphonse Louis Constant, using the pen name of Eliphas Lévi, became not only a similar demonographer, but an adept as well.

Contemporary times have produced a number of demonographers, who have surveyed the field with dispassionate objectivity and a critical, rational attitude. They have dissected the conflict of myth and indurated legend as survivals after the imposition of newer cults. They have examined the field of magic historically, or with literary emphasis, treating the matter itself as a rich, suggestive *corpus vile*. But one notable demonographer, who writes not only with spirit but with an almost personal animus, is the Rev. Montague Summers. His prolific series of studies in witchcraft, lycanthropy, and analogous phenomena through the ages down into the present are uniformly pervaded by a profound conviction not only of the blasphemous nature of the Black Arts, but of their continuous import and impact on society.

Formal prohibitions against witchcraft were of a religious, political, and social nature. Again and again the Old Testament prescribes the death penalty, by stoning, for necromancers, astrologers, wizards. Similarly severe penalties were imposed for practicing magic among the Egyptians, Greeks, and Romans. In 139 B.C. all thaumaturgists were ordered to leave Rome. In 96 B.C. Roman law forbade human sacrifice in magic rituals. By order of the first Emperor, Augustus, all books on magic were burned publicly. In the following reign, under Tiberius, magicians were banished, and until far into the second century decrees were promulgated against astrologers and diviners. In the fourth century again, and in the fifth, thaumaturgy was punishable by severe fines, while the Emperor Theodosius, in 385 A.D., enacted the death penalty for magic operations.

In the fifth century, the Salic Laws imposed fines for association with vampires. In the fourteenth century, both ecclesiastical and secular authorities repeatedly issued decrees against witchcraft, which was officially a heresy.

Under Henry VIII, in 1542, conjuration, witchcraft, sorcery, and enchantment were prohibited. Which means that the practice was rife, for intangibilities cannot be prohibited. A few years later, in 1563, a Bill was passed, in Queen Elizabeth's reign, against wizardry: another in 1601, another in 1604, and again in 1649. All of which indicates that witchcraft was no phantasmic imaginative diversion, but an evil of which the state took official cognizance as a menace to its existence.

During the Middle Ages, in fact until well into the eighteenth century, condemnation of witchcraft was implemented by witch hunts and witch trials. The records and archives of numberless mediaeval cities, in Hungary and Spain, in Italy, Denmark, and Scotland, are packed with circumstantial trials, imposing in their cumulative testimony, yet essentially based on whimsical figments, putative and unverifiable evidence, although on sinister factual effects. In England the last witch to be tried was Alice Molland, convicted of casting spells to destroy three victims, and executed in 1685. In Scotland, the last execution for witchcraft occurred in 1722. Among notorious witch-hunters were, dominantly, Cotton Mather, the eighteenth century Boston minister, whose activities involved the witch trials of Salem in Massachusetts. In this connection, an interesting and unique historical footnote is in order. In 1692, in Salem, Goody Ann Pudeator, the "Hag of Hell," was hanged as a witch. In 1957 her trial was re-enacted on a New York television show, and in that year she was also rehabilitated, somewhat belatedly, by the lower house of the Massachusetts State Legislature. A rare instance of witchcraft exonerated, or, perhaps, of acquittal due to paucity of palpable evidence. In England, Matthew Hopkins, a century earlier, had acquired the formal, official designation of Witch-Finder General. He was instrumental in the execution of hundreds— according to some estimates, thousands—of convicted witches.

Witch hunts, trials, and executions were usually carried out en masse. Thousands of witches were executed, throughout Europe, under anonymity. But records survive of individual trials: names have been preserved and personal circumstances detailed. In Ireland, Lady Alice Kyteler, in the fourteenth century, was tried on charges of poisoning four husbands by sorcery. Gilles de Rais, a fifteenth century French noble, was put to death for occult practices. Marie Balcoin, in Henry IV's reign, was a French sorceress condemned to the stake. In the sixteenth century, Pierre Bonnevault, a French sorcerer, was similarly condemned for Satanic associations. In the same century Madeleine Amalaric, also French, was put to death for causing the death of three persons by witchcraft, while Gilles Garnier, also French, was doomed for lycanthropy. Louis Gaufridi, known as Prince of Sorcerers, was executed in 1611. Early in the seventeenth century Dr. John Lambe, an English wizard, was stoned to death by a London mob in 1628. In France, Urbain Grandier, a Loudun priest, accused of sorcery, was burnt alive in 1634. The roster is long and sinister, and extends through the centuries; and specific names and the formalities of the trials are abundant in public and state archives, historical records, personal memoirs, and similar data.

In England in particular, in the sixteenth and seventeenth centuries, Lancashire was the locale of many investigations and witch trials. Such investigations were intimately associated with religious persecution, particularly persecution of Roman Catholics. Politically, in fact, Catholicism and witchcraft acquired synonymous connotations, as contemporary testimony indicates in pamphlets state trials, and parliamentary records.

Mass executions characterize all periods, and every century had its sudden, wholesale cleansing of occultism from the community or state by means of equally wholesale massacres. In England, as a result of a law passed in 1604 against witchcraft, 70,000 were put to death. In France, under Charles IX, some 130,000 wizards were estimated as populating the country, of whom thousands were executed on charges and conviction of sorcery.

Given such factual, established premises, it would be fatuous, irrational, and naive to assert that witchcraft was merely a phantasmal, exclusively conceptual notion. It had, on the contrary, reality. It produced ascertainable impacts. It became dangerous to the stability of the state. For a non-existent phenomenon does not need to be attacked or legislated against. No laws need be passed against acts that do not exist. Yet from the remotest days, from the Biblical Exodus onward, through the centuries that were marked by the cultures of Babylonia and Greece, Egypt and Rome, in Malaya as well as in the Mediterranean littoral, throughout mediaeval Europe and far down into the eighteenth century, imperial and royal decrees, state laws and parliamentary acts, senatorial promulgations and ecclesiastical prohibitions, have continuously, clamorously, categorically enunciated: Thou shalt not practice witch-craft. Further, they have repeatedly banished, punished, or put to death every such practitioner; and you cannot punish what does not exist. And the state, in whatever form, in whatever age, has never been an unrealistic metaphysician making quixotic thrusts at visionary windmills. It deals with palpabilities, with hard, earthy, material situations. And nothing was ever more material, more earthy, than wizardry.

Accusation of Witchcraft

If a man has laid a charge of witch-craft on another man and has not justi-fied it, he upon whom the withcraft is laid shall go to the holy river, and if the holy river overcome him, he who ac-cused him shall take to himself his house.

Code of Hammurabi, dating in second millennium B.C.

Condemnation of Magic

If either a man or a woman have made magical preparations and they have been seized in their hands and charge and proof have been brought against them the maker of the magical preparation shall be put to death.   Assyrian Law.

Condemned to Death

Two harem conspirators were con-demned to death because they made magical writings to lead astray and work mischief, and made certain gods of wax and certain medicines to weaken the limbs of man.

Egyptian Papyrus, 19th Dynasty.

WAX: the reference is to images of wax, a form of sympathetic magic.
MEDICINES: potions or philtres.

Condemnation of Witches

Thou shalt not suffer a witch to live.

Exodus 22.18.

Enchantment Forbidden!

Neither shall ye use enchantment nor observe times.

Leviticus 19.26.

OBSERVE TIMES: the reference is to astro-logical computations.

No Magic!

Do not turn to mediums or wizards; do not seek them out, to be defiled by them: I am the Lord your God.

Leviticus 19:31.

Magic Forbidden!

The soul that shall go aside after ma-gicians and soothsayers, and shall com-mit fornication with them, I will set my face against that soul, and destroy it out of the midst of its people.

Leviticus 20.6.

Death to Witches!

A man also or woman that hath a familiar spirit, or that is a wizard, shall surely be put to death: they shall stone them with stones: their blood shall be upon them.   *Leviticus 20.27.*

Punishment for Sorcery

But the abominable, and murderers, and whoremongers, and sorcerers . . .

shall have their part in the lake which burneth with fire and brimstone.

Revelation, 21.8.

Sorcery as an Evil

For without are dogs, and sorcerers, and whoremongers . . . and whosoever maketh a lie. *Revelation, 22.15.*

Beware Magicians!

There shall not be found among you anyone that maketh his son or his daughter to pass through the fire, one that useth divination, a soothsayer, or an enchanter, or a sorcerer.

Or a charmer, or one that consulteth a ghost or a familiar spirit, or a necromancer.

For all that do these things are an abomination unto the Lord; and because of these abominations the Lord thy God doth drive them out from before thee.

Deuteronomy 18.

Divine Condemnation of Sorcery

And a command has gone forth from the presence of the Lord concerning those who dwell on the earth that their ruin is accomplished because they have learnt all the secrets of the angels, and all the violence of the Satans, and all their powers—the most secret ones—and all the power of those who practice sorcery, and the power of witchcraft, and the power of those who make molten images for the whole earth: And how silver is produced from the dust of the earth, and how soft metal originates in the earth. For lead and tin are not produced from the earth like the first: it is a fountain that produces them, and an angel stands therein, and that angel is pre-eminent. And after that my grandfather Enoch took hold of me by my hand and raised me up, and said unto me: "Go, for I have asked the Lord of Spirits as touching this commotion on the earth." And he said unto me: "Because of their unrighteousness their judgement has been determined upon and shall not be withheld by Me for ever. Because of the sorceries which they have searched out and learnt, the earth and those who dwell upon it shall be destroyed."

Book of the Secrets of Enoch,
edited by R. H. Charles.

Hanging of Witches

Rabbi Simeon ben Shetah, in the first century B.C., went to Ashkelon. There, helped by eighty students, he caught eighty witches in the act of witchcraft, and hanged them all in one day.

Talmud.

The Law Versus Witchcraft

Whoever chanted an evil spell . . . whoever bewitched the crops.

Twelve Tables, ancient Roman Laws whereby maleficent magic was banned by the State.

[254]

Law Against Spells

If anyone cast a spell or made an incantation to bring shame or criminal reproach on another . . .

Twelve Tables, ancient Roman code of law.

Roman Laws Against Magic

Is it not written in the Twelve Tables: If a man enchants the crops. And elsewhere: If a man utters an evil incantation.

Pliny the Elder (1st century A.D.). Roman encyclopedist. Author of *Natural History.*

TWELVE TABLES: ancient Roman code of laws including laws against witchcraft.

Punishment for Witchcraft

Decrees of the senate were promulgated in regard to the expulsion of magicians from Italy. Among these was Lucius Pituanius, who was hurled from the Tarpeian Rock, and Publius Marcius, who was stripped and lashed to death outside the Esquiline Gate.

Tacitus (c. 55-c. 116 A.D.), Roman historian. Author of *Annals.*

Soothsaying Taboo

The Emperor Tiberius forbade soothsayers to be consulted secretly and without witnesses.

Suetonius (c. 69.-c. 140 A.D.), Roman historian.

Condemnation of Magic

What need is there to mention the miraculous deeds of these deceitful beings: spirits reproducing the fact of Castor and Pollux, the water carried by a vestal priestess in a sieve, the beard suddenly changed to red? All these phenomena have been achieved to induce worship of stone images. If the magicians produce demons, if they make children, goats, tables utter oracles, if they imitate miracles like the wily charlatans that they are, if they are skilled in sending dreams through angels and demons invoked, all the more will these seductive powers do on their own account what they perform for the interest of others.

Tertullian (160-c. 225 A.D.), Church Father. Author of *Apologeticus.*

State Condemns Witchcraft

The Lex Cornelia condemned 'those who killed men by magic incantations.'

Institutes of Justinian.

LEX CORNELIA: old Roman law.

Astrologers Banished from Rome

It was decreed that astrologers, magicians, soothsayers and others who practiced the same profession be interdicted from fire and water.

Ulpian (died 228 A.D.), Roman jurist.

Interdiction from fire and water was the formal Roman declaration of banishment. The year was 17 A.D.

[255]

Punishment for Concocting Philtres

Those who give a philtre to induce abortion or love, though they act without malice, yet commit an act of evil example. The lowly shall be banished to the mines, the more honorable ones to an island, with loss of part of their property.

Iulius Paullus (3rd century A.D.), *Sententiae.*

Edict against Alchemy

In the fourth century A.D. an edict of the Roman Emperor Diocletian ordered a search to be made in Egypt for all treatises dealing with alchemy, which were to be consigned to the flames.

Decree against Divination

Curiosity in regard to divination shall cease, for all men, and for ever.

Decree against Astrology

Let no astrologer enter any house except his own, for any reason. Let friendship with men of this kind, although of long standing, be rejected.

Theodosian Code (4th century A.D.).

Condemnation of Magic

Of those who pay divine honours to certain Angels, and evil-doers, soothsayers, poisoners, charmers, diviners.

Theodore, Archbishop of Canterbury. *Liber Paenitentialis* (7th century), *Theodosian Code* (4th century A.D.). earliest ecclesiastical law in England.

Punishment for Witchcraft

If witches or diviners, perjurers or foul, defiled, notorious adulteresses, be found anywhere within the land; let them then be driven from the country and the people cleansed, or let them totally perish within the country, unless they desist.

Laws of Edward and Guthrum, England, 8th century.

Early Edicts against Witchcraft

In England, royal decrees against magic practices were promulgated as early as the eighth century and as late as the seventeenth century. Among early edicts, these were notable: laws passed in 901 in the reign of Edward I, punishing diviners with banishment; the decree of the death penalty for acts of witchcraft, issued in 940 by King Ethalstan; the edict against enchantments, necromancies, and divination, issued in 959 by Edgar.

Punishment for Associating with Sorcerers

Those who seek divinations and follow the custom of the nations and bring into their homes men of this kind, for the purpose of finding or atoning for anything by magic art, shall be penalized for five years, according to rule.

Herard, Archbishop of Tours (9th century), *Capitularia.*

Evils of Sorcery

There is no doubt, as is generally known, that by certain sorceries and demoniac illusions they—magicians, soothsayers, seers, sorcerers, diviners, enchanters, interpreters of dreams—so affect the minds of certain people by love philtres, food, and prophylactics as to render them mad.

Herard, Archbishop of Tours (9th century), *Capitularia*.

Condemnation of Witchcraft

And, in regard to witches, enchanters, seers, astrologers, interpreters of dreams, and those who contrive divers portents, let them be punished.

Herard, Archbishop of Tours (9th century), *Capitularia*.

Punishment for Witchcraft

Death penalty decreed against agents of the Devil who arouse tempests.

Capitularia, Laws of Charlemagne (9th century).

Punishment of Witch

A woman who bewitches men or beasts or other things, if it is proved against her, shall be burned.

Laws of Forum Turolii (Spain), 12th century.

Condemnation of Sorcery

Those who practice the evil arts of magic and divination were ordered to be excluded from court: for all these operations or rather sorceries arise from the pestilential familiarity of demons and men.

John of Salisbury (1115-1180), *Policraticus*.

Punishment of Astrologers

If astrologers and diviners refuse to cease their practices, they shall be excommunicated.

Gratian (12th century), *Decretum*.

Punishment of Magician

If a man happens to be a magician, and it is proved against him, he shall be shaven in the form of a cross and scourged and banished.

Laws of Forum Turolii (Spain), 12th century.

Condemnation of Astrology

The father of lies taught astrology. Astrologers descend alive into hell.

John of Salisbury (1115-1180), *Policraticus*.

FATHER OF LIES: i.e., Satan.

[257]

Edict against Magic

In 1398 the University of Paris promulgated an edict complaining that the practice of witchcraft had become more frequent and more widespread than at any former period.

Chaucer on Witchcraft

Whylom there was dwelling in my
    country
An archdeacon, a man of high degree,
That boldly did execution
Or punishing of fornication
Or witchcraft.

Geoffrey Chaucer (c. 1345-1400),
English poet. Author of *Canterbury
Tales* (*Friar's Tale*).

Excommunication for Witchcraft

Likewise enchanters, soothsayers, diviners, augurs and magicians, of whatever kind or sex, masters of the magic art and professing that art and those who seek counsel or aid from them, shall be excommunicated.

Statutes of Guillaume, Bishop of Béziers (14th century).

Attack on Sorcerers

They have falsely associated themselves with divination and sorcery.

Pope John XXII (14th century).

Punishment for Witchcraft

Astrologers should be hanged or not allowed to live another day. Some are burned alive and their goods confiscated. Diviners should be put to the sword.

John of Freiburg (14th century)
Summa Confessorum.

Law against Alchemy

In 1404, in the reign of King Henry IV, an Act of Parliament decreed that the making of gold or silver was a felony.

Law Encouraging Alchemy

In the fifteenth century in the reign of King Henry VI, patents were issued for the encouragement of the transmutation of inferior metals into gold.

Magic Books Condemned

Furthermore it condemns all books and treatises on the magic arts and divination.   Council of Rouen, 1445.

Attack on Sorcery

It has come to our ears that numbers of both sexes do not avoid to have intercourse with the infernal fiends, and that by their sorceries they afflict both man and beast; they blight the marriage-bed, destroy the births of women, and the increase of cattle; they blast the corn on the ground, the grapes of the vineyard, the fruits of the trees, and the grass and herbs of the field.

Bull, issued by Pope Innocent VIII, in 1484, giving power to "imprison, convict and punish" all such as might be charged with these offences.

Condemnation of Magic

The art of incantation, divination, augury is abominable to the Lord.

Council of Eichstadt (15th century).

Magic Must Be Punished

Diviners or soothsayers of this kind, enchantresses and enchanters ought to be punished and banished or otherwise severely castigated.

Johann of Frankfurt (15th century).

Elizabethan Condemnation

If any person or persons after the said first day of June shall use, practise or exercise witchcraft, enchantment or sorcery, whereby any person shall happen to be killed or destroyed, they shall suffer pains of death as a Felon or Felons.

Act of Queen Elizabeth I of England, 1563.

Papal Condemnation of Witchcraft

For many devote themselves to Geomancy, Hydromancy, Aeromancy, Pyro-

mancy, Onomancy, Cheiromancy, Necromancy, and other means of divination and magic practices, not without at least secret association with Demons, or silent pact.   *Constitution*, Sixtus V, 1586.

GEOMANCY: Divination by examining handfuls of earth.
HYDROMANCY: Divination by gazing into water surfaces.
AEROMANCY: Divination by atmospheric conditions.
PYROMANCY: Divination by fire.
ONOMANCY: Divination by interpreting letters in a name.
CHEIROMANCY: Evaluation of lines in a person's hand.
NECROMANCY: Evocation of spirits of dead.

Interrogation of a Witch

Berta was present at a gathering of witches when you received from the Prince of Darkness an ointment intended to bewitch Sempronius.

Peter Binsfeld, Bishop of Trier. *Tractatus de Confessionibus Maleficorum et Sagarum*, 1589.

No Mercy for Witches

It is like sparing mad dogs, that everyone knows are incurable.

Nicholas Rémy. *Daemonolatria*, 1595.

Proofs of Witchcraft

Well-known evidences of witchcraft are: pots, ligatures, locks, feathers, and such like, that, in accordance with the pact entered into with the demon, the magician uses to harm a victim by means of witchcraft.

Martin Delrio. *Disquisitionum Magicarum Libri Sex*, 1599.

Torture for Witchcraft

But if the accused is convicted, it is more advisable for the judge not to subject him to questioning, because torture is wont to purge previous evidence, and even purges full proof.

Martin Delrio. *Disquisitionum Magicarum Libri Sex*, 1599.

The reference is to the ecclesiastical trials for witchcraft, prevalent during the Middle Ages.

Kill a Witch!

Witches must be put to death even though they killed no one by poison: even though they did no harm to crops and beasts; even though they were not necromancers—only because they are leagued with the demon.

Martin Delrio. Disquisitionum Magicarum Libri Sex, 1599.

King James VI of Scotland on Witchcraft

The fearfull abounding at this time in this country, of these detestable slaves of the Divel, the Witches or enchaunters, hath moved me (beloved Reader) to dispatch in post this following Treatise of mine, not in any wise (as I protest) to serve for a shew of my learning and ingine, but onely (moved by conscience) to preasse thereby, so farre as I can, to resolve the doubting hearts of many, both that such assaults of Satan are most certainely practised, and that the instruments thereof merits most severely to be punished.

King James VI of Scotland. *Daemonologie*, 1599.

Testimony to Witchcraft

Barnes, or wives, or never so diffamed persons, may serve for sufficient witnesses and proofes in such trialls; for who but Witches can be prooven, and so witnesses of the doings of witches.

King James VI of Scotland. *Daemonologie*, 1599.

Aid in Witch Trials

There are two other good helps that may be used for their trial: the one is, the finding of their marke and the trying the insensibleness thereof: the other is their fleeting on the water: for, as in a secret murther, if the dead carkasse be at any time thereafter handled by the murtherer, it will gush out of bloud, as if the bloud were crying to the heaven for revenge of the murtherer, God having appointed that secret supernaturall signe, for triall of that secret unnaturall crime, so it appears that God hath appointed (for a supernaturall signe of the monstrous impietie of Witches) that the water shall refuse to receive them in her bosome, that have shaken off them the sacred water of Baptisme, and wilfully refusea the benefite thereof: No, not so much as their eyes are able to shed teares (threaten and torture them as ye please) while first they repent (God not permitting them to dissemble their obstinacie in so horrible a crime).

King James VI of Scotland. *Daemonologie*, 1599.

MARKE: the Devil's Mark was believed to have been impressed by Satan on some part of the witch's body.

Parliament Condemns Witchcraft

If any person shall use, practice, or exercise any invocation or conjuration of any evil and wicked spirit, or shall consult, covenant with, entertain, employ, feed or reward any evil and wicked spirit, to or for any intent and purpose: or take up any dead man, woman, or child out of their grave, or the skin, bone, or any part of any dead person, to be used in any manner of witchcraft, sorcery, or enchantment, or shall use any witchcraft, sorcery, or enchantment, whereby any person shall be killed, destroyed, wasted, consumed, pined or lamed in his or her body, or any part thereof: that then every such offender, their aiders, abettors and counsellors shall suffer the pains of death.

Act of Parliament, 1st year of reign of King James VI of Scotland.

Magic in Satire

A leger to the devil sent,
Fully empower'd to treat about
Finding revolted witches out.
And has he not, within a year,
Hang'd threescore of 'em in one shire?

Samuel Butler (17th century English satirist), author of *Hudibras*.

The reference is to Matthew Hopkins, Witchfinder General, who in 1647 published *The Discovery of Witches*.

Punishment of Witches

1645, when so many Vassals of the Devil were Detected, that there were Thirty try'd at one time, whereas about Fourteen were Hang'd, and an Hundred more detained in the Prisons of Suffolk and Essex.

Cotton Mather, *The Wonders of the Invisible World*, London 1693.

Punishment for Magic

Magicians who doom men by curses should be destroyed by fire or sword.

17th century Teutonic Law.

Interrogation of Witches

Under torture, the accused was asked:
Has she any pact with the devil?
Of what kind?
When did it take place?
For how long?

[261]

Was it written or verbal?

At what place?

On what occasion?

Were others present?

What was the pact, or has she a mark?

What led her to it?

Has she practiced sorcery?

Of what kind and in what manner?

With what words and acts?

Seventeenth century Austrian Ordinance.

Punishment for Witchcraft

Those who harm men or beasts by their evil incantations are burnt alive.

17th century Teutonic Law.

Satanic Pied Piper

They gave the Commissioners very strange Instances of the Devil's Tyranny among them; how by the help of Witches he had drawn some Hundreds of Children to him, and made them subject to his power; how he hath been seen to go in a Visible shape through the country, and appeared daily to the people; how he had wrought upon the poorer sort, by presenting them with Meat and Drink, and this way allured them to himself. The Inhabitants of the Village begg'd of the Lord's Commissioners to root out these Witches.

An Account of what Happened in the Kingdom of Sweden in the years 1669 and 1670 in relation to the persons that were accused for Witches. Anthony Horneck, London, 1681.

VILLAGE: Mohra, in Sweden.

Punishment for Satanic Pact

Those who have made a verbal or written pact and have likewise had abominable intercourse with Satan are wont to be punished by fire.

17th century Statute.

The reference is to the ecclesiastical courts that tried witches during the Middle Ages.

Activities of Magicians

Magicians and witches are to be execrated who by their magic practices not change bodies, by charms and philtres only by sorcery but in strange ways entice men, bewitch by their incantations, drive mad and destroy the unwary, kill brute beasts, contrive disease, hail, noxious air, with the help of a demon, harm cattle and crops, prevent connubial intercourse between man and wife, contrive every kind of harm not by the power of the stars or magic arts, but by a pact and intercourse with demons.

17th century Papal Bull.

Scottish Witch Trial

The confession of certain Scotch Witches, taken out of an authentick copy of their Trial at the Assizes held in Paisley in Scotland Feb. 15, 1678.

The Tenour of the Confessions taken before justices: At first of Annabil Stuart of the age of fourteen years, or thereby; who declared that she was brought in the presence of the justices for the crime of Witchcraft; and declared, that on Harvest last, the Devil in the shape of a Black man came to her Mother's House, and required the Declarant to give herself up to him; and that the Devil promised her that she should not want any thing that was good. Declares, that she being enticed by her mother Jannet Mathie, and Bessie Weir, who was officer to their several meetings, she put her Hand to the crown of her Head, and the other to the sole of her foot, and did give herself up to the Devil.

John Glanvil. *Saducismus Triumphatus*, 1681.

Punishment for Witchcraft

If anyone is convicted of having made a pact with Satan, the enemy of the human race, or of having had any other commerce, even if he has harmed no one, and all the more so if he has injured men or beasts with his sorcery, or occasioned other damages by his evil art, it is decreed that he be burnt alive and driven from our midst in the avenging flames.

Jus Prutenicum, 18th century Teutonic Law.

Capital Punishment for Witchcraft Abolished

In 1736 a statute was passed in England, repealing the law against witchcraft made in the first year of the reign of King James VI of Scotland: and enacting that no capital prosecution should for the future take place for conjuration, sorcery and enchantment, but restricting the punishment of persons pretending to tell fortunes and discover stolen goods by witchcraft, to that appertaining to a misdemeanour.

Witch-Burning

For approximately four centuries, throughout the Middle Ages and later, witch-burnng was prevalent in Europe and America, fostered by ecclesiastical and secular investigations. The items that follow offer a general conspectus of the intensity and the distribution of the practice. The information is derived from mediaeval chronicles, records of witch trials, compendia on magic activities, particularly in Germany, France, and Spain.

1347-1400: Carcassonne, France—67 persons burnt for witchcraft.

1399: Berlin—woman burnt for sorcery.

1446-7: Savoy—3 men burnt for sorcery and Sabbat gatherings. Heidelberg and Thalheim—witch burnings.

1459: Arras, France—large number of inhabitants tortured into confession of witchcraft, Sabbat gatherings, levitation. Many were burnt.

1470: Burgundy—2 witches burnt.

1482-1486: Constance—48 witches burnt.

1485: Chauncy, France—2 women burnt for witchcraft.

1507: Calahorra, Spain—30 witches burnt.

1510: Saxony—woman burnt for witchcraft.

1515: Geneva—more than 500 persons executed for witchcraft.

1521: Besançon—2 men burnt as were-wolves.

1524: Near Lake Como—1000 persons burnt for witchcraft.

1589: Saxony—133 witches burnt in one day. Wurtemburg—44 women and 4 men burnt for witchcraft.

1590: Franconia—54 witches burnt in 8 months.

1591-1600: Bern, Switzerland—300 executions for witchcraft.

1591: Ghent—1 witch burnt.

1598: Ghent—1 witch burnt.

1599: Vaud, Switzerland—77 executed for witchcraft.

1627: Dieburg—85 witches executed.

1640-1651: Lindheim—30 witches burnt.

1664: Bury St. Edmund's—Amy Duny and Rose Cullender hanged for witch-craft.

1670: Mohra, Sweden—70 women and 15 children executed on confession of witchcraft. 136 other children between ages 9 and 16 were condemned to "run the gauntlet, and to be whipped on their hands at the Church door for a year together."

1674-1677: Sweden—71 persons beheaded or burnt for witchcraft.

1685: England—last witch executed was Alice Molland, condemned for using spells.

1722: Salzburg, Austria—Man executed for lycanthropy. In Scotland—the last execution for witchcraft took place in this year.

African Decree

The worship of invocation by the juju known as Atinga is hereby prohibited.

Government of Nigeria, 1951.

ATINGA: also known as Anatinga and Alatinga. A witch-finding oracle, prevalent in West Africa.

African Law against Witchcraft

Jail imprisonment for six months is now imposed in Nigeria on
any person who represents himself to be a witch or have the power of witch-craft.

Nigerian Law.

BIBLIOGRAPHY

Aeschylus. *The Persian Women.*

Albertus Magnus. *De Secretis Mulierum.*

Ancina, Johannes Laurentius. *De Natura Daemonum.* Venice, 1581.

Apuleius. *Metamorphoses. Apologia de Magia.*

Arabian Nights.

Audollent, A. *Defixionum Tabellae.* Paris: Fontemoing, 1904.

Augustine. *City of God.*

Baring-Gould, S. *The Book of Were-wolves.* London: Smith, Elder and Co., 1865.

Barrett, Francis. *The Magus.* 3 volumes. London, 1801.

Becker, J. E. de. *Nightless City.* New York: Wessels Bissel, 1905.

Benveniste, E. *Les Mages dans l'ancien Iran.* Etudes iraniennes, xv. Paris, 1938.

Bernard of Cluny. *Denunciation of Magic and Astrology.* Edited by H. C. Hoskier. London: Bernard Quaritch, 1929.

Bodin, Jean. *De La Démonomanie des Sorciers.* Paris, 1580.

Boguet, Henri, *Discours des Sorciers,* 1609. *An Examen of Witches,* translated and edited by M. Summers. New York: Walter V. McKee, 1929.

Bouinais, A. and Paulus, A. *Le Culte des Morts dans le Céleste Empire.* Paris: Musée Guimet, 1893.

Book of Ballymote.

Book of Enoch. Translated by R. H. Charles. Oxford, 1912.

Boylan, P. *Thoth the Hermes of Egypt.* Oxford, 1927.

Brognolus, R. P. *Manuela Exorcistarum ac Parochorum.* Venice, 1702.

Budge, E. A. W. *Egyptian Magic.* London, 1899.

Bulwer Lytton. *A Strange Story.*

Carus, Paul. *History of the Devil and the Idea of Evil.* Chicago: Open Court Publishing Co., 1900.

Cellini, Benvenuto. *Autobiography.*

Cicero. *De Divinatione.*

Contenau, G. *La Magie chez les Assyriens et les Babyloniens.* Paris: Payot, 1947.

Cooper, Thomas. *Mystery of Witchcraft.* London, 1617.

Crowley, Alesteir. *Magick in Theory and Practice.* Paris: Lecram Press, 1929.

Daiches, S. *Babylonian Oil Magic in the Talmud and later Jewish Literature.* London, 1913.

Danaeus, Lambertus. *De Veneficiis.* Cologne, 1575.

Davenport, John. *Witches of Huntingdon. London, 1646.*

David-Neel, Alexandra. *With Mystics and Magicians in Tibet.* London: Lane, 1934.

David-Neel, Alexandra. *Magic and Mystery in Tibet.* New York: Crown, 1937.

Davies, T. W. *Magic and Divination among the Hebrews.* London, 1898.

Davis, R. T. *Four Centuries of Witch Beliefs.* London: Methuen, 1947.

Delrio, Martin. *Disquisitionum Magicarum Libri Sex.* Louvain, 1599.

Digest. Ulpias.

Doutté, E. *Magie et Religion. Algiers,* 1909.

Eckels, R. P. *Greek Wolf-lore.* Philadelphia, 1937.

Elworthy, F. T. *The Evil Eye.* New York: Julian Press, 1958.

Evans-Pritchard, E. E. *Witchcraft, Oracles and Magic among the Azande.* New York: Oxford University Press, 1937.

Fairfax, Edward. *Daemonologia.* 1612.

Festugière, A. J. *La Révélation d'Hermès Trismégiste.* 4 vols. 1949-1953.

Fossey, C. *La Magie Assyrienne.* Paris, 1902.

Frooman, J. C. *De Fascinatione.* Nuremberg, 1674.

Gaisseau, P. D. *The Sacred Forest.* New York: Knopf, 1954.

Gaster, Moses. *Studies and Texts in Magic, Mediaeval Romance, Hebrew Apocrypha and Samaritan Archaeology.* 3 vols. London: Maggs Bros., 1925-1928.

Gerson. *De Erroribus circa Artem Magicam.* Strassburg, 1494.

Gervase of Tilbury. *Otia Imperialia.*

Giffard, George. *Discourse of the subtill practices of Devilles,* 1587.

Givry, Grillot de. *Witchcraft, Magic and Alchemy.* London: Harrap, 1931.

Glanvill, J. *Saducismus Triumphatus*. London, 1681.

Godwin, William. *Lives of the Necromancers*. London, 1834.

Grataroli, Guglielmo. *Turba Philosophorum*. Translated by A. E. Waite, 1896. Most ancient treatise on alchemy in Latin.

Grimoires: *Black Hen*, or *Black Pullet*.
 Constitution of Honorius.
 Great and Powerful Sea Ghost, by Dr. J. Faustus.
 Great Grimoire.
 Grimoire of Pope Honorius
 Hell's Coercion.
 Key of Solomon.
 Lesser Key of Solomon.
 Little Albert.
 Red Dragon.
 Sanctum Regum.
 Sword of Moses.
 Sworn Book of Honorius.
 Testament of Solomon.

Gross, Henning. Editor. *Magica*, 1600.

Guazzo, Francesco. *Compendium Maleficarum*. Milan, 1608.

Henry, V. *La Magie dans l'Inde antique*. Paris: Dujarric, 1904.

History of the Devil, 1814.

Holy Bible.

Homer. *Odyssey*.

Howey, M. O. *The Cat in the Mysteries of Religion and Magic*. New York: Castle Books, 1956.

Hutchinson, Francis. *Historical Essay concerning Witchcraft*. London, 1718.

Iamblichus. *The Mysteries of the Egyptians, Chaldeans and Assyrians*. Translated by Taylor. Chiswick, 1821.

James I, King. *Daemonologie*, 1599.

James of Vitry. *Exempla*.

King, Leonard W. *Babylonian Magic and Sorcery*. London: Luzac and Co., 1896.

Lacnunga. *Anglo-Saxon Magic and Medicine*. Edited by J. H. G. Gratton and C. Singer. Oxford, 1952.

Lenormant, François. *La Magie des Chaldéens.* Paris, 1874.

Lowe, J. A. *Magic in Greek and Latin Literature.* Oxford: Blackwell, 1929.

Lowell, P. *Occult Japan.* Boston: Houghton, Mifflin, 1895.

Lucan. *Pharsalia.* Translated by E. Ridley. London, 1870.

Map, Walter. *De Nugis Curialum.* Translated by M. R. James. New York: Oxford University Press, 1914.

Mason, J. *Anatomie of Sorcery,* 1612.

Mathers, S. L. M. Edited. *Key of Solomon the King.* Redway, 1889.

Mathers, S. L. M. Edited. *Book of Sacred Magic of Abramelin the Sage,* 1898.

Maury, F. A. *La Magie et l'Astrologie dans l'Antiquité et du moyen âge.* Paris: Didier, 1877.

Mengus, Hieronymus. *Flagellum Daemonum.* Venice, 1683.

Merejkowski, D. *Romance of Leonardo da Vinci.*

Michelet, J. *La Sorcière.* Translated by L. J. Trotter, 1863.

Molitor, Ulrich. *De lamiis et phitonicis muliebribus.* Constance, 1489. Written at the request of Sigismund, Archduke of Austria; one of the earliest printed books on witchcraft. Deals with witchcraft, demoniac possession, sorcery, the Sabbat.

Montgomery, J. A. *Aramaic Incantation Text from Nippur.* Philadelphia: University of Pennsylvania Press, 1913.

Naudé, G. *Apologie pour les Grands Hommes Soupçonnez de Magie.* Amsterdam, 1712.

Nock, A. D. Greek Magical Papyri, in *Journal of Egyptian Archaeology,* Vol. 15. London, 1929.

Nyauld, J. de. *De la Lycanthropie.* Paris, 1615.

Papus. *Traité élémentaire de Magie Pratique.* Paris, 1893.

Patritius, Franciscus. *Magia Philosophica.* Hamburg, 1593. Contains Chaldean oracles and philosophy of Hermes Trismegistus.

Perdrizet, R. *Negotium Perambulans in Tenebris.* Etude de démonologie Greco-Orientale. Strasbourg: Publications de la Faculté des Lettres, 1922.

Petronius, *Satyricon.*

Peucer, Gaspar. *Les Devins ou Commentaire des Principales Sortes de Divinations.* Antwerp, 1584.

Pico della Mirandolo, Giovan Francesco. *Libro detto Strega.* Venice, 1556.

Pipernus, Petrus. *De Magicis Affectibus*. Naples, 1634. Deals with demonology and magic medicine.

Plantsch, Martinus. *Opusculum de sagis maleficis*. 1507.

Porta, John Baptista. *Natural Magick*. New York: Basic Books, 1957.

Psellus, Michael. *De Operatione Daemonum*. On the Operation of Demons. F. Boissanade, 1838.

Rémy, Nicholas. *Demonolatria*. Lyons, 1595.

Ricardus, A. *De Praestigiis et incantationibus Daemonum*. Basel, 1568.

Rockhill, W. W. *Ethnology of Tibet*. Washington, 1895.

Roskoff, G. *Geschichte des Teufels*. Leipzig, 1869.

Scott, Sir Walter. *Letters on Demonology and Witchcraft*. London: John Murray, 1831.

Seymour, St. J. D. *Irish Witchcraft and Demonology*. Dublin: Hodges, Figgis and Co., 1913.

Sharpe, C. K. *A Historical Account of the Belief in Witchcraft in Scotland*. London, 1884.

Skeat, W. W. *Malay Magic*. London: Macmillan, 1900.

Storms, G. *Anglo-Saxon Magic*. The Hague: Nijhoff, 1948.

Summers, M. *History of Witchcraft and Demonology*. New York: Knopf, 1926.

Talmud. Kissuf.

Tartarotti. *El Congresso Notturno delle Lamie*. Libri Tre. 1749.

Tavenner, E. *Studies in Magic from Latin Literature*. New York: Columbia University Press, 1916.

Theocritus, Bion and Moschus. Andrew Lang. London: Macmillan, 1901.

Thompson, C. J. S. *Mysteries and Secrets of Magic*. New York: Lippincott, 1928.

Thompson, R. C. *Reports of the Magicians and Astrologers of Nineveh and Babylon*. London, 1900.

Thorndike, Lynn. *History of Magic and Experimental Science*. 6 vols. New York: Columbia University Press, 1923-1941.

Turmel, Joseph. *Histoire du Diable*. Paris: Editions Rieder, 1931.

Vergil. *Aeneid*.

Waite, A. E. *The Mysteries of Magic*. 2nd edition. London, 1897.

Waite, A. E. *The Book of Black Magic and of Pacts*. London, 1898.
Wall, J. C. *Devils*. London: Methuen and Co., 1904.
Westermarck, E. A. *Ritual and Belief in Morocco*. London: Macmillan, 1926.
Winstedt, R. *Malay Magician*. London: Routledge, 1954.
Wright, T. *Narrative of Sorcery and Magic*. 2 vols. London: R. Bentley, 1851.

Zohar.

ACKNOWLEDGMENTS

Grateful acknowledgment is made, in the case of the following books, for the use of relevant material:

Butler, E. M. *Ritual Magic.* Cambridge University Press, 1949.

Davis, R. T. *Four Centuries of Witch Beliefs.* London: Methuen, 1947.

Grimble, Arthur. *Return to the Islands.* London: John Murray, 1957.

W. F. Kirby. *Kalevala.* London: J. M. Dent, 1907.

Morgan, Lawrence, *Flute of Sand.* London: Odhams Press, 1956.

Thompson, R. C. *Semitic Magic.* London: Luzac and Co., 1908.

Trachtenberg, Joseph, *Semitic Magic and Superstition.* New York: Behrman House, 1939.

There is a vivid, detailed description of magic rites in D. Merejkowski's *Romance of Leonardo da Vinci.*

A contemporary English novelist, many of whose themes involve the Black Arts, is Dennis Wheatley. His numerous novels include: *The Devil Rides Out* (Satanism in London), *The Ka of Gifford Hillary, Strange Conflict, To the— Devil—a Daughter.*